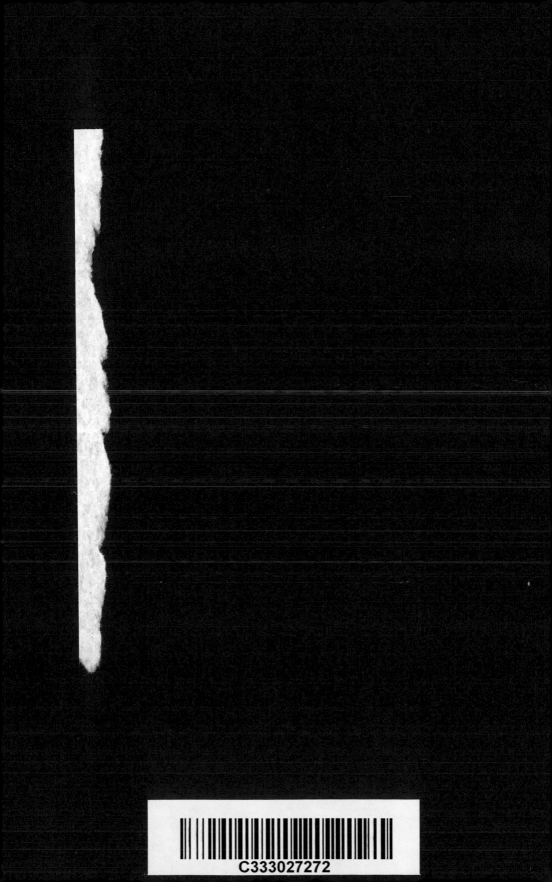

MOLL

Moll

The Life and Times of Moll Flanders

SIÂN REES

Chatto & Windus
LONDON

Published by Chatto & Windus 2011

2 4 6 8 10 9 7 5 3 1

Copyright © 2011 by Siân Rees

Siân Rees has asserted her right under the Copyright, Designs
and Patents Act 1988 to be identified as the author of this work

First published in Great Britain in 2011 by
Chatto & Windus
Random House, 20 Vauxhall Bridge Road,
London SW1V 2SA
www.randomhouse.co.uk

Addresses for companies within The Random House Group Limited can be found at:
www.randomhouse.co.uk/offices.htm

The Random House Group Limited Reg. No. 954009

A CIP catalogue record for this book
is available from the British Library

ISBN 9780701185077

The Random House Group Limited supports The Forest Stewardship Council® (FSC®), the leading
international forest certification organisation. All our titles that are printed on Greenpeace approved
FSC® certified paper carry the FSC® logo. Our paper procurement policy can be found at:
www.randomhouse.co.uk/environment

MIX
Paper from
responsible sources
FSC® C016897

Typeset in Dante MT by Palimpsest Book Production Limited,
Falkirk, Stirlingshire
Printed and bound in Great Britain by
Clays Ltd, St Ives plc

For Felix and Nicolas

Contents

Acknowledgements

I am grateful to my editor, Jenny Uglow, and my agent, Andrew Lownie, for their support and advice. Particular thanks go to Matthew Symonds for allowing me to read his unpublished thesis, 'Grub Street Culture: the newspapers of Nathaniel Mist, 1716–1737', and to Professor Paula Backscheider for replying so promptly to my queries about interpretations of Daniel Defoe's life. As always, the suggestions of my father Tom Rees and friend Tristan Palmer have been invaluable.

List of Illustrations

Introduction:
the life and times of Moll, 1613–83

The Fortunes and Misfortunes of the Famous Moll Flanders, Etc. Who Was Born In Newgate, and During a Life of Continu'd Variety For Threescore Years, Besides Her Childhood, Was Twelve Year a Whore, Five Times a Wife (Whereof Once To Her Own Brother), Twelve Year a Thief, Eight Year a Transported Felon In Virginia, At Last Grew Rich, Liv'd Honest, and Died a Penitent was written by Daniel Defoe and published in 1722. It is one of the most famous English novels. Have you read it? You may think you have, because the book is so often referred to and has been adapted for stage, television and cinema. Kim Novak played the role in the first film adaptation in 1965. That version was called *The Amorous Adventures of Moll Flanders*, advertising its interests up front and displaying its heroine spectacularly décolletée. 'A pat, labored charade of sex by one-dimensional players' was the verdict of Howard Thompson, reviewer for the *New York Times*. Ten years later the BBC cast the British actress Julia Foster in an unremarkable series. It was more similar in tone to Defoe's original (inasmuch as it relied more on character than sex), but as far as plot went departed from the novel as much as the Americans' busty wench.

In April 1993 along came British actress Josie Lawrence in a stage musical version which stayed remarkably true to Defoe's plot. *Independent* critic Paul Taylor described it as mingling 'saucy romp with darker social criticism', which goes some way towards what Defoe was aiming to achieve, although the words 'saucy' and 'romp' were

outside his eighteenth-century lexicon. In 1995 a second British television version starred Alex Kingston as Moll and Daniel Craig as her
lover. This series told the story of a successful and amoral eighteenth-
century prostitute, the 'wickedest woman in Britain', and her excur-
sions into high society and lesbian love. It was gripping and well acted,
and featured the required plunging necklines, but since Defoe's heroine
was neither amoral, eighteenth-century, lesbian nor a prostitute, it too
had little to do with his novel. In 1996 American actress Robin Wright
took her turn, in a version which was billed as 'loosely based on' the
novel but had virtually nothing in common with it. Raised by nuns,
a stint as an artist's model, another in a bordello . . . 'We were sure,'
wrote one acid online reviewer, 'that no Defoe adaptation could
possibly be worse than 1965's *Amorous Adventures* . . . we were wrong.'

The typical costume of an English countrywoman: this is how the young Moll
Flanders would have dressed

   If, therefore, you saw any of these adaptations, you would be
surprised by Defoe's original work. I confess I had turned forty before

I actually read *Moll Flanders*. Until then I had vaguely pictured Moll (as the screen versions suggested) as a woman of wit but little virtue, tumbling curls and bulging breasts, who drifted seductively around eighteenth-century London, working the Covent Garden brothels and picking the pockets of fuddled clients in Soho. When I finally read the book, I realised that I had failed to grasp facts of fundamental importance in Moll's life and character. The first is her date of birth. Although Defoe published the book in 1722, the narrator's final words are 'written in the year 1683', at which date Moll is nearly seventy years old. She is not an eighteenth-century heroine, linked to Gin Lane, William Hogarth, Fanny Hill and the bawdy 1700s. She is born, instead, in 1613 or 1614, which links her to the utterly different ideas and experiences of Puritan England: an overriding concern with morality; civil war, religious dissent, the execution of Charles I, the Protectorate of Oliver Cromwell and the foundation of the American colonies; the restoration of Charles II, *Pilgrim's Progress*, plague and fire.

The second revelation was the number of years she lives in the colonies, or 'His Majesty's plantations' as they were termed at the time. Moll spends as much time in the tobacco fields of America as she does in the London underworld: eight years in Virginia with one husband and nine in Maryland with another. But the third, perhaps greatest, surprise was Moll Flanders' sexual behaviour. Adaptations have unsurprisingly homed in on the easiest versions of 'whorish' behaviour: low-cut dresses, brothel interiors, whips and stockings, heaving breasts and buttocks – all shorthand for historical sex. Fun to watch, for a while at least, but this was not the world of Moll Flanders. When Defoe described his heroine as having been 'twelve year a whore', he did not mean she was a prostitute but simply a woman who had sex outside marriage. She came close to prostitution in the modern sense only during one brief period, in her fifties, and even then it was with one regular client whom she hoped would set her up as his mistress. The rest of her life was devoted to a series of monogamous relationships in which marriage and respectability were always the aim.

If adaptors, commentators and critics have persisted in shifting Moll forward a century, sending her out to walk the streets and ignoring the subtleties of her sexual challenge, it may be because Defoe concentrated exclusively on her personal and domestic circumstances, excising historical context. The principal aim of this book is to restore Moll to that context. She lived at a time when England, Scotland and the American colonies were dominated by Puritanism: the burning quest to live a godly life and erect a godly state by imposing a strict Protestant discipline on all.[1] Against this forbidding background, Defoe's Moll is not a tart with a heart but a real threat to society. For Puritans the only legitimate tool to attain marital or worldly success was godliness, which among other things meant a scrupulous observance of Old Testament strictures on sexual continence. Moll Flanders takes precisely the opposite route: the manipulation of allure, wit, greed, opportunism and sexual desire. Godliness is mocked by her success.

Moll Flanders' story is fascinating enough to have retained a hold on our imaginations in the nearly three centuries since it was written. Equally fascinating, however, are other, lesser-known stories which I explore in this book: that of Daniel Defoe, her creator, and those of the real-life women who inspired him.

Daniel Defoe was born in or around 1660 and died in 1731. Despite his fame – and several scholarly biographies – he remains an obscure figure. By the time he began the series of novels on which his posthumous fame chiefly rests (*Robinson Crusoe*, *Moll Flanders* and *Roxana*) he was in his early sixties and had been many things and many men: husband and father, merchant and bankrupt, soldier and spy, member of a banned religious sect, pamphleteer and writer for hire, convicted criminal and adviser to royalty – and these are just the lives we know about. As Defoe also wrote under a variety of pseudonyms to disguise his various purposes, his biographers have not even been able to draw up a definitive list of his writings, let alone come to any conclusion as to his character. As one recent biographer, Maximilian Novak, says in *Daniel Defoe, Master of Fictions* (2001),

> he has been viewed by some as an amusing scoundrel and by others as a crusading spokesman for a free press and the emerging power of the writer. He has been listed in a dictionary of radical writers and accused of resembling the worst propagandists working for Nazi Germany . . . Both his life and his writings lend themselves to what seems to be limitless interpretation and misinterpretation.

---

1 A Puritan has also been defined as 'a person who pours righteous indignation into the wrong things' (G K Chesterton) and Puritanism as 'the haunting fear that someone, somewhere, may be happy' (H L Mencken).

'Interpretation and misinterpretation' might also describe the vast body of criticism and comment which has grown up around *Moll Flanders* over the centuries, along with the guessing game played over the real identity of its principal characters. Some commentators have suggested that Moll's story was an exercise in 'spiritual biography', a form of literature popular in the seventeenth century which consisted of following a sinner through the tribulations which strewed his or her path to grace. (The most famous spiritual biographies are John Bunyan's *Grace Abounding* and *Pilgrim's Progress*, both written during Moll's lifetime.) Others have seen the book as primarily a political work: a means to condemn capitalism, point up the inequity of the criminal justice system or comment on the political and social status of women. Our own prurient age regards it primarily as an erotic novel.

While *Moll Flanders* contains elements of all these things, I believe any analysis of the novel must start from the fact that its creator was an exceptionally busy man with a large family, financial worries and deadlines. Like any other writer, he had to get down his daily quota of words. For some, it's 500 and for others it's 2,000, written in fits and starts, with shootings-off here and deletions there until a fruitful plot line is reached or an interesting character emerges. Defoe got down some of the day's quota over his first cup of coffee, then he rushed off to St Paul's Churchyard to check on his various newspapers, rushed to another coffee house for another reviving dose and some work on the latest pamphlet, rushed home to see how preparations for his daughter's wedding were coming along and wrote a few more words before falling into bed. In part, at least, *Moll Flanders* was a hastily written money-spinner, constructed around three themes which required little extra research on Defoe's part as he had already written a great deal about them. These were matrimony and how it was managed; the analysis and description of criminal behaviour; and, most of all, the need to colonise and exploit England's plantations in the New World. A dollop of sex and violence was added to leaven the mix, and off it went to press.

Moll's suggested progenitrices are numerous, but my guess is that Defoe had three particular women in mind. The first is thief, brothel keeper and receiver Mary Frith, better known as Moll Cutpurse, who died in 1659 and was the subject of various sensational biographies.

The second is Mary Carleton, a bigamous thief and fraudster also known as Kentish Moll and the German Princess, who was hanged before a London crowd when Defoe was about thirteen. A more obscure woman called Moll King alias Gold alias Gilstone probably provides the most direct inspiration for Moll Flanders' criminal adventures. Mrs King was not only a notorious London pickpocket at the time Defoe was actually writing *Moll Flanders*, but also one of a dozen women transported into penal servitude in the American colonies in January 1722, the month the novel was published.

If clues to the identity of Moll Flanders lie with these three women, the best idea of Defoe's purpose in shaping Moll's story is gleaned from his own introduction. In this he recommends that the reader take away two lessons from Moll's life. The first is a brief plea – a nod to piety after the come-on of the title – to learn how he or she may avoid being robbed or defrauded. The second is a longer manifesto:

> [Moll's] application to a sober life, and industrious management at last in Virginia, with her transported spouse, is a story fruitful of instruction, to all the unfortunate creatures who are oblig'd to seek their re-establishment abroad; whether by the misery of transportation, or other disaster; letting them know, that diligence and application have their due encouragement, even in the remotest part of the world, and that no case can be so low, so despicable, or so empty of prospect, but that an unwearied industry will go a great way to deliver us from it, will in time raise the meanest creature to appear again in the world, and give him a new cast [throw of the dice] for his life.

What follows, then, is the story of Moll's throw of the dice: her life and times, her genesis in the mind of an extraordinary man, and the women who inspired her creation. For the sake of clarity I have used the present tense when talking about Moll's story, and the past tense when explaining the historical context in which she and her creator lived.

Part I

1614–43

I

Moll's mother is sent to Jamestown, Virginia, 1614

In April 1619 an Englishwoman called Elizabeth Handsley appeared at the Old Bailey, London's principal court. She was found guilty of 'stealing divers goods of Mary Payne' and sentenced to be hanged. Shortly after sentence had been pronounced, however, Elizabeth learnt she was to go not to the gallows, but to America: in the Latin of the courts, *po se cull ca null Repr pt. judiciu' pro Virginia.* To an early seventeenth-century Londoner, exile to America can have been a fate only slightly less dreadful than death. There is no record of Elizabeth's reaction. She was put aboard an ocean-going vessel some time that spring and sent to expiate her sins on His Majesty's plantations.

Elizabeth Handsley is the closest we can come to the fictional character who is the mother of Moll Flanders. Daniel Defoe never tells us her name, or much else of her early life; we know only that she was a thief who bore an illegitimate child in prison. She was born an Elizabethan and lived in Shakespeare's London: beams and plaster, church spires, narrow alleys, chamberpots emptied from windows; mudbanks, jetties and boatmen, sheep and chickens, goodwives in white bonnets, a pervading stench of fish, rich men in absurd breeches, plague, recusants and priest's holes, old women with goitres, bear pits and cockfights. This London was not yet a metropolis, despite the influx of immigrants trekking in from the provinces. It was three crowded towns and a palace, with a population of perhaps 200,000 souls. The Borough of Southwark lay south of the River Thames,

Westminster and the City to its north, and the three were connected by a few roads, many fields and a single bridge which sagged beneath the weight of tenements on its sides. Wherrymen touted for custom on the water.

Shipyards were scattered along the river to Redriff (now Rother-hithe),[2] and ships sailed upriver laden with foreign goods. London was 'the mart of the world', proclaimed John Speed's famous atlas of 1611, enticingly called *The Theatre of the Empire of Great Britaine: Presenting An Exact Geography of the Kingdomes of England, Scotland, Ireland, and the Iles adioyning: With The Shires, Hundreds, Cities and Shire-townes, within ye Kingdome of England.* To its docks 'were brought the silk of Asia, the spices from Africa, the balms from Grecia, and the riches of both the Indies East and West'. The arcades of the Royal Exchange were full, for the new activity of 'shopping' was something of a craze. There were warehouses along Poultry and Cheapside, all the way to St Paul's. Anything could be bought and sold in London, even – the common saying went – by those who did not own it. In 1613 or 1614 Moll Flanders' mother steals 'three pieces of fine *Holland* [Dutch linen] . . . of a certain draper in *Cheapside*' and is caught, convicted and sent to Newgate Gaol.

Newgate had been a prison since the twelfth century. Its high unbroken walls on the very edge of the City backed on to the Old Bailey Sessions Yard in a grim synergy of crime and punishment. Moll's mother takes her place here, like Elizabeth Handsley, among the crowd of ill-doers and recusants who came before the judges at 'Sessions of Oyer and Terminer concerning divers treasons misprisions [refusal to acknowledge the monarch as head of the Anglican Church] murder homicides rebellions riots routs and trespasses'.

According to the Calendar of the Middlesex Sessions, a total of 318 people were accused of capital and ninety-three of non-capital offences at the Old Bailey in 1614. There were two categories of offence. Misdemeanours, the less severe, could be punished by fines, the pillory, whipping or imprisonment. Felonies, on the other hand, attracted sentences of exile, execution, branding and forfeiture of possessions. Theft under the value of one shilling was a misdemeanour; murder, manslaughter, rape, burglary and larceny were felonies. Ninety-one more people

2 The name has not disappeared: Redriff Road leads east from Surrey Quays Tube towards the river, and there is a Redriff School in Rotherhithe.

were indicted as recusants (Roman Catholics who refused to attend services of the Anglican Church), a very serious matter when this not only undermined the authority of the King but might call down the vengeance of a Protestant God upon the whole nation.

Newgate Gaol, London

The hearings provide a snapshot of petty crime in London. Non-capital crimes principally threatened public order. First, the various categories of assault: 'with battery', 'with sword' and 'of officers', thereby 'hindering them in the execution of their duty &c'. These accounted for thirty-eight wrongdoers – although only three of them with a sword, the weapon of a gentleman; others presumably used more plebeian weapons like fists and sticks. Eight were accused of 'assembling riotously', one was indicted of 'cheating and cosening' (obtaining something deceitfully) and another of 'extortion by colour of office' (probably some constable or watchman charging protection money). One kept an alehouse without a licence, another was running an illicit bowling alley and eight were accused of keeping brothels. Then there were those whose neglect of property was endangering the public: eight had 'neglected to repair public ways' and one had not repaired 'a ruinous cottage, likely to fall on a public way'. Three constables appeared in the dock for 'permitting vagrants to escape without punishment' (possibly through compassion, probably in return for cash), and ten shopkeepers were hauled up for selling bread by short weight or beer by short measure, along with five brewers caught 'supplying unlicensed keepers of alehouses with ale and beer in excess of their lawful requirements'. There was also one vagabond, three trespassers and two pigeon shooters.

The majority of the 318 wretches who stood accused of capital offences, on the other hand, were thieves, their crimes sometimes aggravated by housebreaking or burglary. Theft of livestock was separately considered: forty-five people were accused of stealing cattle, horses, sheep and pigs. One man was accused of rape and another of sodomy ('an unnatural offence'), eleven of murder and twelve of manslaughter. One hundred and thirty-four of the 318 were convicted, and of these seventy-two men and four women were sentenced to be hanged. One, housebreaker William Backe, 'stood mute' (refused to plead), and was sentenced to the ordeal of *peine forte et dure*. He was to be spreadeagled on the floor of a cell, chained, and have weights of gradually increasing size placed upon him until he spoke or was crushed to death.

The hangings took place on the gallows which stood at Tyburn, a bucolic spot on a road leading west out of London and now the site of Marble Arch. This is where Moll Flanders' mother is bound when she leaves Newgate, for her theft of Dutch linen has been adjudged grand larceny and she has been sentenced to death. Not yet, however. 'My Lord,' she has told the judge, 'I am with quick child.'

No pregnant woman was executed, for in so doing an innocent life would be killed along with a guilty. Most capitally convicted women between the ages of twelve and fifty therefore claimed to be pregnant, and if there were no real foetus in the womb, various strategies were adopted to hoodwink the court. The simplest, reported by 'Captain' Alexander Smith in his *General and True History of the Lives and Actions of the Most Famous Highwaymen* (1714), was 'cramming a Pillow in her Petticoat to make her look big', but there was also 'the old stratagem of drinking new Ale very plentifully, to make her swell', and probably gurgle like a drain. These might have deceived the judge and jury (all men) but a stiffer test had also to be passed: the Panel of Matrons.

A matron was defined in Daniel Defoe's time as a 'prudent and virtuous, motherly woman, also one of the grave women that have the over-sight of children in an Hospital'. Twelve of them had to be found to examine each woman claiming pregnancy. It was thought that the soul only entered the unborn child when it started moving – or became 'quick' – and therefore the job of these twelve women was to lay hands on the claimant's belly and feel for movement. Swollen breasts, a claim that menstruation had stopped or anecdotes of nausea were not enough: the child within had to move. The examination was a notoriously distasteful affair. Until the open Sessions Yard at the Old Bailey was converted into the enclosed Sessions House in 1737, with doors that could be shut, trapping matrons before they fled, the court often had difficulty laying hold of twelve appropriate women to form a panel. In the interests of decency no unmarried woman could be asked to take part, and although Sessions Papers do not record such matters, rounding up twelve protesting mothers and grandmothers must often have brought the court to a halt while ushers went out to shanghai suitable females and summon gaolers' wives from the lodge. In such circumstances, it was possible for a well-connected criminal to pack the panel. If a dozen ladies on the payroll of the accused placed themselves firmly in the usher's view and stepped up, then a verdict favourable to the prisoner was assured.

Moll's mother, however, is not lying when she claims to be with quick child, although she may have lain with one of the Newgate Wags to achieve the state. These were studs, sometimes prisoners and sometimes free men who bribed the gaolers for entrance. They touted

their services round the women's wards, offering (for a fee) to insem-
inate any of childbearing age up on a capital charge. However begotten,
Baby Moll emerges onto the bare boards of a Newgate cell a few
months after her mother's trial, to be suckled, weaned and abandoned.
Her mother, seven months after giving birth and 'being about again,
was call'd down, as they term it, to her former judgment'. The death
warrant is sent to Newgate Gaol, listing the names of all those to
hang, and at dawn the bell of St Sepulchre's Church starts its dreadful
toll. Shoes are banged on floors, there are shouts and screams in the
dim prison corridors, and the condemned emerge to mount their ox-
cart, posies in hand. Cheered by the gathering crowds, they begin their
last journey west. Moll's mother, however, is not among them. She
has escaped death twice: first for her unborn child and then for 'the
favour of being transported to the plantations'.

Moll's mother is not the only one to avoid the noose. Although the
death sentence was passed for crimes which now seem trivial, the
harshness of penal law was tempered by compassion, caprice and acci-
dent. The question of what to do with offenders who were condemned
to hang but did not quite deserve to die was obliquely addressed at
each sessions, and courts had evolved many ways of reducing capital
to non-capital crimes. Compassionate judges would nominally observe
their sentencing obligations and then set about briskly subverting
them. In 1614, for example, the indictments of all but ten of those
accused of grand larceny (a capital offence) were reduced by
connivance of the court to petty larceny (a non-capital offence), saving
them from the noose. It would be pretended that a length of cloth
really worth ten shillings was actually worth less than one, or that a
house had not been broken into, but the householder must have
forgotten to lock the windows. Of the 134 convicted of capital crimes
that year, only seventy-six were sentenced to hang, and of those only
fifty-five actually went to the gallows. Twenty-one were reprieved,
twenty-four were on the loose somewhere in London and the rest
'pled benefit of clergy'.

There were two parallel and separate systems of justice in seventeeth-
century England. Clergymen were answerable not to the courts of the
King but to those of the Church, and judges in the King's courts used
this special status as a way of extending mercy to literate men. Any
accused male criminal who could read was officially regarded as a cleric,

even if judge, jury and everyone else knew he was nothing of the sort. Psalm 51 ('Oh God, have mercy upon me, according to thine heartfelt mercifulness') had become known as the 'neck verse', and while every woman indicted of a capital offence turned to a Newgate Wag, every man committed the first two lines of Psalm 51 to memory. If he could mumble his way through them in court while clutching a Bible, he would be branded with a T for thief on his left thumb and let go – ostensibly to be retried by a Church court, although this rarely happened. During the years in which Elizabeth Handsley and Moll's mother faced the court, however, a new way to save criminals from the noose was emerging. Send them to Virginia.[3]

The end of the sixteenth century – the time of Moll's mother's birth – had seen an explosion of contact with the New World. In 1606 King James I had chartered the Virginia Company to explore and settle American land. This organisation consisted of two elements: the London Company, assigned settlement between the 34th and 41st parallels (approximately Cape Fear and Philadelphia), and the Plymouth Company, allotted land between the 35th and the 48th (Philadelphia to the Canadian border). The reasons for planting these settlements have been well rehearsed, most recently by Benjamin Woolley in *Savage Kingdom* (2007). Principal among them were the desire to find precious metals, such as the Spanish had found in South America, and to discover a route to the east for trade. Various propagandists also cited the necessity of finding raw materials for English manufacturing, new markets for English products and land on which a growing British population could settle.

The overriding political concern in London was that if English settlements were not made, then the Spanish, England's implacable enemies, would move up from Florida and seize the land. Gold, however, was the first goal of the 'adventurers' who put up the money for the scheme. 'Gold is more plentiful there than copper is with us,' claims Captain Seagull in Ben Jonson's *Eastward Ho*, staged in 1605; 'all their dripping pans and their chamber pots are pure gold; and all the chains with which they chain up their streets are massy gold; all the prisoners they take are fettered in gold'.

---

3 Defoe commits a minor historical mistake here: the statute allowing certain capital offenders to be 'reprieved for Virginia' was not passed until 1617. That year, King James I proclaimed that any felon except those convicted of murder, witchcraft, rape or burglary might be sent to Virginia or the West Indies.

A one-armed war hero named Captain Christopher Newport was given command of the three ships which left England in November 1606 and reached America in May 1607. Of the 104 men and boys on Newport's little fleet, some went willingly, others because their masters told them they must, and a few, Benjamin Woolley writes, were procured by an order from the Royal Council authorising Newport to 'round up suitable candidates from taverns and play-houses, or buy them off gangmasters'. They found a fertile country of marsh, streams and unbroken forest. While some dreamed of trekking inland to make their fortune, others set about cutting down the trees and planting the first crops. The rudimentary village of Jamestown began to emerge on a promontory in the newly named James River. After a first attack by the Powhatan, wooden fortifica-tions went up; there was also soon a storehouse, a church and a handful of huts. At first the place seemed delightful. 'Heaven and earth never agreed better,' wrote Captain John Smith, the ebullient if quarrelsome soldier who considered himself the expedition's natural leader. The Virginia Company, enthusiastically promoting the venture in London, advertised free passage aboard its ships, promising 'houses to live in, vegetable gardens and orchards and also food and clothing . . . for men as well as women . . . who wish to go out in their voyage for colonising the country with people'.

Jamestown's first settlers were all male. The first two known females to arrive were Mistress Forrest, who came to join her husband in September 1608, and her teenage maid Anne Burras. Anne was Virginia's first bride, marrying a carpenter three months after her arrival (at the age of fourteen) and doing her bit for the colony's future by swiftly bearing four daughters. Fifty-seven women arrived in autumn 1609, but most of them soon died of disease and malnutrition. What the Jamestown garrison needed to stabilise it, soothe its angry inhab-itants and turn it into a colony was skilled male labour and a supply of wives and mothers. In response to these needs and as a way of finding another alternative to the death penalty, English courts were beginning to fumble their way towards a system of penal trans-portation. By 1618, Sir Thomas Smith, the Virginia Company's treas-urer in London, was doing deals with the courts to send out the mother country's rejects. The first on record as being 'reprieved for Virginia' was tried at the Old Bailey on 3 April that year: Stephen

Rogers, convicted of manslaughter, was 'reprieved after judgment at the instance of Sir Thomas Smith knt. for Virginia because he is of the carpenter's art'. Moll Flanders' mother is another of these: taken from Newgate when her baby is weaned, loaded onto a Company ship with seed, cattle, cloth and dispatches and sent to save Virginia. Elizabeth Handsley went the same way.

They found themselves in a hellhole. Captain Smith's optimistic words had scarcely been uttered before Jamestown was hit by a spate of almost biblical plagues: insects, heat, unhealthy water, disease, dissension and attack. A First and Second Supply were sent out from England in 1608 carrying seed, clothes, livestock, timber, but also more mouths to feed. In 1609 the colony nearly died. The nine ships of the Third Supply, full of the excited but inappropriate colonists who had responded to the Company's advertisements, were caught by a hurricane before they reached the American mainland. Their flagship, *Sea Venture*, was wrecked on Bermuda, and the others limped into Jamestown full of sick and wounded passengers. The next few months became known, in a phrase of utter bleakness, as the 'starving time'. Captain Smith, the only man who seemed able to negotiate with the native inhabitants, was injured and returned to England. Cruelly misled by the men who took command in his absence, the 'lesser sort' starved. The colony's few provisions were reserved for their feckless betters, for Virginia had been settled with the English class system intact.

Captain Smith included the bitter comment of one anonymous settler in his *Generall Historie of Virginia* in 1624.

> Our hogs, hens, goats, sheep, horse or what lived, our commanders, officers and savages daily consumed them. Some small proportions sometimes we tasted, till all was devoured ... by their [the Native Americans'] cruelties, our Governors' indiscretion, and the loss of our ships, of five hundred [settlers] in six months after Captain Smith's departure, there remained not past sixty men, women and children, most miserable and poor creatures. .... so great was our famine, that a savage we slew and buried, the poorer sort took him up again and ate him, and so did diverse one another boiled and stewed with roots and herbs.

When the survivors of the *Sea Venture* managed to build two vessels

from the wreck and sail from Bermuda to Jamestown, they found a
ghost town. It did not seem possible that the colony could continue,
and so old residents and new arrivals packed themselves on to two
ships and sailed for England. They had sailed only ten miles downriver when they met the advance party of the next relief convoy,
bringing supplies and yet more colonists. When that convoy's
commander, Lord de la Warr, ordered them to return, resentment
and bitterness were added to the hunger and disease which already
poisoned the settlement. De la Warr returned to England, taking with
him the story of shipwreck and island adventure which some critics
believe inspired Shakespeare to write *The Tempest*.

By the time Moll Flanders' mother arrives in 1614 or 1615 conditions
are, if anything, worse. Protestant notions of sin and divine vengeance
crossed the Atlantic with the first settlers, and the desperate state of
Jamestown after the starving time was adjudged, at least in part, to
be a consequence of its inhabitants' depravity and indiscipline.
Governor Gates and Deputy Governor Dale, two hard men, were sent
to take charge, and ruled the colony according to a new code called
the Laws Divine, Moral and Martial. It was ferocious, far outdoing
English law: sodomy, adultery, fornication, sacrilege, theft, slander and
desertion were all punishable by death. So were being noisy 'where
silence, secrecy and covert is required' and slaughtering livestock
without permission. Should a man doing guard duty 'swagger', he
must beg pardon on his knees of every officer on duty at the time for
a first offence, and spend a year as a galley slave for his second.

'If today three hundred men should come,' wrote a Spaniard who
had drifted in a couple of years before – wrecked, he said, although
everyone knew he was a spy – 'this same year would destroy more
than one hundred and fifty, and there is not a year when half do not
die. Last year there were seven hundred people and not three hundred
and fifty remain, because little food and much labor on public works
kills them and, more than all, the discontent in which they live seeing
themselves treated as slaves with cruelty.'

Women were not exempt from this 'cruelty', as Mistress Isabell
Perry recalled in 1625. Governor Dale had ordered a group of women,
Mistress Perry among them, to sew shirts for the colony and had given
them a certain amount of thread to do so. Mary Beth Norton quotes
her in *Founding Mothers and Fathers* (1996) as stating that 'yf they did

not performe [their task], They had no allowanc of Dyett [food]'. When the thread ran out, two of the women, Ann Leyden and Jane Wright, made shorter shirts than Sir Thomas approved, and 'were whipt', said Mistress Perry, 'And Ann leyden being then with childe [the same night miscarried]'.

Beatings, dysentery, malaria, 'agues and distempers', attack by natives, not to speak of the dangers of childbirth, which would almost certainly follow a woman's 'dominion' by whatever settler acquired her – these were life's realities for the first Virginians, and the English government which sent out Moll's mother and Elizabeth Handsley was well aware of the risks run by the pioneers it sent to establish New World settlements. Two earlier attempts to settle an American colony – one at Roanoke and the other at Sagahadoc (Maine) – had, after all, both swiftly failed. And even if Jamestown itself survived, most settlers would not.

Moll Flanders' mother and Elizabeth Handsley disembarked to a hostile reception. Necessary as these 'fallen women' might be, bringing the possibilities of breeding, domesticity and sexual release, many in Jamestown did not want them. Among the already forsaken and degraded colonists, the women brought from London's gaols were considered the lowest of the low, and greeted with godly contempt. They were 'corrupt', said one critic, and brought contamination into the infant village. They were, reported Robert Beverley's *History of Virginia*, in 1722, 'of soe bad choyse as made the Colony afraide to desire any others'. This, then, is Moll's mother's new home, and these are her new comrades, one of whom will soon acquire her as wife or servant. She will probably not survive long.

2

Moll emerges into provincial England,
1614–35

When Moll's mother is taken away to Virginia, Moll is left in London, a nameless gaol baby 'about half a year old' and in the most unpromising circumstances. 'My true name,' she writes at the end of her life, 'is so well known in the records, or registers at *Newgate*, and in the *Old-Baily*, and there are some things of such consequence still depending there, relating to my particular conduct, that it is not to be expected I should set my name or the account of my family to this work.' We never know her name at birth, therefore; the only thing we can be sure of is that she is called neither Moll nor Flanders. (I, for ease of reference, will nonetheless refer to her as Moll throughout her life.)

Between a third and a half of all seventeenth-century children died before their fifth birthdays; a gaol baby had to be born tough merely to survive infancy. Some abandoned infants were claimed and adopted by relatives. Others might be 'put out to nurse' by families which did not want to take the child into their home but were willing to bear the expense of fostering. In London the Royal Hospitals took in some of the rest until such age as they were deemed able to support themselves. One can imagine other writers rubbing their hands over the possibilities offered by such a childhood but Daniel Defoe, hurrying his heroine to a point when more adult adventures might start, was not interested. Had he wished, he might have brought Moll to Virginia very soon after her mother, for when his heroine was four or five years old, the first gangs of 'kidnappers' (literally child stealers) were sent onto the streets of London to round up children for the new colony.

Sir Thomas Smith, treasurer of the Virginia Company, was a tireless evangelist of American opportunity but found his colonising work impeded by stories of misfortune and cruelty leaking back across the Atlantic. Too few people were crossing voluntarily to America for the new plantations to thrive, and those who survived the sea voyage then had to get through the dreaded 'seasoning': the first bout of malaria which, added to the scurvy which killed in wintertime, the typhus brought across the sea by lice, attacks by the Powhatan and regular outbreaks of smallpox, made for a short life expectancy. The colony needed a larger supply of labourers, and preferably one which was healthier, more malleable and uncontaminated by immorality. Children were perfect, and there was a perfect plague of them in the poorer parts of English cities. Sir Thomas talked with the City of London aldermen,[4] who were seeking some solution to the infestation on their streets, and they hatched a plan of mutual advantage. The City would pay five pounds per child shipped to Virginia as an 'apprentice'. It was a plan, said its promoters, devised to benefit the poor creatures involved while doing incidental good to the plantations. In the summer of 1618 City constables went out to 'apprehend all such vagrant children, both boys and girls, as they shall find in the streets and in the markets or wandering in the night'. In February of the following year, ninety-seven of those apprehended were picked out by a Company official and dispatched on three ships to Virginia.

Their arrival, unlike that of Moll's mother, was apparently welcomed, for later that year the Company prayed His Lordship the Mayor of London 'in pursuit of your former so pious actions to renew your like favours and furnish us again with one hundred more for the next spring'. Hundreds of poor children would disappear in this manner during the 1620s, sold into colonial slavery with the approval of both City and Privy Council.

The Virginia Company asked its administrators to conduct a census

---

4 The post of alderman was founded in the Middle Ages and still exists. Aldermen are senior officials in the City of London, serving as Justices of the Peace, governors and trustees of schools, hospitals, charitable foundations, etc.

in 1623, listing the names of those alive and those who had died since April the previous year. On the 'List of the Livinge and the Dead' sent to London on 16 February, the 'Dead since April last' accounted for more than 20 per cent of the colonial population. Elizabeth Handsley did not figure on the list at all. Either she had died before April 1622, or she was married. Don Jordan and Michael Walsh, authors of *White Cargo: The Forgotten History of Britain's White Slaves in America* (2007), have calculated from musters that of the 300 children shipped between 1619 and 1622 only twelve were alive in 1624. One of them, Elizabeth Abbott, was an indentured servant. She had survived longer than most who worked in the tobacco fields. In October 1624, however, her master beat her to death for staying away from her work in the fields without leave.

Little Moll is taken up instead by a different pack of kidnappers, one which drifts in sinister fashion across the pages of various seventeenth and eighteenth-century romances, snatching small children as they go. 'The first account that I can recollect,' she writes, 'or ever could learn of myself, was, that I had wandr'd among a crew of those people they call *gypsies*, or *Egyptians*; but I believe it was but a very little while that I had been among them, for I had not had my skin discolour'd or blacken'd, as they do very young to all the children they carry about with them.' Defoe drops another tantalising narrative prospect, however: instead of introducing her to witchcraft, communion with the Devil, theft and all the other sins of which Gypsies were regularly accused, Moll's kidnappers simply leave her in Colchester when she is three years old.

Colchester, in the north-east corner of the county of Essex, was then a pretty and thriving market town, a prosperous little place whose wealth derived from cloth. Defoe knew the town well. In 1722, the year of *Moll Flanders'* publication, he optimistically rented a large estate there, one of the many impetuous and bad business decisions which obliged him to keep writing. Here, the abandoned child is taken before the magistrates, whose task it is to determine who is obliged to support her. Enquiries are made for the Gypsies, but they have disappeared; and she is 'not a parish charge upon this, or that part of the town by law (being born elsewhere)'. The infant has fallen between the cracks in the Poor Laws.

The Poor Laws were early attempts to alleviate poverty through

L'ENTRÉE DE LA REYNE DANS LA VILLE DE COLCHESTER

Colchester in 1637, when Queen Henrietta Maria visited the town

state intervention, passed at a time of alarm that the population was not only visibly increasing but also becoming poorer. This poverty was a result of a series of bad harvests and the new phenomenon of inflation, which sixteenth-century economists struggled both to explain and to control. The first Poor Law was passed in 1547, devolving care for the poor upon the newly created Anglican parishes, and a series of later sixteenth-century statutes refined and extended the system.

(Punishment is another way of looking at it. Under the 1547 act, beggars and vagrants were to be put in the stocks and then enslaved for two years. A law of 1572 enacted that, for a third offence, they should be executed.) The measure which most directly affected Moll Flanders was the 1601 Elizabethan Poor Law, although Daniel Defoe – who was not terribly concerned with historical accuracy – was probably thinking of the 1662 Poor Relief Act, which introduced the concept of 'settlement' in a parish as a necessary qualification for receipt of poor relief.

Poor relief was the fund established to provide food, clothes, shelter and sometimes training or apprenticeship for paupers. It was collected from richer inhabitants in each parish and administered by the Overseers of the Poor, a group of men chosen from local ratepayers. These men made a careful distinction between those made destitute by their own fecklessness on the one hand and the 'poore by impotency, defect or casualtie' on the other, the latter being deemed to have fallen into destitution through no fault of their own. One unintended consequence of Poor Law legislation was that it led some impoverished folk to leave their own parishes and seek relief in a richer or more generous one. Overseers swiftly grew wise to this, and took care to reserve money for their own poor, and support no one else's.

Little Moll, born within the walls of Newgate, belongs to no parish. Strictly speaking, no one, anywhere, is under any obligation to provide for her. It is not the recent institution of the Poor Laws which comes to her rescue, but the ancient one of charity. 'As my case came to be known,' she recalls, 'and that I was too young to do any work, being not above three years old, compassion mov'd the magistrates of the town to order some care to be taken of me, and I became one of their own, as much as if I had been born in the place.' Thus adopted, she has some of the security of a parishioner for the first time in her life. Security, however, goes hand in hand with restrictions. Moll has left the freedom of Gypsy wanderings for a place inside the social edifice, and gender, class and illegitimacy all destine her for its lowest storey. Above her rises a vertiginous, crushing tower of others, all entitled to tell her what to do.

Early seventeenth-century Colchester had a population of about 11,000 – enough for it to be regarded as a sizeable town – of whom perhaps 1,500 were Dutch, mainly from Flanders. These immigrants were textile workers, and their presence had invigorated the town and shaped Colchester's particular brand of parochial compassion. Tiny children were fostered by townsfolk who received a fee from the parish for doing so. From the age of seven or eight, however, children were expected either to go into domestic service or learn some skill by which they could start earning their own bread. In East Anglia those skills tended to be within the textile trade: spinning, carding, combing, flax- or hemp-beating. One Norfolk parish ordered that 'poore children' be 'put to schoole to knitting and spinning dames'. In another, children of poor labourers were ordered to 'be taught to knit and spin by some honest women in the Towne that are fit to teach them'. In Sparkenhoe, Leicestershire magistrates bought in 'hemp flaxe & wool for the setting of work of such as are not able to sett themselves to worke and for the ymployinge of little children not yet able to be putt to apprentizes or to service'. This is Moll's fate: she is put out to nurse with a 'dame' who 'got a little livelihood by taking such as I was suppos'd to be; and keeping them with all necessaries, till they were at a certain age, in which it might be suppos'd they might go to service, or get their own bread'.

Moll is a good and amenable little girl. By the age of eight she has acquired sufficient expertise in domestic crafts to be placed as maid in a local family and taken off parish expenses. When news comes from the magistrates that this is to happen, however, Moll is terrified. Domestic service, she recalls in old age, is an idea to which she always had 'a thorough aversion'. Fortunately she has learnt to spin and sew so well that after some pleading her dame allows her to stay on and pay her way by taking in piecework, the staple of female employment in towns such as Colchester. So she continues until the age of about thirteen, when the old lady dies. At this point Moll is homeless and can no longer support herself. However, being a pretty little thing and already well known to Colchester's 'middling sort' for her dainty ways and the neatness of her seams, she is taken in by a family which treats her as something between a companion to the daughters and an upper servant. She has experienced gaol, Gypsy camp and dame school; now, for the first time, Moll becomes part of a family.

In the seventeenth century the words 'family' and 'household' were interchangeable. They meant not the small nuclear unit of modern times, but all those living together under one roof or set of inter-dependent roofs: husband, wife and children, but also apprentices, servants and journeymen, poor relations and other dependants. Moll's Colchester family consists of a father (scarcely mentioned), a mother, three daughters, two sons and an unspecified number of indoor and outdoor servants. One of Colchester's more prosperous clans, the household probably belonged to the emerging merchant class, which lived well, played an important part in local and sometimes national administration, but kept itself distinct from gentry and aristocracy.

The name given to Moll in her new life is Mrs Betty (Betty, in Defoe's time, being a generic name for a chambermaid, in particular a wanton one). Her duties are not onerous. She has succeeded in escaping the miserable life of skivvy – single servant to a small household – which would probably have been her lot had she left her dame as a child. Instead, she is made rather a pet by the young ladies, attending their lessons and learning some of their accomplishments: French, a little music and writing. She also grows into a notably handsome girl, a fine singer and a fair dancer. 'Thus far,' as Moll writes, 'I have had a smooth story to tell of myself, and in all this part of my life I not only had the reputation of living in a very good family . . . but I had the character too of a very sober, modest, and vertuous young woman.'

This pretty picture changes, however, when the elder of the family's two sons, 'young gentlemen of very promising parts', begins to cast covetous glances in her direction. Although the younger son will turn out to be the better man, the older one, a 'gay gentleman that knew the town as well as the country', is far more attractive. He is also practised in seduction, and

> had too much judgment of things to pay too dear for his pleasures; he began with that unhappy snare to all women, viz. taking notice upon all occasions how pretty I was, as he called it, how agreeable, how well-carriaged and the like; and this he contrived so subtly, as if he had known as well how to catch a woman in his net as a partridge when he went a-setting; for he would contrive to be talking this to his sisters when tho' I was not by, yet when he knew I was not so far off but that I should be sure to hear him.

Despite the family's relative wealth, their Colchester house would have been a crowded place. Moll would have shared a bed either with one of the sisters or with upper maidservants, for young women did not sleep alone. Privacy was not a requirement of living; indeed, it was considered indecent to allow young ladies in particular to conduct a private life hidden from their parents. Family life therefore allows few opportunities for the young man to be alone with Moll.

A steady 20 per cent rate of bridal pregnancy throughout the sixteenth and early-seventeenth century attests that considerable sexual licence was allowed in those cases where it was presumed that a young couple would marry and both sets of parents were happy with that prospect. Anne Hathaway, for example, who became Mrs William Shakespeare in 1582, gave birth to her first child five months after the marriage. Lawrence Stone, influential chronicler of family life in the seventeenth century, has uncovered a mass of evidence to show that parents of courting couples routinely allowed, even made space and time for, 'bundling'. This could be kissing and cuddling – the practice now unattractively known as heavy petting – but could also be full sexual intercourse. But Moll, however pretty and accomplished, is an illegitimate maidservant and certainly not marriage material for the young master. His family will not countenance bundling, and there is nowhere it can be enjoyed in secrecy. They cannot go below stairs, for there will be cook and pot boy; they cannot linger on landings or outside closets, for they will be seen by inquisitive maidservants; they cannot sneak into the parlour, for there will be one sister practising the virginals and another stitching at her tapestry; they cannot even find a quiet space in the little garden, for there will be cook again, gathering her vegetables; or in the yard, for that is home to the stable boy and the groom; or any little outside alley, lest they are seen by the neighbours or the neighbours' servants. The young man's seduction must therefore begin in brief and stolen moments. 'I scarce ever look'd towards him in publick, or answer'd if he spoke to me, if any body was near us, but for all that, we had every now and then a little encounter, where we had room for a word or two, and now then a kiss; but no fair opportunity for the mischief intended.'

One evening, however, when Moll and two of the sisters are sitting in the garden, he slips a note into her hand, explaining a plan to get her alone on the morrow. He will request she run an errand for him

to the other side of town; he will follow her and they will tryst in the
house of a friend. It all goes as planned, and once they are alone
together

> he began to talk very gravely to me; and to tell me, he did not bring
> me there to betray me, that his passion for me, would not suffer him
> to abuse me; that he resolv'd to marry me as soon as he came to his
> estate, that in the mean time, if *I* would grant his request, he would
> maintain me very honourably, and made me a thousand protestations
> of his sincerity, and of his affection to me; and that he would never
> abandon me.

His 'request', naturally, is that she will sleep with him, and his promise
is that she and any child will be looked after if she is so unfortunate
as to become pregnant. His suit is backed up by a bag containing a
hundred guineas. Despite the money, Moll always maintains that she
began the affair for love of the young man. However, the wage of an
average chambermaid was about two pounds a year so the money he
dangles in her face represents a fortune. Poor Moll: only seventeen or
so, she does not yet know that promises made by sexually frustrated
young men to their maidservants are not to be believed. She acqui-
esces. Pregnancy may be averted if the young man is careful and
knowledgeable, but there is also the risk to her reputation if rumours
of their involvement get out. Not only will she be dismissed from her
family, making it almost impossible to get work locally, but she may
even be hauled up before a Church court.

    Church courts had jurisdiction over matters of sexual morality:
fornication, illegitimacy, adultery and the general mass of sexual behaviour known at the time as incontinence, a catch-all category into which
Moll's teenage love affair falls. We can catch glimpses of Moll's seducer
in young men called before the Church courts of Essex in the 1620s.
A butcher called John Nash, for example, quoted by Geoffrey May in
'Experiments in the Legal Control of Sex Expression' (1929), appeared
in 1621, charged with 'incontynencie with sundrey persons . . . in particular he doth nowe harbour in his howse one Elizabeth Sweetinge [his
very own Mrs Betty] and doth keepe her as his common strumpet for
the space of these two or three months last past'. Nash, the court
noted, had 'formerly bene presented for other offenses and because

this court hath dealt favorably with him, and forgiven him the fees, therefore he doth but laughe and deride at your courte, and swears you shall never get a penny of him, doe what you can'.

The penances ordered by Church courts could usually be converted into payment of a 'fee', or fine: in some cases help mending the church roof, in others a contribution to local charity and occasionally a straight-forward bribe. John Nash clearly made a decent living from his trade and had enough money to pay a fine. Furthermore, as a marriageable young man, he did not suffer the loss of sexual credit which would afflict a female similarly accused. He might well laugh at the court. Moll, on the other hand, is a young woman with no family, money or trade. She would suffer worse. Historian G R Quaife conducted a survey of the penalties handed out in the diocese of Durham during this period and found that the smallest fine for incontinence, imposed on Marie Darnell, a 'housekeeper', was twenty pounds plus eight pounds costs, and on top of this Marie had to make public confession of her sins on four occasions. Even this was lenient; Mistress Darnell might have been given a public whipping. Moll, humiliated and dismissed, would have become one of the outcast provincials heading for London and doing whatever they could to survive in its swelling anonymity.

On the other hand, Moll may have missed a trick here. Church courts investigating goings-on between a young unmarried couple frequently ordered them to marry, for this, under Old Testament rules, was the only moral solution to incontinence. If the couple married, accusations of lewd behaviour would be immediately dismissed. Moll, however, may be unaware of this, or perhaps the planning and cunning necessary to get news of the affair out without her being identified as its source, followed by all the manoeuvres and negotiations with court, family, employers and lover himself to get him into church are beyond her resources. And as no nosy neighbour goes running to the churchwardens with news that the young master is tumbling Mrs Betty, the opportunity passes, and so does the chance of Moll Flanders becoming a stout contented merchant's wife, settling into a peaceful provincial life, attending church, quarrelling fondly with her husband, producing a brood of sons and daughters and becoming a pillar of the community.

Instead, the affair continues in secret for over a year. A spoke is

finally thrust into its wheel not by Church spies but by the family's
younger son, Robin, when he also falls in love with Mrs Betty. Robin's
love is of a more respectable character. He really does want to marry
Moll, whereas his elder brother had spoken of marriage only to get
the maid into bed. When Robin's sincerity becomes obvious to
everyone and even his mother's reservations over her son's marrying
a servant are overcome, Moll turns to her lover to ask his help and
advice. No one, she says, will believe I am in earnest when I say I do
not want to marry Robin, and I cannot tell them it is because of you.
What shall I do? The perfidious elder brother gently releases himself
from his promises, counselling his cast-off mistress to marry the other
brother and make the best of it. Now he knows of Robin's feelings
for her, he says, their own love affair is at an end and can never be
resumed.

This untrustworthy young man is Moll's first love, and she suffers
greatly from his rejection. For a time she refuses to let him go,
reminding him again and again of his promises.

> The bare loss of him as a gallant was not so much my affliction as the
> loss of his person, whom indeed I loved to distraction; and the loss of
> all the expectations I had, and which I always had built my hopes upon,
> of having him one day for my husband, these things oppressed my
> mind so much that, in short, I fell very ill; the agonies of my mind, in
> a word, threw me into a high feaver, and long it was, that none in the
> family expected my life.

He will not relent, however, spying his way out of an imbroglio which
is becoming tiresome. Secretly visiting her in her weakened feverish
state, he presses his case. First he assures her that 'what has happened
between us . . . may be buried and forgotten', and offers her 'five
hundred pounds in money, to make you some amends for the free-
doms I have taken with you'. Next he paints a frightening picture of
what might befall her if their secret gets out. 'Being turned out to the
wide world a meer cast-off whore', which is, of course, in his power
to cause, 'terrified me to the last degree, and he took care upon all
occasions to lay it home to me in the worst colours that it could be
possible to be drawn in.' When he offers an extra £300 if she will
become his brother's wife – the payment, naturally, to remain their

secret – she consents, though bitterly, to the new arrangement. And so, as Moll herself puts it, her lover 'shifted off his whore into his brother's arms for a wife', and the marriage with Robin is duly celebrated.

When Daniel Defoe wrote his own treatise on marital harmony in 1715, *The Family Instructor*, he made clear his belief that unions such as Moll's with Robin were only slightly less sinful than fornication: 'He or She,' he wrote, 'who, with that slight and superficial Affection, Ventures into the Matrimonial Vow, are to me little more than legal Prostitutes.' Moll may now be legally married, but she has only stepped from one ungodly union into another. Robin was, as she said,

a tender, kind, good humour'd man as any woman could desire; but his brother being so always in my sight . . . was a continual snare to me; and I never was in bed with my husband, but I wish'd my self in the arms of his brother . . . in short, I committed adultery and incest with him every day in my desires, which without doubt, was as effectually criminal in the nature of the guilt, as if I had actually done it.

3

Moll is a widow and a wife again, 1635–7

Early-modern England abounded with treatises or 'conduct books' (mainly written by men) on the management of the household. The period after the Reformation was particularly rich in these, perhaps because the huge and bewildering changes in demography, religious observance and political allegiance produced a yearning for order and hierarchy. One of the best known at the time of Moll's childhood was *A Godlie Forme of Household Government*, written in around 1598 by the Puritan divines John Dod and Robert Cleaver. This laid out very clearly the hierarchy and duties of a family ordered as God wished (or at least as the Reverends Dod and Cleaver interpreted his wishes). If every household conformed to the divine plan, Dod and Cleaver taught, not only would the morality and stability of the family be ensured, but so would that of the nation.

The proper structure of a household was most commonly illustrated by comparing it with that of the state. The husband/father was the ruler, both temporal and spiritual, and his authority was absolute, for he stood in relation to the rest of the household as God did to the Church. Indeed, he was God's representative within the walls of his own house, however mean or grand a dwelling that might be. The rest of the family was made up of 'those that must be ruled', and each of these lower orders was to be governed differently: 'there is one rule to governe the wife by, another for children, another for servants. One rule for young ones, another for olde folks.'

Moll, born outside wedlock and outside the parish, now also finds herself outside the norms of the godly family: despite her newly married status, she is still sidling along on her own lonely path. The conduct books worried a great deal about the subversion of the father/husband's authority by over-educated wives, ambitious sons, disobedient daughters and servants who did not understand their place in God's scheme. The influence of servants on more susceptible members of the household was, they thought, particularly pernicious. Given that children in wealthy families often had more contact with servants than with their own parents, *A Godlie Forme of Household Government* warned that they could be taught to 'sweare, blaspheme, and use all manner of uncleane speeches' and even be 'allure[d] to stage plaies, to dice houses, and other like places, which are the very bane of youth'. Too late for Robin; he has married the maid, unaware she has already been polluted by his own brother.

The writers of family handbooks also dwelt at length on the relationship between husband and wife, for harmony or the lack of it between these two set the tone for relations among all other family members. Dod and Cleaver made it clear to the husband that although the law allowed him a free hand over his wife and her property, it was in his interests to use her gently. 'The husband that is not beloved of his wife', continues the book, 'holdeth his goods in danger, his house in suspision, his credite in ballance, and also sometimes his life in perill: because it is [reasonable] to believe that she desireth not long life unto her husband, with whom she passeth a time so tedious and irksome.'

Here too poor Robin has no chance. This passage could have been written for Moll, sighing with boredom in her Colchester parlour, yearning for the lover she has lost and struggling dutifully to love and obey the one she has accepted. Robin, fortunately for him, does not survive long enough to see John Dod's full list of calamities brought upon his house, but dies of unspecified causes in the mid-1630s. He leaves Moll a widow about twenty-three years of age, with two small children who are 'taken happily off my hands, by my husband's father and mother'. This leaves her free to begin casting about for a little fun and a second husband. She is fortunate in that she has saved over a thousand pounds from the elder brother's gifts and bribes, for without this her marital prospects would be very limited. Even with this large dowry, she knows she cannot look above the rank of tradesman, for her birth will always count against her. She is determined, however, to have a mate with some refinement: no dirty fingers or soiled aprons for her.

> I was not averse to a tradesman, but then I would have a tradesman forsooth, that was something of a gentleman too; that when my husband had a mind to carry me to the court, or to the play, he might become a sword [wear a sword becomingly], and look as like a gentleman, as another man; and not be one that had the mark of his apron-strings upon his coat, or the mark of his hat upon his periwig.

At length she finds such a man, a handsome shopkeeper with premises in London, and her second marriage begins pleasantly. It too is brief. A child is born but swiftly dies, its short life passed over in one sentence, and Moll realises she has been unwise in her second choice of mate. The couple moves to London, but spends little time minding the shop and more bouncing about the country in expensively hired coaches, pretending to be aristocrats. 'What I got by that,' she writes,

> was, that I had the pleasure of seeing a great deal of my money spent upon my self, and as I may say, had some of the spending it too.
>   Come, my dear, *says he to me one day*, shall we go and take a turn into the country for about a week? Ay, my dear, *says I*, whither would you go? I care not whither, *says he*, but I have a mind to look like quality for a week; we'll go to OXFORD *says he*: How *says I*, shall we go, I am no horse woman, and 'tis too far for a coach; Too far, *says he*, no place is too far for a coach and six: if I carry you out, you shall travel like a dutchess; Hum *says I*, my dear 'tis a frolick, but if you have a mind to it I don't care.

The money is soon spent.

Just as Moll, by acquiring the security of a parishioner, lost the freedom of her Gypsy sisters, she has now, by reacquiring the status of a married woman, lost the freedom of the widow. A *feme seule*, a single woman, was permitted to own property, write a will and make contracts in her own right, but all property rights of the *feme covert*, or married woman, were subsumed in those of the husband. Married women lost rights even over the property they had brought to the marriage: all their goods, even their persons, belonged to the man who acquired them at the altar. According to law, therefore, Moll, once more a *feme covert*, can do nothing to stop her husband spending her money. And according to the advice of the conduct books, she cannot even reprimand or advise him, but must submissively bear with his mistakes and keep smiling as he ruins them both. A wife, lectures John Dod, must be not only obedient, but 'cheerfully and willingly' obedient, 'proceeding from an holy fear and reverence' of her husband, who is to her 'in God's stead'.

Moll, however, holds her feckless second husband in no more divine awe than she held the dullard who was her first. 'I had foreseen *sometime*,' she recalls, 'that all was going to wreck.' The only thing she can do is secrete funds or property somewhere out of her husband's reach and knowledge, and thus manage 'to reserve something . . . *tho' it was not much* for myself'. In just over two years their joint coffers are emptied and her husband is arrested for debt. 'He got,' Moll writes, 'into a *spunging-house*, being arrested in an action too heavy for him to give bail to.' One or other of his creditors laid a complaint before the sheriff; the sheriff sent a bailiff to arrest him, and that officer took him to his own home until he paid off the debts. This was the 'spunging-house', and there were dozens of them in London, noticeable by the iron bars across the windows, the thugs guarding the doors, the weeping families outside and the emanating smell of too many bodies in too small a space. If his debts are not paid and bail is not granted, Moll's husband will be removed from here to one of the dreaded debtors' prisons. There he will languish (and possibly die), until his debts are redeemed by someone on the outside, for he himself will not be allowed out to work them off.

Moll comes to find him at the bailiff's house. He apologises to her for his thoughtlessness, castigates himself for letting himself be arrested, and tells Moll to save what she can from the wreck of their life together and forget him. She should, he says, 'go home, and in the night take away everything I had in my house of value, and secure it; and after that, he told me that if I could get away 100 *l*. or 200 *l*. in goods out of the shop, I should do it; only *says he*, let me know nothing of it, neither what you take nor whither you carry it'. It is the last time she ever sees him. A couple of days later she hears he has broken out of the bailiff's house and escaped to France.

It is at this point that Moll's 'adventures and misadventures' really begin. She has already been a whore inasmuch as she has had sexual relations outside marriage, but has managed to keep that secret and not become pregnant by her first lover. As a wife, then widow, then wife once more, she is no worse off than she would have been had she not been swayed at the age of seventeen by a pretty face and a bag of guineas. But now, in the mid-1630s, she finds herself, as she says, 'a widow bewitched; I had a husband and no husband, and I could not pretend to marry again, though I knew well enough my husband would never see *England* any more, if he lived fifty years: *thus I say*, I was limitted from marriage, what offer soever might be made me.'

It is the worst position a woman can find herself in, and it is this misfortune, rather than any moral deficiency, which sets Moll off onto the path of fraud, identity change and serial bigamy which will characterise the rest of her life.

With her usual resourcefulness, however, as soon as she hears her husband has disappeared she sets about 'casting things up' to see what she has and how long it can be expected to support her. Now her money is spent, her wealth takes the form of saleable or pawnable possessions: items she must carry from place to place and rented room to rented room, constantly guarded against theft by some fellow lodger, visiting 'friend' or opportunistic burglar. They are lengths of cloth from the shop, tableware, a little cash, some jewellery. A letter from her vanished husband 'let me know where he had pawn'd 20 pieces of fine *Holland* for 30l. which were really worth above 90l., and enclosed me the token, and an order for the taking them up'. Adding to these 'a parcel of fine muslins, and some plate, and other things', she reckons she has goods worth a total of £500. This is a good sum – although less than half what she had a year ago – but she knows she may never again be able to count upon the earnings of a husband, and legitimate employment for females brings in very little money. Needlework, millinery, domestic service – these are the sorts of tasks Moll might take up, as she did in her childhood, but they will not support her in the manner to which she has become accustomed. Nor is she secure even in the possession of her bits of cloth and tableware, for if the bailiffs find out who and where she is, they will take them away to pay her husband's debts. Briskly, she does what she must. She packs her belongings, gathers her courage and crosses London Bridge.

Crossing the bridge is not a step taken lightly, for it means leaving behind the relative safety of the City and entering the Borough of Southwark. The Borough had an appalling reputation: 'better termed a foule dene then a faire garden', complained Puritan Donald Lupton in *London and the Country Carbonadoed and Quartred* (1632); 'here come few that either regard their credit or loss of time'. This was the home of the poor, the vagrant, the fallen, the foreign and the fugitive from justice. Adventuring blades from the City and Westminster crossed to Southwark to find their dirtier fun: cards, women, brawls, bear baiting, cock fights and cheap liquor, plays at the Globe, 'dicying houses, bowling allies and brothel howses'. Breweries, tanneries and dye works kept the air foul, and the narrow streets were full of rowdy apprentices and beggars. Living alone in such a place is a frightening prospect for a young woman like Moll, but she has little choice. Within the heaving dissolute Borough are two areas which have become a vital part of London's criminal architecture: the Liberty of the Mint and its depraved neighbour, the Clink Liberty. These enclaves are areas of judicial and administrative anomaly, where debtors and other criminals can live unmolested if – unlike Moll's unfortunate husband – they can get there before their creditors lay hold of them.

When Southwark bought 'titles of independence' from the Crown in 1550 and became a borough, the titles excluded four areas: the Mint, the Clink, Suffolk Place and Paris Garden. Before the Reformation the Church of Rome had governed these places, but they had since become effectively lawless and therefore refuges for anyone evading justice. Each of the four areas attracted its particular brand of criminal or degenerate. Paris Garden had lately been notorious as the home of London's most famous brothel, Holland's Leaguer, run by the extraordinary Bess Holland. This was housed in the Garden's old manor house, which still had its moat, drawbridge and portcullis. These had been brought back into use a few years before Moll fled south when the brothel was besieged by a troop of the King's soldiers sent to close it down. Mrs Holland had defied them all, sending her girls to empty their chamberpots onto the men's heads as they crossed the moat. The area to which Moll flees acquired its name when King Henry VIII established a royal mint in Southwark in about 1543. That had long since ceased to operate, and by the time Moll takes up residence there it specialised not in making money but in sheltering debtors.

The Mint was not a picturesque part of olde worlde London, but an area of disease and squalor housing a dangerous criminal subculture with its own laws, rituals and customs. South of the prison known as the Clink and opposite St George's Church, small heavily guarded gates led into a tight-packed ghetto of dirty lanes and tenements. It was built on marshy land, below the level of the river, and every species of waterborne filth seeped into the northernmost streets. Its only recommendation as a place to live was the safety from pursuit it offered its inhabitants. Creditors who managed to enter by force or subterfuge would, if discovered, find themselves at best insulted and at worst beaten up. Bailiffs and informers fared worse: made to 'utter blasphemies, eat parchments, drink salt and water', or be 'pumped' – have their head held under a street pump – or be dipped in a sewer until ready to kiss a brick covered in human faeces and repeat after their tormentors, 'I am a Rogue, and a Rogue in Grain, and damn me, if ever I come into the Mint again.' Some of the Mint's inhabitants had been there for years. No work was to be had, and they could not leave to find any outside to repay their debts, for the roads all around were lined with debt collectors ready to catch them if they emerged. Despite these restrictions, some men managed to enjoy life there.

Drink and gambling were common and Moll 'soon got,' she writes, 'a great deal of company about me', for ladies were scarce in that place and eagerly sought. 'I kept myself safe yet,' wrote Moll, 'though I began, like My Lord Rochester's mistress, that loved his company, but would not admit him farther, to have the scandal of a whore, without the joy.' (Rochester was a rake who made his way through the beds of society ladies in the 1660s and 1670s, a few years before Moll wrote her memoir.) The company is not, however, to her taste. 'There was something horrid and absurd in their way of sinning, for it was all a force even upon themselves: they did not only act against conscience, but against nature.' Sometimes their sadness and guilt 'would break out at their very mouths when they had parted with their money for a lewd treat or a wicked embrace. I have heard them, turning about, fetch a deep sigh, and cry, *What a dog I am!* Well, *Betty*, my dear, I'll drink thy health tho', *meaning the honest wife*, perhaps had not a half-crown for herself and three or four children.' Each day the debtor's family suffers more, 'he flyes to the same relief again, *(viz.)*

to drink it away, debauch it away, and falling into company of men in just the same condition with himself, he repeats the crime, and thus he goes every day one step onward of his way to destruction'.

Moll is not ready to immerse herself in this world of depravity. When she emerges from the Mint a few months later she is a new woman, a widow operating under an alias which will deflect her husband's creditors from her scent. For the first time she is going by the name of Mrs Moll Flanders.

4

Moll goes to Virginia, 1637

The new 'Mrs Flanders' is able to leave the Mint because she has made a useful and affectionate friend while she is there, 'a very sober, good sort of woman, who was a widow too, like me', but in better circumstances. Her husband, a sea captain, had been ruined by an unfortunate business venture and killed himself, leaving her at the mercy of his creditors. With the help of friends, however, she has paid off her debts. Ready to return to the world outside, she invites Mrs Flanders to be her guest, 'till I could put myself in some posture of settling in the world to my mind; withal telling me, that it was ten to one but some good captain of a ship might take a fancy to me, and court me, in that part of the town where she lived'.

The captain's widow lives in Redriff, a village half-encircled by a curve in the Thames just east of Southwark and opposite Wapping. Redriff is a village devoted to commerce and seafaring. This is the home of shipwrights, merchant officers, chandlers, indenturers and contractors: anyone connected with the business of making money overseas. Captain Christopher Jones, who ferried the Pilgrim Fathers to New England aboard the *Mayflower* in 1620, has been recently buried in its church. Men with land or clients in Virginia, Barbados and the just-established American colony of Maryland have their agents and warehouses here. A vast dock and arsenal stand at the river's edge, and the marshes to either side, 'noisome' at low tide and under continual reclamation, are littered with the debris of boatbuilding. The main street of the village runs along the wharf, with views of the hamlet of Ratcliff on the river's north bank and, in the foreground, all the noise, confusion and energy of business: ships being loaded and unloaded; men staggering up the mud with bundles on their heads; horses (and more men) pulling carts to the warehouses to unload spices, wine, furs, skins, tobacco; clerks with their lists and inventories; ladies holding their skirts out of the way as sailors splash towards the Angel Tavern, built on stilts in the marsh. And Moll, walking wistfully down to the wharf each time a merchantman comes in and hoping its captain – or at least its first officer – back from a trip to Virginia, Barbados or the Indies, might notice the pretty lady, make enquiries and come calling.

She is finding it hard to enter the marriage market again. Men in London, she has discovered, particularly ambitious men who might make good husbands, want only a bride with money. Moll's looks, wit and accomplishments do not compensate for her lack of dowry.

> Men chose mistresses indeed by the gust [taste] of their affection, and it was requisite to a whore to be handsome, well-shaped, have a good mein [manner] and a graceful behaviour; but that for a wife, no deformity would shock the fancy, no ill qualities the judgment; the money was the thing; the portion was neither crooked nor monstrous, but the money was always agreeable, whatever the wife was.

For Puritans this was a lamentable state of affairs. Another of John Dod's conduct books, the *Duties of Husband and Wife* of 1603, ranked love first among their 'common duties'. 'They must love one another,' he wrote, 'with a pure heart, fervently.' Love will preserve them from 'unchaste actions and strange lusts'; it will bring patience with each other; it will encourage them to 'seek the good of one another' and it will arm them 'against jealousy and unjust suspicions'. The poor had always been able to form relationships based on affection, for there was no property involved, and as the seventeenth century progressed, fewer and fewer propertied families outside the monarchy and aristocracy forced daughters into matches they found personally abhorrent. But despite increased recognition that affection between spouses was desirable, a marriage still had to be economically appropriate: a girl might not be pushed into the arms of a rich but repellent suitor, but neither would she be permitted to marry one with charm but no prospects. Matters had changed little when Daniel Defoe came to write his own treatises on marriage and family life. 'Ask the ladies why they marry,' he wrote sadly; 'they tell you 'tis for a good settlement. . . . Ask the men why they marry, it is for the money . . . How little is regarded of that one essential and absolutely necessary part of the composition, called love.'

A marriageable woman was negotiated for by prospective and actual master – husband, and father or guardian – and her price was determined by status, prospects, personal attractiveness, age and so forth. Father would provide a dowry and husband would agree a 'jointure', the pension to support her in widowhood. Those such as Moll, who have no one to negotiate for them, are obliged to carry on the matter themselves (if they want to marry), and this is what Moll is setting out to do with the help of her new friend. In one way she is better off without the 'protection' of male kin: widows can own property and are thus in a position to negotiate its disposal, and widowhood is the status Moll decided on when she left the Mint. It is a reminder that the neatly ordered patriarchal world advocated by conduct books, the Church and the law was frequently subverted by the awkward facts of life, death and personality. All seventeenth-century theorists had difficulty fitting widows in particular into their schemes, as women were considered to have one of only two statuses: married or yet to be married. A widowed woman fitted neither; in modern parlance, she was a loose cannon.

Family break-up and remarriage were common in a period of low life expectancy. In Southwark during the 1620s 16 per cent of households were headed by a woman, a calamity so dire that the conduct books could not even bring themselves to address it. Many, perhaps the majority, of households also contained step-relatives, inevitable when so many died young. Twenty-five per cent of marriages contracted that decade by London tradesmen, for example, were to widows, bringing about all the upheavals of adoption, reclassifications of status, income and so forth, which rippled disturbingly through entire extended families.

The resources with which Moll has to negotiate, however, are not enough to secure her entry into the sort of new family she seeks. As soon as her friend's acquaintances realise the pretty widow is poor, she 'began to be dropt in all the discourses of matrimony'.

> Being well bred, handsome, witty, modest and agreeable; all which I had allowed to my character, whether justly, or no, is not to the purpose; I say, all these would not do without the dross [money], which was now become more valuable than virtue itself. In short, *the widow*, they said, *had no money*. I resolv'd therefore, as to the state of my present circumstances; that it was absolutely necessary to change my station, and make a new appearance in some other place, where I was not known.

So begins a game which will become wearily familiar to Moll. It is orchestrated by her friend, and the plan is this: that lady's new husband must be brought to believe that Moll is his wife's cousin, and 'had at least £1500 fortune, and that after some of my relations [died] I was like to have a great deal more'. That the husband should happily accept the arrival on the scene of a cousin whose existence he has never heard of might suggest he is easily hoodwinked. However, people leaving their parishes could so easily and casually lose touch with birth families because of distance, bereavement, disgrace, change of status or apathy that it is entirely possible the new husband has never met any of his bride's relations before marrying – as a widow, she made her own arrangements – and thus happily accepts Moll as some cousin 'up from the country'.

> It was enough to tell her husband this; there needed nothing on my side. I was but to sit still and wait the event, for it presently went all over the neighbourhood that the young widow at Captain —'s was a fortune, that she had at least 1500 *l.* and perhaps a great deal more; and *that the captain said so*; and if the captain was ask'd at any time about me, he made no scruple to affirm it .

And now, when a whiff of money is added to looks, greedier fish approach the bait. 'I presently found myself bless'd with admirers enough, and . . . had my choice of men . . . I who had a subtile game to play, had nothing now to do but to single out from them all the properest man that might be for my purpose; *that is to say*, the man who was most likely to depend upon a *hear say* of a fortune, and not inquire too far into the particulars.' In other words, a suitor who is rich but a bit thick.

A likely candidate soon comes along. His name is Humphrey, and he declares prettily that 'he loved me above all the world; that if I would make him happy, that was enough'. Knowing this is all flannel, and that the hook must lodge deeper in the gullet before she can bring Humphrey in, Moll plays him skilfully. 'This was my man; but I was to try him to the booms, and indeed in that consisted my safety; for if he baulk'd, I knew I was undone, as surely as he was undone if he took me . . . I pretended on all occasions to doubt his sincerity, and told him, perhaps he only courted me for my fortune. He stopped my mouth in that part with the thunder of his protestations.'

And on and on it goes as Moll teases information from her lover about his situation while maintaining a close silence on her own. He is a man of some charm and distinction, 'very well to pass in the world'. He is not a ship's captain, after all, but an American planter, a little younger than she: one of those sunburnt, work-hardened, increasingly glamorous colonials who can entertain the ladies with talk of empty lands and clean rivers, spice, skins, furs and savages. His income comes principally from estates in Virginia, he tells Moll, 'which brought him in a very good income, generally speaking, to the tune of £300 a year, but that if he was to live upon them, would bring him in three or four times as much'.

They marry, and Moll drops the name Flanders and assumes Humphrey's family name, although we never learn what that is. It is her sixth or seventh name so far. So in love is he, and so cleverly has Moll kept her distance from rumours of her fortune, that Humphrey cannot reproach her when the truth of her financial affairs comes out. However, it becomes clear that in order to live as they wish, they will have to move to Virginia. England is too expensive, and the American estates will only be brought to yield properly under the firm hand of a master living in the big house and supervising his workers. The matter is settled, and the couple turns to preparations for the voyage to Humphrey's homeland.

Marchants wife of London

Civis Londinensis melioris qualitatis Vxor

The typical dress of a merchant's wife in the 1640s: this is how Moll would have dressed at the time of her marriage to Humphrey

In 1635 a manual was written for people in Moll and Humphrey's situation, preparing to travel out to the Chesapeake and set themselves up as landowners. From the long specific list of apparel, household items, weapons, fishing and fowling equipment and farm tools, it is clear these were scarcely to be found in America (and particularly in Maryland, the newest American colony); everything of this nature had to be imported from Britain. Livestock and seed, however, were to be purchased in the Chesapeake. To barter for these, the new settler was advised to take

a superfluitie of woolen, or linen cloth, calicoes, stayes, hatts, shooes, stockings, and all sorts of clothing; of wine, Sugar, Prunes, Rasins, Currance, Honey, Spice, and Grocery wares, with which hee may procure himselfe cattell there, according to the stocke he dealeth withal, About 4 or 5 Pound laid out here in commodities, will there buy a

Cow; and betweene 20 and 30 shillings, a breeding Sow. The like
Commodities will furnish him either there, or in Maryland, with
Hogges, Poultry, and Corne. Hee may doe well also to carry a super-
fluity of Knives, Combes, and Bracelets, to trade with the women
Natives; and some Hatchets, Howes and Axes, to trade with the men
for Venison, Fish, Turkies, Corne, Fawnes to store a Parke, etc.

There was one other vital item of cargo which no new settler sailed
without. 'In the taking of servants', the manual instructed, the settler

may doe wil to furnish himselfe with as many as he can, of usefull
and necessary Arts:

A Carpenter, of all others the most necessary; a Mill-wright, Ship-
wright, Boate-wright, Wheele-wright, Brick-maker, Brick-layer, Potter:
one that can cleave Lath and Pale, and make Pipe-staves, etc. A Joyner,
Cooper, Turner, Sawuer, Smith, Cutler, Leather-dresser, Miller, Fish-
erman and Gardiner. These will be of most use; but any lusty young
able man, that is willing to labour and take paines, although he have
no particular trade, will be beneficiall enough to his Master.

These servants were indentured: they put their name or cross on a
contract agreeing to serve a certain number of years' labour – usually
four or seven – in return for the cost of their passage to America and
occasionally some help in setting themselves up independently at the
end of that period. Most indentured men and women were not taken
across the ocean for personal service. A few might be kept by whoever
paid their passage, but most were auctioned off on arrival to other
labour-starved planters. The price they fetched repaid the costs of the
settler who brought them out, usually with a good profit on top. This,
then, is the cargo, human and otherwise, that Moll and Humphrey
are busy procuring, although Moll does not itemise it. 'We put,' she
writes, 'on board the ship *which we went in*, a large quantity of good
furniture for our house, with stores of linnen and other necessaries,
and a good cargoe for sale, and away we went.' It sounds so carefree,
and yet undertaking a sea voyage to America was a frightening
prospect, one which had to be carefully timed and properly planned.

It took about two months to reach Virginia from London, and ships
tended to leave as late as they dared in autumn, knowing that winter

would be spent unprofitably holed up in the Chesapeake, sitting out
the storms. Weather was only one of the hazards, however; ships
sailed armed and in convoy against the constant threat of pirates. Four
years before Moll and her husband set off for America, the Jesuit priest
Andrew White had made the same voyage. His *Briefe Relation of the
Voyage unto Maryland* of 1634 suggests what a perilous enterprise a
transatlantic passage aboard a seventeenth-century vessel was.

Maryland was a new colony, acquired by royal gift and settled by
aristocratic decree. In 1625 King Charles I had inherited the throne on
the death of his father, James. Charles believed utterly in divine right:
that his authority as monarch derived directly from God. Subjects
might advise and petition, but no authority existed which could veto
his decisions. He had resolved to govern alone in 1629, dismissing the
Parliament at Westminster when its members defied his demands for
more money and warned him against any creeping introduction of
'Romish rites' to the Anglican Church. (Charles was married to a
French Catholic queen, Henrietta Maria, and was thought to be dangerously under her influence, both political and religious.) In 1632 he
unilaterally detached a large chunk of Virginian territory and handed
it over to his friend and servant, the Roman Catholic George Calvert,
first Lord Baltimore. Lord Baltimore's annual rent to the Crown was
one fifth of all gold and silver found, and two Native American arrows,
to be delivered to Windsor Castle each Easter.

Lord Baltimore intended his American lands to be in part a money-
making machine, along the lines of the increasingly successful Virginia,
and in part a sanctuary for his fellow Catholics, who were feared and
hated in England and Scotland. What he and Charles ignored, however,
was the fact that Catholics were also unwelcome in English America.
This was especially so when they arrived clutching titles of possession
to land already cleared, occupied and seeded by Virginian colonists
who now found themselves on the wrong side of a new border.

Lord Baltimore named his American bounty Maryland after Queen
Henrietta Maria and sent out a first party of colonists under the lead-
ership of his son Leonard. Father White was with the little convoy,
which left the Solent late in the year, on 22 November 1633, and White's
vessel almost went aground in a winter gale before she even reached
the Cornish coast. To the relief of all aboard, a large armed London
merchantman appeared as they rounded the Cornish peninsula, for,

said Father Andrew, they had feared they 'might meet with Turkes or other pirates'. Another north-westerly gale, however, sent the merchantman racing back to Falmouth while the settlers' ship carried grimly on under 'such a sea of winde as if they would have blowen our ship under water at every blast'. In a wild black night the main-sail split 'from top to toae and cast one part of it into the sea this amazed the stoutest hearte, even of the sailours, all the Catholiques fell to praier, Confessiones and vowes'. They rode the storm out, praying they would not be pushed onto the rocks of the Irish shore, 'till we were with milder weather freed from all those horrours'.

Sweeter winds took them south, and they sailed down the Spanish coast looking out nervously for the 'Turkes', but 'saw none, it seems they were returned home to celebrate their Tamisom [Ramadan], a great feast which happeneth about that time'. By Turkes Father White meant the North African pirates, more colourfully known as Barbary corsairs from Algiers, Salé, Tunis and Tripoli, a string of city-states along the north coast of Africa and part of the vast Turkish Ottoman empire. They terrorised the Mediterranean and adjacent seas, preying on the rich cargoes shipped between Spain, France, Italy, the Levant and the Americas, and raiding coastal towns in the Mediterranean countries, Britain, Ireland and even Iceland, carrying away thousands of Christian slaves for sale. Only three years before, they had attacked Baltimore, the Calverts' seat in Ireland, and abducted 108 people. Hundreds of English ships were lost to the Barbary pirates during the seventeenth century, and captives could expect a life at best wretched and at worst extremely short.

As the Maryland ships left Madeira behind them and headed into the ocean, lookouts saw three ships approaching. Fearing they were manned by corsairs, Ramadan behind them and plunder on their minds, the colonists 'made readie for fight, neither wanted some [there were some] who imprudently wished the master to make towards them', but those hotheads were quelled, and the prudent commander 'answered he could not iustifie that to the owners of the ship'. Happily, the 'pirates' turned out to be Canary merchantmen and passed with a friendly salute.

The ocean passage was fair; even the dreaded calms of the doldrums did not catch them. There was some inevitable seasick-ness, but the greatest pain of the voyage was self-inflicted. Wine was

'so immoderately taken' on Christmas Day 'as the next day 30 sick-
ened of fevers, whereof about a dozen died afterward'. As they
approached the American coast in February, the settlers discussed
how best to procure the corn seed they needed to plant their first
fields. It was unlikely, the first Marylanders thought, that the
Virginians would sell them any, for they came not only as competition for land and market but as members of an abhorrent religious
sect. The ship was therefore diverted to Barbados to buy seed and
found that island in an uproar. The indentured servants there, mainly
deported from Irish lands seized by colonising English landlords,
'conspired to kill their masters and make themselves free, and then
handsomely to take the first ship that came, and soe goe to sea'.
This was the last of the threats packed into the three-month voyage,
and the Marylanders escaped it when the conspiracy was discovered
and its leaders were hanged. Father White's ship entered the Potomac
River three months out from England, seven weeks and two days
of which had been spent at sea, which 'is held,' he said, 'a speedy
passage'.

However cautious a master might be in sailing with the seasons
and along a well-frequented route, most vessels which made the voyage
to the New World came back with some anecdote of misfortune: a
failure in the fabric of the vessel, a brush with furious elements or a
near encounter with a human enemy. The coasts of Bermuda, Spanish
Florida, Barbados and the lands north of Virginia were already dotted
with European wrecks. This is what Moll and Humphrey face as they
board their ship at Gravesend, and Moll will have heard plenty of talk
in Redriff about such dangers. She knows no one sets off for America
without making a will and saying a prayer.

She does not dwell on the voyage in her memoir. It was 'long', she
writes briefly, 'and full of dangers . . . after a terrible passage, frighted
twice with dreadful storms, and once with what was still more terrible,
I mean a pirate,' they approach the American coast. When word comes
that there are clouds on the horizon and birds in the air, she and the
other passengers climb on deck and gaze west, where land will soon
appear. When the lead touches bottom and brings up mud mixed with
reddish sand, the tallowed stump is cut off and pinned to the mizzen
mast for all to see: the Capes of Virginia are dead ahead.

5

Moll meets her mother-in-law in America, 1639

The Capes of Virginia are Charles, to the south, and Henry, to the north, named after the sons of James I. Prince Henry, a bright young Protestant prince, died in 1612 of typhoid fever. His surviving younger brother Charles, less bright and apparently less Protestant, will soon plunge Britain into civil war. Inside the Capes, Moll's ship passes the tiny settlement of Kecoughtan (now Hampton) and the passengers gaze up the magnificent prospect of the Chesapeake Bay. Out of sight to the north-east is the village of St Mary's, where Lord Baltimore's Marylanders are sowing their first tobacco fields.

Moll's ship turns into the York River, an estuary on the Chesapeake's western shore. Fields and occasional houses slide by either side, between trees bigger than any an Englishwoman has ever seen. The boxes, bundles and servants which make up Moll's cargo are unloaded at jetties along the shore, and the empty spaces in the ship's hold are filled with tobacco. Moll and Humphrey disembark at the river's narrowest point, a straggle of huts which will become Yorktown. Humphrey's plantation lies on this tongue of land between two rivers, in what is now known as Virginia's Historic Triangle between Jamestown, Yorktown and Williamsburg. Stepping thankfully ashore, they find a colony which has not changed greatly since Moll's mother arrived a quarter-century ago. Then it was one fortified outpost on the edge of a vast unknown continent, living under threat; now it is a collection of fortified outposts, scattered across the little peninsula and still living under threat: less from the old enemy, the Spanish, than a new one: the Powhatan Confederacy.

In the earliest years of settlement planters had optimistically made clearings among the great trees some miles up- and downriver from Jamestown, and worked on what were planned to be new towns: Henricus, out in the west, named for dead Prince Henry; Wolstenholme, downriver, a collection of wattle and daub huts on the clay. Expansion had inevitably brought them into conflict with the local inhabitants, and raids, retaliations and abductions had become common. The young Powhatan princess known as Pocahontas was abducted by English traders in 1613 and held for ransom in Henricus against English colonists and tools taken by her people. It was here that she met and married the English widower John Rolfe and helped bring about an eight-year truce between incomers and indigenes. The marriage was brief: Pocahontas, converted to Christianity and baptised Rebecca, died at Gravesend after a trip to England with her husband. The peace lasted little longer: on 22 March 1622 the Powhatan rose and the outlying pioneers bore the brunt of their fury. About 400 colonists (one third of the white population of Virginia) were killed that day, and Henricus and Wolstenholme were practically destroyed.[5] The terrified settlers retreated to Jamestown, abandoning their plans of expansion, and another period of draining, embittering guerrilla warfare began. Native property was destroyed wherever it was found; crops were burnt and the settlers' dogs turned loose on Powhatan villages. Men who left Jamestown to go hunting did not return, or were found scalped by other foraging parties.

The colonists had only recently ventured east again, building a nervous line of farms as far as the native village of Kiskiack. They had been induced to leave the security of Jamestown by the promise of land: 'fifty acres per poll [i.e. per head] for all . . . persons who ye first yeare and five and twenty acres who the second yeare, should adventure or be adventured to seate and inhabit on the southern side of the Pamunkey River, now called York, and formerly known by the Indyan name of Chiskiack, as a reward and encouragement for this

5 A recent archaeological dig showed that 'the Englishmen were in full metal armor like medieval knights and the heavy armor and a closed helmet hampered movement, restricted vision and muffled warning signs of approaching enemies. It is no wonder they were no match for the Indians.' http://cnx.org/content/m17800/latest/

their undertaking'. This was probably the area in which Moll's dead father-in-law had obtained the plantation to which Humphrey was now taking her. The area covered by land grants had soon been pushed further out, to encompass all the lower peninsula, and a fortified wooden wall was built from river to river to keep the natives out. Marshy at the edges, the enclosed peninsula rose to a healthy ridge in the centre, where the colony's physician, Dr Potts, had been given the beautiful land he called Middle Plantation, now Williamsburg. From here, the land fell away towards the rivers, where less favoured colonists lived among the mosquitoes.

There had been other changes. When Moll's mother arrived twenty years before, the colony had been engaged in subsistence agriculture. The gold sought by the earliest explorers was never found, although there were still hopes that somewhere in the vast hinterland great gold-digging, gold-working cultures might exist and be conquered for English gain. Instead, tobacco had all but ousted any other crop, and the demands of this labour-intensive, land-intensive plant shaped Virginia's development. John Rolfe reaped his first, small harvest of Spanish tobacco in 1612. Somehow he had obtained the seeds of the sweet *Nicotiana tabacum* plant from South America despite strict restrictions on its export to protect the Spanish monopoly, a historical mystery that has never been satisfactorily explained, and probably never will be. Two years later he and Pocahontas visited London to discuss how best to exploit the crop. When it became immediately clear that London merchants would buy as much tobacco as Jamestown could produce, fields were cleared beyond the palisades, colonists marched out of town with hoes over their shoulders, and every few yards between the houses was planted up by those left behind. 'The colony,' wrote its governor, 'creeps from this marshbound island, up the stream plantation by plantation.' A list of the farms and tiny villages contains evocative, lonely names: 'the Neck of Land', 'Jordain's Jorney', 'the Plantation over against James Cittie', 'Captain Berkley's Plantation, seated at Falling Creek'. When Moll's mother took up the hoe, planters were exporting about 20,000 pounds of leaf to England; by the time Moll herself arrived, 1.5 million pounds were leaving each year.

Tobacco is, however, a voracious weed. The crop could only be grown three or four times on the same land before the soil became exhausted, so new fields had constantly to be cleared and sown. Winter was the clearing time, when men and women went out into below-zero temperatures to cut the bark off trees to kill them, then burn the land around, drag the leaves, branches and undergrowth away, break and turn the frozen soil. In February or March the beds were planted, with charcoal or ash worked in, and formed into a myriad tiny mounds. Planting took place in May, and as the temperatures rose remorselessly, men and women worked a twelve-hour day in the fields. Each seed in each damp mound must be tended: watered, watched, cleared painstakingly of the tiny tobacco worms which settled and clung in their thousands. As the plants grew, flowering tops must be snapped off, bottom leaves removed and suckers cut from stems, and weeds attacked with the hoe. In August the crop was brought in and hung to cure; as winter approached, it was taken down and packed, ready for the tobacco ships. And when the long labour in the fields and barns was done, there was all the other work: cooking, cleaning, mending, nursing children, tending livestock, grinding corn in the mortar, gathering firewood. This relentless toil, as far as Moll knows, has been her mother's life.

An engraving of tobacco cultivation in colonial America

Among the many things which Moll has not confided to Humphrey is that her mother may be one of the five or six thousand people living hereabouts.[6] The chances of her survival, after all, are slim. However large a profit the tobacco plantations yield, those who work them die young, and Moll has little fear of bumping into an embarrassing middle-aged relative. Not, it transpires as she gets to know her new mother-in-law, that the relationship would be held against her, for that lady herself arrived in difficult circumstances.

Tobacco required a constant supply of labourers, and the Virginian workforce, struggling with disease, malnutrition, maltreatment and overwork, was not yet self-perpetuating, let alone able to generate increase. A few bullish colonists had suggested the mass enslavement of the Native Americans as an answer to the labour problem, but some were squeamish about the proposal, and others recognised that it simply would not work, indeed could cause more difficulties than it resolved. Immigration from Britain still seemed the only answer, and the Virginia Company and the English government had tried various means to encourage it.

In the earliest days Company informers seem to have hung around the Old Bailey or paid the clerks and gaolers for information each sessions. Who among those on the death warrant was a handy fellow? Who a healthy fertile lass? Sir Thomas Smith intervened to spirit Stephen Rogers away to Virginia in April 1618; that August Ralph Rookes appeared before the court and 'on his conviction of incorrigible vagabondage' was also reprieved 'so that he should be sent to Virginia'. Presumably he had some useful skill he refused to practise, or perhaps he was just considered a potential field hand who might as well die after tilling the soil of Virginia as do nothing in England. In April the following year they were joined by Elizabeth Handsley, our model for Moll's mother, and in May by Jane Goodwyn 'for the theft of a petticoat'. In 1621 William Hill, convicted 'of stealing Richard Atkinson's bull . . . asked for the book' [the Bible] and was also 'respited for Virginia'.

As Moll gains her new mother-in-law's confidence, it emerges that she had come here the same way, reprieved from death in London to be branded and sent to America. 'Here's the mark of it, CHILD, *says she*, and pulling off her glove, look ye here, *says she*, turning up the

_____
6 A census of 1634 returned 5,119 colonial inhabitants.

palm of her hand, and shewed me a very fine white arm and hand, but branded in the inside of the hand, as in such cases it must be.' Nor is she ashamed of it. Many of her friends and neighbours arrived the same way. 'You need not think such a thing strange, *daughter*, for as I told you, some of the best men in this country are burnt in the hand, and they are not asham'd to own it; there's Major – *says she*, he was an eminent pickpocket; there's Justice *Ba*——*r* was a shoplifter and both of them were burnt in the hand, and I could name you several, such as they are.'

Indeed, 'the greatest part of the inhabitants,' she claims, arrived in Virginia 'in very indifferent circumstances'. And whatever the unhappinesses of her own first years in America, 'I look back on them with a particular satisfaction, as they have been a means to bring me to this place': wealthy, respected and mistress of her own farm. She was one of the lucky ones, having been placed in service with a 'good family, where, behaving herself well, and her mistress dying, her master married her, by whom she had my husband and his sister, and . . . by her diligence and good management after her husband's death, she had improv'd the plantations to such a degree as they then were.'

Despite all the recruitment drives in England, Scotland and Ireland, there had never been enough women to go round in the colonies. Britain's gaols and bridewells never disgorged enough to maintain the colonial population; nor had convict women ever become popular. Campaigns were therefore launched in England to supply a more virtuous strain of breeder, and a non-convict boatload had come up the James River in 1619 (the same year as the first negro servants): ninety 'young maids' to provide the essential domestic and reproductive element. More arrived in 1621. In tune with the times, they were godly girls.

There hath been especial care had in the choice of them, for there hath not any one of them been received but upon good commendations . . . we pray you all therefore that at their first landing they may be housed, lodged, and provided for of diet till they be married . . . and in case they cannot be presently married, we desire they may be put to several householders that have wives till they can be provided of husbands. There are fifty more which are shortly to come [as it is believed] that the plantation can never flourish till families be planted, and the respect of wives and children fix the people on the soil.

Respected though wives and their future children might be, there was a whiff of cattle dealing in the arrangements recommended for their distribution. Price per wife (paid to the Virginia Company to offset its costs in transporting the women out) was 'i20lb weight of the best leaf tobacco for each of them, and in case any of them die, that proportion must be advanced to make it up upon those that survive'. Boatloads of young women, whom the colonists were assured had been 'selected with care', continued occasionally to arrive, along with tragic cargoes of children kidnapped on Cheapside and the banks of the Fleet, and groups of indentured servants like those that Moll and Humphrey have themselves brought out and sold along the river.

Few women, therefore, arrive in the colony in such comfortable circumstances as Moll, protected by her status as a planter's wife and welcomed by a wealthy and affectionate mother-in-law in possession of a big house and servants of her own. Cushioned from the harsher aspects of colonial life, Moll settles in and bears two more children. She is not particularly in love with Humphrey – the passion felt for her Colchester seducer has never been replicated – but she, he, the children and his cheerful old mother live very well on their planta- tion. Certainly it is much better than anything an illegitimate gaol baby could have imagined she would achieve. 'I thought myself,' she would recall wistfully, 'the happiest creature alive'.

6

Moll learns a shocking truth, 1643

If a comfortable life, it is also a strange one for a young woman who knows only England. Alien sights confront Moll both inside and outside her house. Outside is the vast forest: trees entwined with creeper form a solid green wall which the colony's labourers fight to bring down, aided by the herd of imported goats which munch their way steadily through the undergrowth. There is neither the open country she knew in East Anglia, nor the streets and wharves of Redriff; only the claustrophobia of her house in its clearing of fields, and closed-in vistas beyond the reach of her servants' hoes and spades. There are no grassy plains on which to rest the eye or gallop, and the only clear spaces except the colonists' plantations are the fields of the Native Americans, falling steadily into the hands of new owners as their old ones retreat into the forests.

Planter families starting out with modest means lived in very simple dwellings, reflections of those left behind in England. Frame houses were quick and cheap to build and were usually of a single storey, with a ladder providing access to a loft, where the family slept. They had roofs of shingles, floors of beaten earth, and wattle and daub chimneys at each end which either carried off smoke from the hearth or failed to do so and burnt the house down. They were dark and cramped, for there were few or no windows, and light only entered through doors left open in summer or cracks between the clapboard nailed to the frame. Hurriedly built from perishable materials, none survives.

Captain Christopher Calthrope and his wife Anne were well-off planters in York County at the time Moll and Humphrey settled there, and would have lived a similar life to them. We know the layout of their house from the inventory Anne submitted to York County Court on her husband's death. The house was made up of three parts: the 'outer room, the chamber and the shedd'. The family – husband, wife and four children – lived, ate and slept in the chamber, where there were two feather beds with bolsters, sheets, blankets, valances and curtains (a gesture towards marital privacy), a couch bed and a couch. The outer room was a store and workroom, where they kept a huge pile of bolts of fabric, probably for barter as well as for their own household use. The 'shedd' was the kitchen, a lean-to with a fireplace, in which Anne listed racks, hooks, bellows, andirons (metal supports for logs in a fireplace), cooking pots, pans, two brass kettles, skimmer, mortar and pestle, and grater. She also had pewter-ware for the table, three dozen napkins and six tablecloths. Outside there was a dairy (ten milk trays, a tub and earthenware pan), beehives, accommodation – not described in the inventory – for the nine indentured servants who worked the Calthrope estate, and stabling for their livestock: four draught oxen, six steers, thirteen milch cows, five heifers, four yearlings, seven calves, three sows, two barrows (castrated male pigs for slaughtering) and four shoats (young weaned pigs).

Perhaps the household Humphrey's parents had built up was slightly grander, more like that of Captain Samuel Mathews and his family, whose estate of several hundred acres at the mouth of the Warwick River resembled the feudal English model of village development. Mathews Manor, later called Denbigh, combined residential dwellings, workshops for various tradesmen and agriculture within a single environment. The Mathews house – still a crowded, one-storey affair – stood at the centre and activity surrounded it. Hemp and flax were sown in one field, and some of the many outbuildings were given over to spinning. When the anonymous author of *A Perfect Description of Virginia* described the Mathews estate in 1649, he recorded that 'forty Negro servants' (probably slaves) worked the tobacco fields and were also taught the trades of a village economy: blacksmithery, joinery, caulking, cooping. Eight shoemakers worked in a tan-house, and there was a large dairy and a butchery, for some of Mathews' cattle were slaughtered and sold to outbound ships.

What happened inside a Virginian household, whether the Calthropes', the Mathews' or Moll's, was little different from life inside a prosperous farmhouse in England, although living conditions were more crowded. The wife ran the domestic economy, supervising servants (if she had them) or doing the work herself: milking cows and making butter and cheese, tending the kitchen garden, preparing food, salting or smoking meat, ensuring the fire did not go out, washing and making clothes. There was a little less technology than in England – only one watermill, for example, and that in Flowerdieu Hundred, so corn grown out of reach of Flowerdieu had to be ground by hand – and no shops. Where Moll's Colchester mistress might have bought in her candles, her linens, her furniture and her soap, Moll's Virginian household has to manufacture these things itself. Social life is scarce, with few women for Moll to visit or be visited by. Households are isolated in their plantation clearings, with everybody obliged to fall back on each other for company. Moll and Humphrey probably share the same chamber as Moll's mother-in-law, with only a bed curtain giving them some privacy at night, and the older lady would, perforce, have become her closest companion. There are no coaches to take her visiting here and there in comfort: even a relatively wealthy woman like Moll either walks or rides a horse, and riding alone through the ancient forest is risky. Wandering bands of artisans and labourers might come knocking on doors and bunk down in outhouses – carpenters, labourers, blacksmiths working job by job or contract by contract on plantations not big enough to employ a servant for every task – but there are few occasions on which Moll can enjoy the company of other women her age, unless she seeks it among her servants.

With four or five times more men than women in the Chesapeake colonies, there were not many forums for women to meet outside the home. Even church attendance – the traditional weekly catch-up at home in England – was observed with difficulty when the nearest place of worship might be miles away down an unmade road. Servant women and lowlier wives could enjoy each other's company in the milking shed or on the banks of the stream where laundry was done, but Moll has servants to milk and wash for her. Perhaps the only time she enjoys a roomful of private female society is at the birth of her children. But if life is lonelier, it is also more secure in others. Moll's dream of a comfortable wifely life with her first lover had been snatched

away by his perfidy and her naivety; here, perhaps, is her second chance
to live it.

Her marriage seems successful. This time she has chosen well,
and her husband is a decent and hard-working man who treats her
with courtesy and provides well for his growing family. As a second-
generation landowner, he is near the top of the colonial social pile.
Whereas his own father might have worked in the fields alongside
his servants, doing the same work in the same conditions as those
he paid and housed, Moll's husband is taking a step back from manual
labour and forward into the life of a colonial gentleman. He can
afford to. The social and economic structure of Virginia has been
calculated and maintained to ensure a concentration of wealth and
power in the hands of a few, and Humphrey is among them.

Colonial employers benefited immensely from a corruption of the
ancient English system of indentured service. Desperate to see more
land cleared and settled, the Virginia Company had fashioned a colonial version of the old English practice. Under a 'headright' scheme
introduced in 1618, one hundred acres of land were allotted with every
new settler in Virginia – not to the settler himself, however, but to
whoever paid his passage to America. In *White Cargo* Michael Walsh
and Don Jordan describe this system as 'an invitation to those with
money to secure great tracts of Virginia by populating it with the
poor'. Immediately, men and women with capital formed syndicates
to buy up areas of American land, call them by comforting English
names and send labouring people out to do the spadework of settlement. The original generous headright was soon scaled back, but each
servant still brought fifty acres of colonial soil for the master and need
only be provided with a leasehold on a twentieth of that at the end
of his or her service. It was a foolproof way for those with capital to
acquire land. The indentured servants Moll and Humphrey have left
here and there along the York River have each brought them fifty acres
of Virginian forest.

'The planters buy them,' Moll's mother-in-law explains, 'and they
work together in the field till their time is out; when 'tis expired, *said
she*, they have encouragement given them to plant for themselves; for
they have a certain number of acres of land allotted them by the
country, and they go to work to clear and cure the land, and then to
plant it with tobacco and corn.'

This was a rosy picture, for many indentured servants were treated appallingly. Firstly, those who did not arrive with money in their pockets (or married to one who did), whether convict or indentured, were generally considered by the older settlers to be idle, immoral and in need of strict supervision and discipline. Secondly, and in order to increase their dependence on their masters, indentured servants were rigorously excluded from the administration of the colony. Even family life was made difficult. Male servants, for example, were not allowed near the 'bridal boats'; those maids were for planters. Nor, with few exceptions, were indentured labourers allowed to bring over spouse and children from Britain without paying a heavy fee to their master or adding years to their term of service. A typical indenture ran as follows:

[The Forme of binding a Servant]

THIS INDENTURE made the ... day of ... in the ... yeere of our Soveraigne Lord King Charles, etc. betweene ... of the one party, Witnesseth, that the said ... doth hereby covenant promise, and grant, to and with the said ... his Executors and Assignes, to serve him from the day of the date hereof, untill his first and next arrivall in Mary-land; and after for and during the tearme of .... Yeares, in such service and imployment, as the said ... or his assignes shall there imploy him, according to the custome of the Countrey in the like kind. In consid-eration whereof, the said ... doth promise and grant, to and with the said ... to pay for his passing, and to find him with Meath, Drinke, Apparell and Lodging, with other necessaries during the said terme; and at the end of the said terme, to give him one whole yeeres provi-sion of Corne, and fifty acres of Land, according to the order of the countrey.

[1635]

All this is of little concern to Moll, however, snug in her house with her babies, her mother-in-law and servants for company and a husband striding manfully about his plantation outside, accumulating money. Her domestic life is – almost – all she desires; a lingering sadness for the lover of her youth may occasionally descend, but she brushes it away. But outside the domestic sphere things in Virginia are less comfortable, even for women in Moll's privileged position. Some of those English-looking timber-framed cottages were built with a telling colonial variation: gun slits in the walls. If the new arrivals ever felt too cosy in their adopted land, they had only to look at the figures living on the margins of their settlements to remind them they were no longer at home: not vagrants or Gypsies, but Native Americans, or 'Indians', as the settlers call them. They are an unsettling presence. They might be friendly; they might be curious or have their minds on trading; they might have come to kill.

The quiet life of Virginian landowners was interrupted during the last year of Moll's residence there. On 18 April 1644 thousands of Native American warriors attacked the colonies' frontiers. Nearly 500 people died in the course of a single morning, and outlying farmsteads were abandoned, just as they had been in 1622. For a time it was thought the Indians would advance and strike at the heart of the colony, but instead, also as in 1622, they retreated to await the colonists' reaction. It came swiftly, and was brutal and thorough. A general assembly declared the English colonists would 'for ever abandon all formes of peace and ffamiliarity with the whole [Indian] nation and will to the utmost of our power pursue and root out those which have any way had their hands in the shedding of our blood and Massacring of our People'. If not a word of this enters Moll's recollections – not her fear for herself and her children, nor her husband's enrolment in the vengeful militia sent to hunt down the attackers, nor the terrified cartloads of old, young and females fleeing their farms and making for Jamestown – it is perhaps because a domestic but to her equally horrific development takes precedence in her memories.

The Reverends Dod and Cleaver, returning to the subject of the love and reverence in which a woman should hold her husband, put her ideal attitude thus: 'Thou art unto me my father and mother, Mine owne deare husband, and well beloved brother'. Moll has been in Virginia five or six years when, talking once again to her mother-in-law about gaolbirds and their happy colonial fates, she realises that she is living a ghastly perversion of this well-meant homily. As the older woman reveals some particular detail about her own life, Moll begins 'to be very uneasy; but coming to one particular that required telling her name, I thought I should have sunk down in the place . . . let anyone judge what must be the anguish of my mind, when I came to reflect that this was certainly no more or less *than my own mother*'.

The woman who was forced to abandon her in Newgate is here, rocking in her chair before her. The labour of tobacco cultivation did not kill her; nor did the Indians, the seasoning, childbirth or any of the other common colonial deaths. Her own mother! And not only hers.

As this appalling realisation bears in upon Moll, she begins to panic. She has unwittingly been in an incestuous relationship for five years and 'had now had two children, and was big with another by my own brother, and lay with him still every night'. It was known that incestuous sexual intercourse could produce deformed babies, and although the first two children of the marriage were born healthy – at least, Moll never tells us otherwise – there was no guarantee that the child in her womb would also be so. But incest was not only a danger to her unborn child; it was also an offence against the 'law of God', and God proclaimed his laws in strident tones in the 1640s.

Incest was named as a capital crime in the first Virginian legal code, laid down in 1610. No one has been convicted under the law and Moll probably has little idea of statutes and statutory penalties anyway. She will be pretty sure, however, that there will be nasty consequences if news of her situation leaks out. She might receive a whipping at the cart-tail, or be forced to undergo the humiliation of public penance: standing on a stool in church, dressed in white and holding a placard with the details of her offence written for all to see. But most of all there is the fear that Humphrey might divorce her on grounds of consanguinity. The Bible and English law both clearly state that sister and brother may not marry. If he divorces her, therefore, Moll's children by him will be illegitimate, and she will have no claim to maintenance during her husband's life nor to any part of his estate on his death.

She can confide in no one and so suffers in silence for months. One step she must take, however, is immediately to break off sexual relations with Humphrey. She now finds him, poor man, repellent, and cannot bear his touch. Naturally this leaves him first distressed, then bemused and finally angered. He is a mild man, but after all she is his property and surrendered all rights over her body when she married him. The situation continues for months. The household, once calm and prosperous, becomes unsettled and wretched. So bad do things become that Moll eventually tells her husband she must return to

England, reminding him he promised when they married that he
would allow her to return if 'I found the country not to agree with
me'. He refuses to consider that idea, even threatening to put her in
the 'mad-house' if she does not mend her ways.

> *He told me*, I did not treat him as if he was my husband, or talk of my
> children, as if I was a mother; and *in short*, that I did not deserve to
> be us'd as a wife: that he had us'd all the fair means possible with me;
> that he had argu'd with all the kindness and calmness, that a husband
> or a Christian ought to do, and that I made him such a vile return,
> that I treated him rather like a dog than a man, and rather like the
> most contemptible stranger than a husband: that he was very loth to
> use violence with me, but that *in short*, he saw a necessity of it now
> . . . and that for the future he should be oblig'd to take such measures
> as should reduce me to my duty.

Threatened with assault, rape or imprisonment, Moll tells her husband
something of the truth: 'that he neither was my lawful husband, nor
they lawful children, and that I had reason to regard neither of them
more than I did'. This mystifies and enrages him more than ever, and
more miserable months pass while he nags at her to reveal the whole
story, and she refuses without his prior permission to leave for
England. Realising at last that she is in earnest, he asks his mother
to try and get at the story and eventually Moll confesses the whole
thing to her. At first the mother is shocked and frightened by the
terrible thing which has happened in the heart of her family. After
much thought, however, she pragmatically comes to what is, for Moll,
an impossible conclusion: 'that I should bury the whole thing entirely,
and continue to live with him as my husband . . . let the whole matter
remain a secret as close as death, for child, *says she*, we are both
undone if it comes out'. Understanding as she does the terror of
poverty and what it may induce a person to do and become, the
mother promises to bequeath a portion of her estate to Moll in her
own right, 'so that if it should come out afterwards, I should not be
left destitute, but be able to stand on my own feet, and procure justice
from [my husband]'.

While acknowledging the good sense of her mother's advice, Moll
cannot bring herself to take it: 'every thing added to make cohabiting

with him the most nauseous thing to me in the world, and I think verily it was come to such a height, that I could almost as willingly have embrac'd a dog, as have let him offer any thing of that kind to me'. On and on the turmoil goes, the son pleading with the mother to get to the root of his wife's hostility, the mother prevaricating, the wife resisting. In the end, sitting calmly on the porch one night, Moll decides the only way out is to tell her husband everything. When he comprehends the horror of what she is saying, the man is so afflicted that he tries to hang himself, but is rescued by a servant. Depression consumes him, he ails in his bed, and while nursing him the thought flits across Moll's mind that maybe there will be a different outcome to this tangled story than the one she had previously aimed at: 'his life was apparently declining, and I might perhaps have married again [in Virginia], very much to my advantage'. England calls irresistibly, however, and as Humphrey starts to mend, she exploits his fragility to extract the promise she wants.

> We agreed that after I arriv'd [in England] he should pretend to have an account that I was dead . . . and so might marry again when he would. He promised, and engaged to me to correspond with me as a sister, and to assist and support me as long as I liv'd; and that if he dy'd before me, he would leave sufficient to his mother to take care of me still, in the name of a sister.

Thus assured of her share – eventually – of her mother's wealth, Moll returns to England in about 1646, after eight years in America. She does not travel light, for no ship returning from Virginia comes with an empty hold, and Moll's cargo of tobacco is designed to provide her with a dowry. Past experience has taught her no husband will take her without one. The voyage home is as miserable as the journey out. When the ship is driven by a storm onto the coast of Wales, she decides to carry on to London by coach rather than sail the shorter distance down the coast to Bristol. Off she goes with her clothes, money, 'bills of loading and other papers', but when she arrives in London three weeks later it is to learn that most of her tobacco has been lost at sea. What she has lost might have allowed her to marry again 'tolerably well; but as it was, I was reduced to between two or three hundred pounds in the whole, and this without any hope of recruit'.

She has changed her name and identity again – for the eighth, ninth or perhaps even tenth time – and reverted to the status of widow. Being completely without friends in London – 'for I found it was absolutely necessary not to revive former acquaintances' – she decides to live elsewhere. 'As I was still far from being old, so my humour, which was always gay, continu'd so to an extream; and being now, *as it were*, a woman of fortune, tho' I was a woman without a fortune, I expected something or other might happen in my way, that might mend my circumstances, as had been my case before.'

With her usual blithe indifference to events outside her own life, off she goes to Bath.

Part II

1646–83

7

Moll returns to England and is an adulteress, 1646–55

Bath is an elegant town on the Avon River in south-west England, celebrated for the thermal springs which bubble up through its limestone. Nearly two thousand years ago the Romans took their pleasures here, building the public baths which survive to this day. 'Taking the waters' became fashionable under Queen Elizabeth I and, although the town would not reach its apogee as a fashionable watering place for another three generations, by the 1640s it was already a place with a name for gallantry, convalescence and expensive leisure: a playground for the seventeenth-century equivalent of elderly millionaires and those who stalked them. This is what Moll means when she hopes 'something or other might happen . . . [to] mend [her] circumstances'. Bath must have been a welcome change after the loneliness and austerity of her Virginian life. But however gay behind closed doors, Moll's new home town was occupied by a Puritan army. Returning to England, she has found a country torn in two by civil war.

The three kingdoms of England and Wales, Scotland and Ireland spent the 1630s under absolute rule. 'Princes,' Charles I declared, 'are not bound to give account of their actions, but to God alone.' Beneath the facade of supreme kingly authority, however, grievances gathered and festered, and were expressed and acted upon as they always had been. The country was increasingly divided by religion: on the one side the Anglican church supported by the King, and on the other the Puritans and the various burgeoning Protestant sects known collectively as

Nonconformists or Dissenters – those who did not conform to, or dissented from, the tenets of the Anglican Church. In particular it was feared that Charles, influenced by his unpopular queen, was in league with Catholic countries in Europe to reintroduce the Church of Rome to England. And with fear of Roman Catholicism came fear of the European model of absolute kingship, which was anathema to most in Britain. When Charles attempted, in 1634, to impose a tax known as ship money, which had not been authorised by Parliament, many towns defied him and refused to collect it. Then, in 1637, there were riots in Scotland when the Church there was ordered to use the Anglican prayer book, which Calvinist Scots refused to accept. Indeed, it was an angry and impromptu Scottish army which forced Charles to recall Parliament again in 1640. The Scots had been stopped on the border but might strike again at any moment. If they did so, Charles knew they would find huge sympathy among the English.

When the King demanded that Parliament vote money so he could fight the Scots, Members responded by insisting that he first sign acts authorising a parliament to be called once every five years independently of royal permission, that certain of his favourites be removed from power and that ship money be declared illegal. A point of no return came on 4 January 1642, when Charles illegally entered the House of Commons and attempted to arrest five Members of Parliament. They had fled, having been warned, but this final piece of kingly disrespect for an ancient English institution triggered declarations 'for Parliament and against Popery'. Negotiations between the two sides failed; Charles sent Henrietta Maria to the Continent to enlist Catholic support and in August 1642 he raised the royal standard at Nottingham, declaring war.

In Moll's old home, Colchester, where her first, forgotten children were now of an age to fight, there was more support for Parliament than for the King. Bath, her new home, suffered badly. When fighting began, the West Country showed itself largely Royalist, and a Parliamentary army was dispatched from London to suppress the King's supporters. The vital port of Bristol was quickly taken and Parliamentary soldiers – Roundheads – occupied Bath. In July 1643, however, they were ejected by Royalist Cavaliers. Troops from both sides descended on the little town; houses, stores and workshops were broken into, and its 2,000 inhabitants were terrorised by drunken warriors who forgot their political differences in the joy of plunder. For two years Bath was Royalist until, in July 1645, the King's garrison surrendered to Parliament, and the Roundheads marched back in.

A quarter of the male population fought in the English Civil Wars, and an equal proportion of the female population, if not more, was directly affected by death, injury, bereavement and destruction. Families were split – in some cases brother fought brother and father fought son. Age-old certainties were called into doubt, and the country was gripped by introspection and revolution as people tried to determine God's will for the nation and for themselves, seeking guidance in prayer and anguished debate. If ever there was an occasion for spiritual reflection, it was Moll's time in Bath. This could have been the chance to set her off on a *Pilgrim's Progress*, a search for her own *Grace Abounding*. Her personal circumstances suggested it, and so did the 'world turned upside down' around her.

Not a bit of it. She is determined to have fun after eight years in the wilderness.

> I liv'd pleasantly enough, kept good company, *that is to say*, gay, fine company; but had the discouragement to find this way of living sunk me exceedingly, and that as I had no settl'd income, so spending upon the main stock was but a certain kind of *bleeding to death*; and this gave me many sad reflections in the intervals of my other thoughts. However, I shook them off, and still flatter'd myself that something or other might offer for my advantage.

If not spiritual exploration, perhaps an interest in the political upheavals around her? Already there were signs that 'the people' were turning out to be more disparate and more unruly than Parliament wished. There were 'unbridled spirits' who talked of extending the franchise, demanded freedom of speech and worship and called for an end to corruption and abuse. If the King's authority could be questioned, why not that of others who claimed divine sanction for their position of social, economic and familial power: aristocrats, bishops, employers, masters, husbands? But Moll is impervious to it all. Nothing in her world has changed. The soldiers on the streets are an inconvenience to be skirted and ignored, and the rantings and levellings of visionary, troublesome men and women do not impinge.

Moll is not concerned with making her way by any of the new routes under discussion: female enfranchisement, education, spiritual enlightenment or the right of women to practise a trade or profession. She is still seeking the safe – in some ways – old status of *feme covert*. Perhaps she knows that this brief burst of revolutionary fire will be put out sooner or later by the old authorities, that the world will return to its conservative senses and revolve about the same axis and that a woman will continue to be destitute without a man to provide for her. And so she determinedly sets off on rounds of 'the Bath', and forms a friendship with a charming gentleman also taking the waters. He is, unfortunately, in possession of a wife, although 'the lady was distempered in her head, and under the conduct of her own relations'. But with no potential husband emerging from the steam to claim her, it seems this is the best Moll can get.

The story of temptation, flirtation, seduction and consummation is played out over about a year, and in the end 'the government of our virtue was broken, and I exchanged the place of friend for that unmusical, harsh-sounding title of whore'. Moll would prefer to marry again, but her lover cannot, for his insane wife still lives. When Moll gives birth to a baby boy, he sets her up as his beloved mistress. He lives in London, sharing a house with his afflicted spouse, while Moll and her son are kept in 'very handsome rooms' a few miles away at Hammersmith.

Hammersmith lay four miles from London on the great western road, a bankside village studded with mansions, river meadows where the cows grazed, almshouses and workers' cottages. It too was thrown into turmoil by the Civil War. London was Parliamentarian (although with an established Royalist resistance movement), the King having withdrawn from the capital at the start of the war and established his headquarters at Oxford. Despite some early Royalist victories, the superior training and determination of the Parliamentary forces told and Cromwell's New Model Army, commanded by Sir Thomas Fairfax, emerged by 1645 as an unbeatable force. The decisive battle was fought in June 1645 at Naseby, where the defeated King fled the battlefield. In 1646 he surrendered to the Scots, who handed him over to the English Parliament. When the New Model Army, now a dangerously independent political force, fell out with Parliament in the summer of 1647, its commanders took possession of the King and occupied

London. Fairfax became one of Moll's neighbours, being quartered in Brandenburgh House in Hammersmith, the riverside home of an evicted Royalist.

As Moll settled into her own Hammersmith lodgings, the New Model Army forcibly prevented certain Members of Parliament from taking their seats in the House of Commons. On 6 January 1649 the purged and intimidated chamber authorised the trial of the King. On 20 January 1649 Charles I was found guilty of treason by a court whose legitimacy he refused to accept. Ten days later he was led across the yard outside Banqueting Hall in front of a silent crowd and executed with a single blow from an axe. On 6 February Parliament voted to abolish the House of Lords, and the next day abolished the monarchy itself. England was a republic and a rogue state, henceforth to be 'Governed as a Commonwealth and Free State by the supreame Authoritie of this Nation, the Representatives of the People in Parliament and by such as they shall appoint and constitute as Officers and Ministers under them for the good of the People and that without any King or House of Lords.'

The nation was convulsed, its constitutional fabric ripped and shredded. Despite a decade of debate and polemic on kingship, parliamentary representation and the rights and responsibilities of ruler and ruled, most people still believed that the King was divinely appointed. The headless corpse in Whitehall was God's own representative, and who knew how God might punish the nation for its actions? When fleeing Royalists brought news of the regicide to Virginia and Barbados, the colonial administrations proclaimed their loyalty to the dead King's son; they wanted nothing to do with this unconstitutional and irreligious republic. Virginia, nonetheless, came to a swift accommodation with Parliamentary forces when an English fleet was sent to 'reduce the colony' in 1651, settling for the right, denied by Charles I, to trade with nations other than England.

Moll's lodgings are only a few miles from the scaffold in Whitehall, and the troops of the New Model Army thunder back and forth between Hammersmith and Westminster each day. They bother her no more in London than they did in Bath. 'Now,' she recalls,

I was indeed in the height of what I might call my prosperity, and I wanted nothing but to be a wife, which, however, could not be in this

case, there was no room for it; and therefore on all occasions I study'd
to save what I could . . . against a time of scarcity, knowing well enough
that such things as these do not always continue . . . I kept no company
but in the family where I lodg'd, and with a clergyman's lady at next
door; so that when [my lover] was absent I visited nobody, nor did he
ever find me out of my chamber or parlor whenever he came down;
if I went anywhere to take the air, it was always with him.

Thus a facade of respectability is carefully preserved, while adultery
and illegitimate births take place behind it. One wonders how many
happy but forbidden real-life ménages survived and defied the moral
violence of the Commonwealth. Was Moll's a fictional exception, or
was England quietly humming with illicit couples getting on with life
and love as they always had? Moll bears two more babies in Hammersmith, but both die. The boy born in Bath survives, however, and
mother and son 'live six years in this happy but unhappy condition'.
Despite the turmoil about her, Moll seems set for a fair passage through
her middle age. However, she is sailing dangerously close to the wind.
Austere men had seized power in England when the King's head rolled.
For them the cosy world inhabited by Moll, her lover and their illegitimate son was an abhorrence, something to be rooted out, held up
for public condemnation and destroyed.

Adultery had been a capital offence in Puritan New England for
nearly two decades. The most famous case was that of Mary Batchellor,
who is believed to be the inspiration for Nathaniel Hawthorne's novel
The Scarlet Letter. In 1650 Mary was sentenced to receive thirty-nine
lashes and be branded with the letter A. In 1652 her husband returned
to England, abandoning his wife and infant child to fend for themselves in America. Mary's petition for divorce – a reasonable request
in the circumstances, one would have thought – was denied, and she
was whipped again. For the men now in control in England, Parliament's first duty was to enforce a similarly strict interpretation of
godly government. In May 1650 it approved an act 'for suppressing the
detestable sins of Incest, Adultery and Fornication'.

Be it enacted by the authority of this present Parliament, That in case
any married woman shall from and after the Four and twentieth day of
June . . . be carnally known by any man (other then her Husband) (except

in Case of Ravishment) and of such offence or offences shall be convicted as aforesaid by confession or otherwise, every such Offence and Offences shall be and is hereby adjudged Felony: and every person, as well the man as the woman, offending therein, and confessing the same, or being thereof convicted by verdict upon Indictment or Presentment as afore-said, shall suffer death as in case of Felony, without benefit of Clergy.

There were a couple of get-out clauses in this infamous and ultimately ineffective act: if a man did not know the woman was married, he would not be prosecuted; if the woman's husband 'shall be continu-ally remaining beyond the Seas by the space of three years, or shall by common fame be reputed to be dead' or had abandoned his wife more than three years before, the woman was off the hook.

If Moll and her lover know of this new law – and the new Parlia-ment made its pronouncements at thunderous, unavoidable volume – they may consider themselves safe nonetheless. Certainly they do not tryst for the last time on Parliament's cut-off day and part for ever on 25 June. Adultery by a married man does not, after all, count for the Puritans, so Moll's lover will not be prosecuted for infidelity to his wife. He also believes Moll to be a widow. The clauses concerning husbands beyond the seas or those reputed dead might give Moll some comfort, although any investigation into her marital history to judge the truth of such claims may turn up severe embarrassments. Even if the couple falls outside the prescriptions of the new rules on adul-tery, however, they are certainly falling foul of the act's third listed offence, fornication.

If any man shall from and after the Four and twentieth day of June . . . have the carnal knowledge of the body of any Virgin, unmarried Woman or Widow, every such man so offending, and confessing the same, or being thereof convicted by verdict upon Indictment or Present-ment, as also every such woman so offending, and confessing the same, or being thereof convict as aforesaid, shall for every such offence be committed to the common Gaol, without Bail or Mainprize, there to continue for the space of three Moneths.

The 1650 Act was the culmination of a long campaign against incon-tinence. For decades petitions had been raised, sermons preached and pamphlets published calling for the Church to concentrate less on time-wasting ceremonies that reeked of Catholicism and more on curbing the sexual immorality of its flock. It might seem that these were times in which people like Moll Flanders could not possibly flourish, let alone continue along their normal path, yet what Parliament decreed and ordered its officers to detect and punish did not always get done. In practice, it seems, juries presented with women on trial for their lives on charges of adultery disliked the harshness of the law. Of twenty-two women charged under the Adultery Act during the eleven years of the Interregnum (it was swept off the statute books in 1660) only one was convicted and hanged. The rest were found not guilty.

Moll, at least, never cites the new morality laws as influencing her decisions or way of life. Her conscience occasionally troubles her, 'yet I had the terrible prospect of poverty and starving, which lay on me as a frightful spectre, so that there was no way of looking behind me'. The new administration knew how to belabour women like Moll with an enormous stick, but not how to provide them with a different way of existence. For six years Moll lives quietly as a citizen of the commonwealth, her way of life an outrage to its guiding principles.

The prevailing atmosphere of disapproval, repression, danger and spiritual terror, however, works its insidious way into her lover's mind. Once more it is not an event of national or colonial importance which wrecks Moll's tranquil life, but one entirely within the domestic sphere. Disaster strikes when her lover falls ill and nearly dies. Unable to ask openly for news of him, Moll disguises herself as a maidservant 'in a round cap and straw hat', sent by her mistress to know how the gentleman is, and gets the servants' gossip. It is a tremendous shock: 'the doctors said there was very little hopes of him', the kitchen maids tell her; indeed, 'they did not expect that he could live over the next night'.

This is terrible news to Moll, whose thoughts revert instantly to how she is going to support herself and the child. However, a fortnight or so later she learns that he has survived, and that 'there was hopes for his life'. She settles into waiting to hear from him. As weeks, then months, go by, and she knows he is alive and recovered, she cannot understand why he has not written to her. Worse, he has stopped sending her money; the rent is due, and they have nothing to eat. Her letters go unanswered, until she pays someone to put one straight into his hands as he sits in a coffee house. To this, he sends a dreadful answer.

> MADAM – I need not acquaint you with what has been my condition for some time past; and how, having been at the edge of the grave, I am, by the unexpected and undeserv'd mercy of Heaven restor'd again: in the condition I have been in, it cannot be strange to you that our unhappy correspondence has not been the least of the burthens which lay upon my conscience; I need say no more; those things that must be repented of, must be also reform'd.

Their relationship is over. Parliament would have been proud: to save his soul, he has turned out his mistress.

> I wish you would think of going back to the *Bath*, I enclose you here a bill for 50 *l.* for clearing your self at your lodgings, and carrying you down, and hope it will be no surprize to you to add, that on this account only, and not for any offence given me on your side, I can SEE YOU NO MORE; I will take due care of the child, leave him where he is, or take him with you, as you please; I wish you the like reflections, and that they may be to your advantage. I am, &c.

Moll writes again in an attempt to shame him into making more provision for her, telling him she 'desir'd to repent as sincerely as he had done, but entreated him to put me in some condition that I might not be exposed to the temptations which the Devil never fails to excite us to from the frightful prospect of poverty and distress'. She will not trouble him further, she pleads, and as a guarantee of that suggests she go back to Virginia if he will put up another fifty pounds to get her there. That suggestion, however, is 'a cheat so far, *viz*, that I had no intention to go to Virginia . . . the business was to get this last 50 *l.* of him, if possible, knowing well enough it would be the last penny I was ever to expect.' It is a lesson she has been learning since her early days in Colchester. Fifty pounds arrives; she signs a 'general release' and thus, 'though full sore against my will, a final end was put to this affair'.

8

Moll meets her one true love in Lancashire, 1654–7

Moll Flanders' relationship with her married lover takes her into the early years of the 1650s. A little later in that decade – Moll is always vague with dates – her life begins to resemble that of the real-life adventuress, Moll's contemporary Mary Steadman, née Moders (or Modders) alias Day alias Carleton alias Countess Maria de Wolway, also known as Kentish Moll, the German Princess and, more vulgarly, Mary the Vulva.

Born Mary Moders in 1642, she was the daughter of a Canterbury tradesman: a shoemaker by some accounts, a maker of violins by others. Little Mary found her pretty ways and genteel habits gave her an entrée to a slightly higher class of children and she acquired a taste for the kind of life which her status at birth did not allow. In the late 1650s she married a shoemaker who could not support her as she wished, and when both children of the marriage died, Mary, now surnamed Steadman, decided she had had enough.

Moll Flanders takes the relatively modest step of going to Bath in order to seek her fortune; Mary Steadman's plan was bolder. Her first attempt to start a new life took her on board a ship at Gravesend bound for Barbados, the richest island in the British Americas and the perfect place for a determined woman to reinvent herself. This was an island made for aspiring bigamists, for men outnumbered women at least threefold, some of them having abandoned wives and children in England for parishes to deal with. 'A Baud,' said one shocked

visitor to the island in 1655, 'brought ouer puts on a demuor comport-
ment, a whore . . . makes a wife for some rich planter.' Unfortunately,
Mr Steadman – or someone else – collared Mary before the ship left
and brought her back. It is from this date – the early 1660s – that her
life begins to provide what seems to be direct inspiration for some of
Moll Flanders' adventures.

What happened to Mary Steadman immediately after her Barbadian
adventure was thwarted is unclear – either she ran away again, or
Steadman abandoned her – but she soon married Mr Day, a Dover
surgeon. Her first indictment for bigamy followed but was dropped
because she convinced the court that she had believed Steadman to be
dead when she remarried. As Steadman turned out to be alive, however,
her life with Day was at an end and Mary Moders-Steadman-Day too
found herself a 'widow bewitched'. She sailed for Europe, to work on
the new identity which would return her to marriageability. According
to an account of her adventures written by the Newgate Ordinary in
1673, she travelled to the German city of Cologne, taking respectable
lodgings there in which to entrap her suitors, and frequenting the baths
for which Cologne, like Bath, was famous. 'Here,' ran the same account,
'our adventuress had the picking of a few feathers from an old gentleman
who fell in love with her' before fleeing back to the Low Countries
and taking a boat to England. Whatever she had plucked from her
German admirer, however, did not keep her going for long.

When she reappeared in England she was, she said, Maria de Wolway,
daughter of Henry van Wolway, Lord of Holmstein, a fictional German
principality. Lord Henry, she explained, had promised her to an aged
suitor whom she was determined not to marry, and for this reason
she had fled to London. More precisely, she fled to the Exchange
Tavern in Poultry, this being the first place she found open when she
came off the early boat from Gravesend in March 1663, disembarking
with the fish and demurely dressed in 'an old black velvet waistcoat,
black silk petticoat, and black hoods drawn over her face'. According
to the Newgate Ordinary's account

> She was got into the aforesaid tavern, in company with some gentlemen,
> who, she perceived, were pretty full of money. These gentlemen
> addressing her in the manner usual on such occasions, she immedi-
> ately feigned a cry, which she had always at command. The tears trickled

down her cheeks, she sighed, she sobbed, and the cause being
demanded, she told them that she little thought once of being reduced
to such a wretched necessity as she was now in, of exposing her body
to the pleasure of every bidder. Here she repeated the history of her
extraction and education, telling them a great deal about her pretended
father, the Lord Henry van Wolway, who, she said, was a sovereign
Prince of the Empire, independent of any man but his sacred Impe-
rial Majesty.

They fell for it. The Lady Maria was given a room in which, she was
assured, the valuables she had brought with her would be safe and
which would afford her the 'secrecy, seclusion and rest' she needed.
After a nap she went to post letters to the Continent concerning, she
said, her affairs, and then engaged in a long sympathetic talk with Mrs
King the landlady.

Mrs King's eighteen-year-old brother John Carleton was a man in
need of both fortune and wife. Alerted to the presence of a distressed
lady with a title and a bag of cash, John hotfooted round from the
Inns of Court, where he was a clerk, and began his seduction.

> He made his addresses to the Princess van Wolway in the most dutiful
> and submissive manner that could be imagined, making use of his
> brother's interest to negotiate the affair between them, till with a great
> deal of seeming reluctance at marrying one of common blood, her
> highness consented to take him to her embraces. Now was Mr Carleton
> as great as his Majesty, in the arms of an imaginary princess; he formed
> to himself a thousand pleasures, which the vulgar herd could have no
> notion of; he threw himself at her feet in transport, and made use of
> all the rhetoric he could collect to thank her for the prodigious honour
> she had done him.

This at least was one version of his behaviour; Mary herself would
later claim that he kept her 'close in the nature of a Prisoner', under
cover of devotion but in reality to exclude rivals and force her hand.
Most contemporary commentators accepted that John had exagger-
ated his status and prospects to make himself more enticing to the
young noblewoman he presumed he was wooing. Either way, the
courtship was brief. Letters arrived for Mary from abroad which

seemed to substantiate her story and they married in April 1663. For a happy fortnight they lived in handsome rooms – the rent forwarded by the Carleton parents in expectation of Mary's own money soon arriving – and dashed round Hyde Park in rented coaches. But something in Mary's story had failed to convince some friend of her new husband's, who wrote secretly to Dover for information. A letter came in return.

DOVER, May the 4th, 1663.

SIR: This morning I received your letter, dated May the 2nd instant, and accordingly have made inquiry. By what I can discover, it is a gentlewoman that is the greatest cheat in the world. She hath now two husbands living in this town, the one a shoemaker named Thomas Stedman, the other a chirurgeon named Thomas Day. She was born in Canterbury, her maiden name is Mary Modders, her father was a musician belonging to Christ Church, Canterbury. She was lately in Dover Castle a prisoner, taken out of a ship bound for the Barbadoes, where she cheated the master of 50 pounds. If it be she, I am sorry for your friend's misfortune. If I shall refer you to Mr John Williams his wife, who liveth near St Saviour's Dock, Newstaires, near Redriff, she is the master's wife of the Barbadoes ship; and if you can prevail with her to go to see her, she will give you full satisfaction whether it be she or no. I pray you send me a line of the appearance of the business, and the man's name that is married to her and his calling; for it is reported a minister took her up at Gravesend. My respects to your-self and father. I remain, your loving friend.

As John Carleton learns he has been duped by his princess, we return to Moll Flanders, also a widow bewitched, twenty years older than Mary and once more experiencing 'the terror of approaching poverty'. The money her former lover has grudgingly put up is not enough to support her for long. 'I cast about for innumerable ways for my future state of life,' she writes, 'and began to consider very seriously what I should do, but nothing offer'd.' She can only fall back on the strategy which has worked for her previously: 'I took care to make the world take me for something more than I was, and had it given out that I was a fortune.' She protests that she does not do this for the love of deception, but is forced to it by circumstances:

I was now a loose unguided creature, and had no help, no assistance, no guide for my conduct: I knew what I aim'd at, and what I wanted, but knew nothing how to pursue the end by direct means; I wanted to be plac'd in a settled state of living, and had I happen'd to meet with a sober good husband, I should have been as faithful and true a wife to him as virtue it self could have form'd: if I had been otherwise, the vice came in always at the door of necessity, not at the door of inclination; and I understood too well, by the want of it, what the value of a settl'd life was, to do any thing to forfeit the felicity of it; nay, I should have made the better wife for all the difficulties I had pass'd thro', by a great deal.

Opportunity comes when a fellow lodger in London, a lady from Liverpool, hears the discreetly fostered rumours that Widow Whatever-name-she-is-going-by is worth a fortune, and begins seeking her friendship. After many little chats on the difficulties of living within one's income in London, the lady proposes that Moll accompany her on a tour of Lancashire, staying with her relations and thereby saving a little money. Her brother James, the lady says, known familiarly as Jemmy, 'was a considerable gentleman, and had a great estate also in *Ireland*'; he would be charmed to offer them his hospitality. With little hesitation Moll leaves for Liverpool with an eye to the gentleman brother. 'It was a base design I went with,' she would confess, 'tho' I was invited thither with a design much worse than mine was, as the sequel will discover.'

It is too dangerous for Moll to carry her money with her while she travels the lonely roads of north-west England but finding somewhere safe to leave it in London proves difficult.

I found my self in great distress; what little I had in the world was all in money, except as before, a little plate, some linen, and my cloaths; but I had not one friend in the world with whom to trust that little I had, or to direct me how to dispose of it, and this perplex'd me night and day; I thought of the bank, and of the other companies in *London*, but I had no friend to commit the management of it to, and to keep and carry about with me bank bills, talleys, orders, and such things, I look'd upon it as unsafe; that if they were lost my money was lost, and then I was undone; and, on the other hand, I might be robb'd and perhaps murder'd in a strange place for them; this perplex'd me strangely, and what to do I knew not.

Eventually she is recommended to a clerk in the bank where she has occasionally cashed bills sent to her by Humphrey. Presenting herself as a widow just arrived from America 'perfectly desolate and friendless', she asks this 'broker's' advice and receives an explanation of how she might deposit her money in London but draw upon it even as far away as Chester. This seems a miraculous operation to her, but the gentleman who explains it is honest, she is sure, and competent; he is also clearly struck by his handsome new client. After a great deal of flirtatious talk about what he might do were he only in a position to do it, Moll gets to the nub of it. Her new friend and admirer is in almost the same fix as she: 'I have,' he confesses ruefully, 'a wife and no wife . . . to be plain with you, I am a *cuckold*, and she is a *whore*.'

A rushed and businesslike courtship follows. He declares his intention to seek a divorce and wants to know if Moll will marry him if he does so; she says she will consider the matter seriously but, with the prospect of Liverpool before her, is unwilling to commit herself further. The banker is honest, true; solvent, decent and clearly enamoured; and with all that a bit dull. Perhaps memories of honest Robin, the Colchester bore, enter her mind.

> In short, I ventur'd to avoid signing a contract of marriage, and the reason why I did it, was because the lady that had invited me so earnestly to go with her into *Lancashire* insisted so positively upon it, and promised me such great fortunes, and such fine things there, that I was tempted to go and try; Perhaps, *said I*, I may mend myself very much, and then I made no scruple in my thoughts, of quitting my honest citizen, whom I was not so much in love with, as not to leave him for a richer.

Knowing her money is in good hands and she has a marital safety net behind her, Moll sets off for Liverpool.

Lancashire is a new county for Moll. She does not burst into it with quite the élan of the German Princess entering the Exchange Tavern, for her cover is that of a rich but sober widow. Her design, however, is exactly the same. Jemmy is, it seems, exactly what Moll has been looking for, driving up 'in his own chariot, and in a very good figure, with two footmen in a good livery'. According to her friend, he is 'a match worth my lissening to, and the last his estate was valued at, was a 1000 *l.* a year, but the sister said it was worth 1500 *l.* a year, and lay most of it in *Ireland.*' The two fortune-hunters size each other up, like what they see and begin the game.

> I that was a great fortune, and pass'd for such, was above being ask'd how much my estate was, and my false friend taking it upon a foolish hearsay had rais'd it from 500 *l.* to 5000 *l.* and by the time she came into the country [i.e. Lancashire] she call'd it 15000 *l.* The Irishman, for such I understood him to be, was stark mad at this bait: in short, he courted me, made me presents, and run in debt like a mad man for the expences of his equipage, and of his courtship . . . He never so much as asked me about my fortune or estate, but assured me that when we came to *Dublin* he would jointure me in 600 *l.* a year good land [leave her land worth £600 per year on his death] . . . this was such language indeed as I had not been used to.

She will have the use of his 'park and his stables, of his horses, his gamekeepers, his woods, his tenants, and his servants', all of which he and his sister take pains to describe to her as well 'as if we had been in the mansion-house, and I had seen them all about me'. The man's prospects seem as enticing as his person, but Moll does not know that this time she has met her match. Both sexes play the game of hooking a rich mate, sometimes by courtship and sometimes by violence. Moll is taking a risk in allowing it to be thought she is a rich widow and leaving the security of a place where she is known.

Although the Scots seem to have been particularly given to the practice of bridal abduction, the kidnapping and forcible marriage of rich women also occurred in England. One famous case took place in 1637, when fourteen-year-old heiress Sarah Cox was snatched from Newington Common by Roger Fulwood, the brother of a school-friend. Roger took the girl to Winchester Palace, residence of the Bishop of Southwark, and asked his mother to look after her overnight. The following morning Sarah was taken to a chapel and found herself summarily married, then stripped and put to bed with her abductor in the presence of witnesses. Fortunately, friends tracked her down and rescued her; eventually the marriage was annulled and Sarah's fortune was saved. As Antonia Fraser describes in *The Weaker Vessel* (1984), Roger Fulwood, initially sentenced to be hanged, was pardoned and released after his mother petitioned Charles I, claiming it had not been a serious crime.

The Fulwood affair attracted notoriety because of Roger's aristocratic connections. A shoemaker operating in the 1670s attracted his women less sensationally but with far more charm. He appeared at the Old Bailey in 1676, 'charged by common Fame with having Seventeen Wives', although he was only indicted for four. Unlike Roger Fulwood, the shoemaker had relied on personal appeal rather than brute force. For five years he had travelled England 'pretending himself a person of quality, and assuming the names of good families, and that he had a considerable Estate per Annum'. Making it his business to find well-off single women, he 'would very formally make Love to them, wherein being of handsome taking presence, and Master of a voluble insinuating tongue, he commonly succeeded to engage their easie affections'. Once married, he 'for some small time injoy'd their persons, and got possession of their more beloved Estates', and vanished 'with what ready mony and other portable things of value he could get'. Although the shoemaker begged at his trial for transportation, his petition, unlike that of the better-connected Fulwood's, was not heard. He was hanged.

Moll, however, is as sure that Jemmy is telling her the truth about his fortune as Jemmy is that Moll is telling the truth about her own. Moreover, the pair have fallen headily in love, and so they marry, Moll under the impression she is going to live like a great lady on estates recently torn from their Irish owners and Jemmy believing his bride is bringing him £15,000, on which he can live like a gentleman wherever he pleases. It is only when they are married and talking of heading for Holyhead to make the crossing to Ireland that Jemmy begins asking pointed questions. Has she no business to settle in London before she leaves England? Is her estate in the Bank of England[7] – in investments – or in some other form? Land perhaps? Moll, safe with a ring on her finger, comes clean, or cleanish at least. 'I seemed to look strange at it, and told him I knew not what he

---

7 Defoe commits one of his occasional historical mistakes here: the Bank of England was not established until 1694.

meant; that I had no effects in the Bank of *England* that I knew of;
and I hoped he could not say that I had ever told him I had: no, he
said, I had not told him so, but his sister had said the greatest part
of my estate lay there.'

So the sister is summoned to explain to her brother and new sister-
in-law exactly what she told whom, and on what authority. When the
bad news is broken to Jemmy that his new wife has approximately
one hundred pounds to her name, fur flies.

> He cou'd not speak a word but pointed to [the sister]; and, after some
> more pause, flew out in the most furious passion that ever I saw a man
> in my life; cursing her, and calling her all the whores and hard names
> he could think of; and that she had ruin'd him, declaring that she had
> told him I had fifteen thousand pounds, and that she was to have five
> hundred pounds of him for procuring this match for him. He then
> added, directing his speech to me, that she was none of his sister, but
> had been his whore for two years before, that she had had one hundred
> pounds of him in part of this bargain . . . *she cried*, said she had been
> told so in the house where I lodg'd. But this aggravated him more than
> before, that she should put so far upon him, and run things such a
> length upon no other authority than *a hear-say*; and then, turning to
> me again, said very honestly, he was afraid we were both undone; for
> to be plain, *my dear*, I have no estate, *says he*, what little I had, this devil
> has made me run out in waiting on you and putting me into this
> equipage . . .
>
> Why, *says I to him*, this has been a hellish juggle, for we are married
> here upon the foot of a double fraud.

The consequences of Moll Flanders' little fraud are very different to
that of the Princess de Wolway's. When the anonymous letter arrived
from Canterbury with accusations against the new Mrs Carleton, her
in-laws immediately acted. They confronted Mary with the claims;
she denied them. They examined the jewellery she had made such a
fuss about keeping safe and found it was counterfeit. News of this
development shot round the City, and various people came knocking
at the Carleton door, saying she was not to be trusted: Mrs Williams
(mentioned in the letter) appeared, as did a shoemaker who had known
Mary during the time she had lived at Mrs Williams' house. Mary

proudly denied it all, her German accent never slipping, but in May 1663 she was charged and sent back to prison, awaiting a second trial for bigamy.

It was one of those cases which grips the popular imagination every so often. On one side there was a pretty lady with a devious brain, a nice line in distressed womanhood and a phalanx of noisy supporters. On the other there was a vindictive, silly, humiliated man – but one who had right on his side. London was enthralled by the scandal and the woman at its centre. The pamphleteers were more cynical. *The lawyer's clerk trepanned by the crafty whore of Canterbury* was on sale within days, then the journal *The Man in the Moon*, forerunner of the modern red-tops, took up the story. 'She spoke Dutch, French, and several broken languages,' it said excitedly, 'telling them her estate was 12,000 a year, and that she had jewels about her worth 3,000 more, and a coach with six Flanders mares besides store of coin coming over.'

By her own account, Mary Carleton, like Moll Flanders, had been very careful to allow rumours of her fortune (if not her birth and single status) to be spread by others and never to allow them to be directly attributable to herself. She had dressed herself to look rich, behaved in the manner of a rich lady, worn jewels only a rich lady might be expected to own and written letters to the Continent (and received some back) which she said were about her estate. Yet never had she explicitly claimed to be rich. It was the innkeeper, she said, who 'conceived such imaginations in his Head that he claimed she was worth £8,000 a year', and as for the Carletons, 'it is sure a greater imputation and shame to them to be found such Cheats and Lyars, than it can be the least slur to me, who never avowed any such thing, nor boasted of my Quality and Fortune'.

It should have been an easy matter to prove Mary Carleton a bigamist, especially as the injured party was a lawyer's clerk. Nonetheless, the prosecution was brought with such extraordinary ineptitude that she was acquitted. She appeared calm and sober in the Old Bailey, behaving herself with a 'grace and gallant deportment' worthy of her claimed upbringing and ready to hear the case against her. The charge was straightforward but the evidence was not. Instead of her first husband, one Mr Knot appeared and said he 'had known Mary from childhood, identified her, and testified that he had given her in marriage to Thomas Stedman.' Instead of the Dover surgeon, there was a letter attesting her marriage to him from some other person. Other prosecution witnesses were confused and unconvincing, and Mary suggested sadly that bribery rather than a love of truth had brought them to London that day. Then she produced five of her own who swore blind that she had been born, to their certain knowledge, in Cologne.

Why, asked the judge, did she come to England? To advance her fortunes, she replied, adding, 'I thought not to cheat anybody, though many went about to cheat me.' What thought ye when ye married Mr Carleton? asked the bench, to which she repeated, 'My Lord, if any cheat was in the business, they went about to cheat me, I not them; for they thought by marriage of me to dignify themselves and advance all their relations, and upon that account were there any cheat, they cheated themselves.' The judge pointed out to the jury that if she really had been married previously, additional evidence of that fact should have been presented, and that if they did not believe Mr Knot's unsupported testimony, they must acquit her. They did so. One last item remained. When the Carletons had rejected Mary, they had taken from her her expensive clothes, her counterfeit jewels and all her other portable wealth.

'My Lord, though I am acquit from all these crimes which is falsely laid against me, what shall I do for my clothes taken from me?'

'We ought not to look for that,' replied the judge; 'you have now a husband to do it.'

Samuel Pepys, in a lively discussion of the case with his friends, was 'high in defence of her wit and spirit, and glad that she is cleared at sessions'. He had no doubt of her innocence but if ever there was a sucker for a pretty face, Pepys was it. Although Mary's marriage to John Carleton had been judged legal, however, it was now over. Maintenance of the wife was supposed to be the flip side of the law by which a married man acquired her property, but the Carleton family had no intention of maintaining Mary. She was on her uppers, and this time so publicly that she could not, like Moll Flanders, simply retire to another part of the country and pull the same scam again. She had to stay in London and do what she could to survive.

It is different for Moll and Jemmy. Despite the way in which each has misled the other, both believe they have truly found the love of their lives, and the cheat does not affect their feelings. Moll offers her husband the twenty pounds and eleven guineas which is (nearly) all she has; he refuses to take it and flings down the fifty guineas which is his entire estate, 'bidding me take it, though he were to starve for want of it'. Each toasts the other ruefully at the valedictory dinner which follows, and then there is a night of what she refers to delicately as 'close conversation'.[8] 'We proposed a great many things, but nothing could offer where there was nothing to begin with. He begged me at last to talk no more of it, for, he said, I would break his heart; so we talked of other things a little, till at last he took a husband's leave of me, and so we went to sleep'.

He is gone when she wakes but returns within hours, as unable to leave her as she is him. They travel south together, agreeing they must harden their hearts and separate in Bedfordshire, from where Moll will go on to London alone. At the final coaching inn, however, she begs a further two weeks with him to see if they might not 'think of something to prevent such a ruinous thing to us both, as a final separation would be'. In unromantic Dunstable she makes her final proposal. It is of the age: when there is nothing left to be done in England, the time has come for the colonies. Skating over the more complicated details, Moll relates to Jemmy how well she lived in Virginia; that her mother is still there, and a wealthy woman; and that her husband has been dead some years.

Then I entered into the manner of peoples going over to those countries to settle, how they had a quantity of land given them by the constitution of the place; and if not, that it might be purchased at so easie a rate that it was not worth naming.

I then gave him a full and distinct account of the nature of planting; how with carrying over but two or three hundred pounds' value of *English* goods, with some servants and tools, a man of application would presently lay the foundation for a family, and in a very few years be certain to raise an estate.

I let him into the nature of the product of the earth; how the ground was cur'd and prepared, and what the usual increase of it was; and demonstrated to him, that in a very few years, with such a beginning, we should be as certain of being rich as we were now certain of being

---

8 'Conversation' was a legal term for sexual intercourse, particularly in the phrase 'criminal conversation', meaning adultery.

poor . . . and added, that after seven years, if we liv'd, we might be in
a posture to leave our plantations in good hands, and come over again
and receive the income of it, and live here and enjoy it; and I gave him
examples of some that had done so, and liv'd now in very good circumstances in *London*.

It was a complete manifesto, the sort which came, printed, from shipping agents and indenturing syndicates. Jemmy is not unreceptive to
colonial adventure but is reluctant to cross the Atlantic to find it. There
is, after all, an easier way for Cromwell's Englishmen to get hold of
land in the 1650s. Just across the sea from Liverpool the fertile fields
of Ireland are ripe for marriage to English capital.

The English (or Norman) conquest of Ireland is a long, sad and
bloody story. It began in the twelfth century, when Henry II installed
an Anglo-Norman elite to rule alongside the Gaelic chieftains, and was
taken up with renewed vigour during the Reformation. Ireland then
posed a Catholic threat to the newly Protestant England which Henry
VIII knew he must neutralise, if not by persuasion or assimilation then
by conquest. The end of his daughter Elizabeth's reign had seen a bloody
nine-year war between English forces and the Ulster Confederacy, an
alliance of chieftains from Ireland's northernmost province. Repression
had continued under James I. The Ulster plantation – a scheme for
forcibly settling Ulster with Protestant landowners – was set in motion
in 1609, just after the Virginia Company was established and with some
of the same English dynasties at the sharp end of conquest and exploita-
tion. Cheap land and labour enticed English and Scots tradesmen,
labourers and capitalists across the Irish Sea, and a plantocracy grew up
in Ulster as it did in Virginia and Barbados, although not without oppo-
sition. Guerrilla warfare plagued the English settlers behind their
palisades and Irish Catholic 'rebels' seized their chance and fell on the
Protestant settlers during the chaos of the English Civil War. In 1649 an
alliance was signed between the Irish Confederates and Charles II, son
of the executed King, who was living on the Continent and plotting his
return to England. When Oliver Cromwell had dealt with his enemies
in England, therefore, he turned with a vengeance to the Irish.

While Moll and her former lover were canoodling in Hammersmith, Oliver Cromwell was suppressing colonial dissent. A fleet was
sent to Virginia and an army crossed to Ireland. Drogheda was besieged

in 1650, its garrison massacred and its commander beaten to death with his own wooden leg. Next came Lisnagarvey in County Antrim, the sack of Wexford and the siege of Waterford, the reduction of Duncannon, Kilkenny, Conmel, Munster and Limerick. When Galway surrendered in 1651, Ireland lay at Cromwell's mercy. Anyone judged to have participated in the rebellion against the Protestant settlers was killed; thousands were sent as slaves to the West Indian plantations, and the land of all Confederates was confiscated. These were the estates which Moll's new husband was proposing to buy and manage. In Ireland, as Jemmy enthusiastically calculated, 'a man that could confine himself to country life, and that could but find stock to enter upon any land, should have farms there for £50 a year, as good as were here [i.e. in England] let for £200 a year; that the produce was such, and so rich the land, that . . . we were sure to live as handsomely upon it as a gentleman of £3000 a year could do in England.'

Husband and wife argue fondly back and forth over whose expropriated lands might yield the greater income, but Jemmy proves immoveable. He tells Moll 'that if he found nothing to be done in *Ireland*, he would then come to me and join in my project for *Virginia*' but would concede no more than that. The lovers part at last, 'though with the utmost reluctance on my side; and indeed he took his leave very unwillingly too, but necessity obliged him, for his reasons were very good why he would not come to London, as I understood more fully some time later'.

Alone once more, Moll returns to London and takes lodgings near Clerkenwell, on the northern edge of the City, where 'being perfectly alone, I had leisure to sit down and reflect seriously upon the last seven months ramble I had made; the pleasant hours I had with my last husband I look'd back on with an infinite deal of pleasure; but that pleasure was very much lessened when I found some time after that I was really with child.'

9

Moll returns to London and encounters Mother Midnight, 1657–62

It is Moll's tenth pregnancy, and she is in her mid-forties. Her situation is nothing out of the ordinary for women of her time. Stevie Davis puts it neatly in *Unbridled Spirits* (1998), her collection of biographies of free-thinking women at the time of the English Revolution. Women, she says, were 'bound into cycles of child-bearing and child-burying, ignorant of contraception except for prophylaxis'. Moll's first two children, born in the early 1630s, were left with their grandparents in Colchester and are now adult. One, born to her brief second marriage, died as a baby. Three more, born in the late 1630s and early 1640s, are in Virginia with her husband/brother. She also bore three to her Hammersmith lover, although only one of these survived, the baby born in Bath in 1649 or 1650 and given up to her former lover when he was a 'fine, lovely boy of above five' and his father found God. Her situation at the time of his birth was very different to that she finds herself in now, for although the boy was a bastard, the father had had the decency to provide for him.

Her Bath landlady had made the arrangements at the time of that birth, with Moll's lover supplying the funds. Moll had somewhat dreaded letting the landlady into the secret of her pregnancy, but in fact she 'made light of it; she said she knew it would come to that at last, and made us very merry about it'. Fortunately they found her 'an experience'd old lady at such work; she undertook everything, engag'd to procure a midwife and a nurse, to satisfie all inquiries, and bring us off with reputation, and she did so very dexterously indeed'. It was just as well that the landlady knew her way around these procedures, for the bearing of children out of wedlock required a sure and delicate touch. Moll's landlady had to come up with a cover story if Moll, a woman in an adulterous relationship, were not to be denounced and hauled before the Church court, which would order her, at the least, to do public penance in church and, at the worst, to be 'whipped at the cart's arse'. The father-to-be was sent away to London, and when he had gone, the landlady 'acquainted the parish officers that there was a lady ready to lye in at her house, but that she knew her husband very well, and gave them, as she pretended, an account of his name, which she called Sir *Walter Cleave* . . . this satisfied the parish officers presently, and I lay in with as much credit as I could have done if I had really been my Lady *Cleave*.'

The father did not cavil at the expenses put to him by the landlady as being necessary and, Moll being Moll, she made a profit on the affair. 'As he had furnish'd me very sufficiently with money for the extraordinary expences of my lying in, I had everything very handsome about me [but] knowing my own circumstances, and knowing the world as I had done, and that such kind of things do not often last long, I took care to lay up as much money as I could for a wet day, as I call'd it.'

Three or four 'of the best citizens' wives of Bath' attended her and suspected nothing, such was the landlady's skill in telling tales. A 'charming child' was born, the bloody, perilous business of childbearing passed over in a sentence of sixteen words. Defoe was probably never present at the birth of his own children, for birthing in the seventeenth and early eighteenth centuries was acknowledged as a matter for women. 'Man-midwives' had not yet taken over.

Childbirth was a stuffy, smoky, smelly and intimate affair in a crowded room with as great a fire as the household could afford and trays of food continually brought to sustain and encourage the labouring woman: perhaps, as recommended in *The Compleat Midwifes Practice, In the most weighty and high Concernments of the Birth of Man* (1656), 'broth, yolk of a poached egg with some bread, a cup of wine or distilled water'. The midwife's first task when she arrived was to check the abdomen to see whether the child had 'fallen down' ('engaged', in modern terminology). If it had, she lubricated her hand with butter or oils and inserted it to check how far the cervix had dilated. Washing is not mentioned in the midwives' handbooks, and the notion of disinfecting would not be introduced for more than 200 years. Women were as likely to die of infection as of complications arising from the birth itself. If the labour was long or troubled, the midwife massaged the abdomen and the perineal tissues with sweet oils and administered an enema to relieve constipation. A suggested recipe included white wine, rosewater, damask prunes, raisins, mace, aniseed and sugar. Various herbal potions were commercially and locally available to speed labour and reduce pain. There was also a terrifying manual method of delivery known as the swathe band: a broad piece of linen wrapped around the labouring woman's abdomen and held on either side by brawny assistants who pulled with all their might when the mother pushed, hoping to pop the child out. In those cases where the membrane refused to rupture, a midwife in a hurry would tear at it with a fingernail, while one with more time sat her mother over a pot of warm water and herbs.

When the baby emerged, it was caught in the midwife's apron and laid on the mother's belly so its sex could be determined and any deformities found. The child was made to breathe and the umbilical cord was cut – close up for a girl, and some inches long for a boy, for a convex belly button was thought to inhibit the growth of the penis. Then the baby was oiled, swaddled, laid in its cradle and offered its first drink. Colostrum was thought to be bad, perhaps because of its unmilky appearance, and so the infant would generally be offered something heartier as a welcome to the seventeenth century: 'mithridate, molasses, wine and cardus water' was one brew recommended.

This treatment is what Moll and her son by 'Sir Walter Cleave' would have received in their comfortable chambers in Bath. A decade later and pregnant by Jemmy, Moll is in different circumstances. Although this time she really is married (if bigamously), she never expects to see her husband again and has no proof of her married status. She and Jemmy did not marry in church; there is no one around to back up the story, and provoking too many enquiries into her married life would, as usual, be unwise. With no one to vouch for her, she is at the mercy of parish informers.

The day-to-day business of the Church courts was to hear cases of morality: accusations of adultery, whoredom, fornication, incest or any other 'uncleanness and wickedness of life'. It was the responsibility of churchwardens to bring such cases before the courts, and of the various sources on whom they relied for their information – neighbours, family members, tavern gossip – midwives, with their privileged access to the secrets of the bedchamber, were among the most important. In recognition of this fact, as well as of their medical skills, they approached the status of professional as closely as any females could. Aspiring practitioners were apprenticed for up to seven years before appearing before a Church court to be examined, sworn and licensed. The licensing examination was performed not by a medic but by a cleric, for its objective was not to determine the woman's midwifery skills but the godliness of her character and her allegiance to the Anglican Church. A book of oaths dated 1649 tells us what the midwife promises to do in the course of her work: help poor women as well as rich, oblige the mother to name the true father of the child and ensure that the child is not killed, hurt or put in danger. She must not use witchcraft, charms or sorcery, nor administer abortifacients or allow a stillborn child to be clandestinely or improperly buried. If she hears of unprofessional practices by other midwives or of women practising without a licence, she must report them to the churchwardens. Finally, she must not allow baptism except as 'appointed by the Lawes of the Church of *Englande*'.

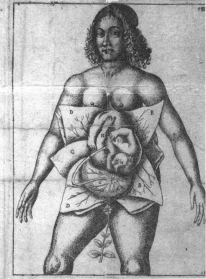

An illustration from *The Midwives Book, or the Whole Art of Midwifery discover'd* by Jane Sharpe, 1671

Some unlicensed women must have helped others give birth in isolated areas where there were no licensed practitioners or when the birth was secret. Some of these women were reported and presumably some were not. There must, similarly, have been midwives who did not tell all they should to the churchwardens. On the whole, however, according to a study of seventeenth-century London midwives by historian Doreen Evenden, the women took their oath very seriously. Why should they not? They were part of the society which produced these rules, respectable women who shared the views on moral and immoral behaviour which the rules enshrined. The conception and bearing of children was not a private matter, a concern only for the parents; it was a matter for parish and state, and midwives were at the birth as representatives of authority.

Moll, without a husband and in a strange place, does not know where she may safely turn for help in bearing her tenth child. 'This was a perplexing thing,' she recalls, 'because of the difficulty which was before me where I should get leave to lye inn; it being one of the nicest [trickiest] things in the world at that time of day, for a woman that was a stranger, and had no friends, to be entertain'd in that circumstance without security.'

This is one of the reasons so many poor girls who found themselves pregnant told no one, gave birth in private and killed the newborn baby. Cases of infanticide belonged not to the Church courts but to secular justice. They were regularly heard at the Old Bailey after 1624, when Parliament passed an act 'to prevent the murthering of bastard children'. Judgments tended to be harsh, both for the immorality of the child's conception and the manner of its death. Sessions Papers record two 'Young Wenches' appearing in 1674 who were

it seems inticed to Folly, and at last got with Child, and to cover one sin with a greater, most Unnaturally, and Barbarously, Murthered their Infants, one of them casting hers into an House of Office [lavatory], and the other endeavouring to Bury hers in a Celler: but being both discovered by certain Symtomes usually visible in that condition (presumably leaking breasts or vaginal bleeding), upon strait search, the whole matter came to be disclosed, and they respectively Commited. They had little to say for themselves besides the common Plea, that their Children were Still-born, but upon Reading the Statute whereby it is provided in such Cases that unless the same be proved by, at least one Credible witness, it shall be reputed and punished as Murder, and they were both Condemned to Dye.

When Moll's landlady notices her lodger's belly is swelling , she gives her notice to leave. When Moll falls ill, however, she relents and proposes, grudgingly, to procure a midwife. As Moll then realises, 'the mistress of the house was not so great a stranger to such cases as mine was, as I thought at first she had been . . . and she sent for a midwife of the right sort, that is to say, the right sort for me'. The midwife is summoned, comes to Moll's chamber and immediately reassures her client by promising secrecy. 'All the ladies that come under her care were married women to her,' she says. 'Every woman, *says she*, that is with child has a father for it, and whether that father was a husband or no husband, was no business of hers; her business was to assist me in my present circumstances, whether I had a husband or no. [And so] I found presently, that whether I was a whore or a wife, I was to pass for a whore here, so I let that go.'

In thieves' cant, the woman brought in to help is known as Mother Midnight. Her business is to run a clandestine lying-in house, or maternity hospital, for prostitutes and unmarried or adulterous women. She has bribed parish officials and Church ministers to turn a blind eye, in return for disposing of the children born in her house in such a way that they will not fall on parish expenses. (Moll's landlady, Mother Midnight tells her, would have liked to set up a similar operation, but 'could not secure the parish', the real reason for her initial resentment of a pregnant woman in her house.) Mother Midnight's clients are advised to spend three months lodging with her: two months before and one after the birth, and she offers a three-tier menu of services. Thirteen guineas, the lowest rate, buys board and lodging, 'a nurse for the month, and use of child-bed linen . . . a minister to christen the child and to the godfathers and clark' and 'a supper at the christening if I had five friends at it', her own services as a midwife and 'the taking off the trouble of the parish'. A more expensive option adds 'linnen and lace' to the child's clothes and crib, as well as sweetmeats at the christening party. The most expensive of all includes bed and board for the lady's own servant, 'the finest suit of child-bed linen' and 'a supper, the gentlemen to send in the wine'.

What complicates an already difficult situation for Moll is that she is still in regular correspondence with her London banker. He, faithful fool, knows nothing of her marriage to Jemmy and approaching accouchement. He thinks she is still in Liverpool, waiting to hear if his own petition for divorce has been successful. Nor is she going to tell him the truth. She writes once a week 'to let him know I was still alive' but has no intention of seeing him until the problem of the child has been resolved. His latest letter, full of 'kind, obliging things', is forwarded from Liverpool and arrives at Mother Midnight's house when Moll is heavily pregnant. It 'earnestly press[ed her] to return to London' because 'he had obtain'd a decree, I think he call'd it, against his wife, and that he would be ready to make good his engagement to me, if I would accept of him, adding a great many protestations of kindness and affection, such as he would have been far from offering if he had known the circumstances I had been in.'

She writes back, addressing her letter from Liverpool and announcing she will be back in London towards the end of the year. Is he sure, she asks – with a certain impudence, given her own circumstances – that his remarriage will be completely legal? She then turns to considering her options, explaining a little of her situation to Mother Midnight and asking her advice. The midwife, no stranger to the dangers arising from an unplanned pregnancy, provides two further services which Moll may find useful. The first she does not so much suggest, as hint at.

> One time in discoursing about my being so far gone with child, and the time I expected to come, she said something that look'd as if she could help me off with my burthen sooner, if I was willing; or, in *English*, that she could give me something to make me miscarry, if I had a desire to put an end to my troubles that way; but I soon let her see that I abhorr'd the thoughts of it; and, to do her justice, she put it off so cleverly, that I cou'd not say she really intended it, or whether she only mentioned the practice as a horrible thing; for she couch'd her words so well, and took my meaning so quickly, that she gave her negative before I could explain my self.

Just as the notion of a 'quickening' foetus could save female convicts from hanging, so it could save other women from the charge of abortion. Until the unborn child quickened in the womb, its soul was believed not to have entered its body and therefore its destruction was not murder. However, as many women must only have realised they were pregnant when they felt those first intimate movements, their quest to abort began only at that moment. More knowledgeable women would have realised earlier, when a regular menstrual pattern was disrupted or they were visited by nausea, and for them there was a plethora of herbal remedies. Some were home-made; others could be bought at apothecaries' shops. These were carefully described as being 'physic' for menstrual problems, designed to 'bring down the menses' or 'provoke the termes' when a regular cycle had been disrupted by illness. Nevertheless, they were widely understood also to be the means of causing an early abortion. The seventeenth-century herbalist Nicholas Culpeper specifically warned midwives to 'give not any of these to any that is with Child, least you turn murderers'. Rue was thought to be particularly effective, as was savin (juniper), perhaps because of their bitter taste, but various other concoctions were confessed to before the Church courts. Alan Macfarlane, in *Abortion Methods in England* (2002), writes that one man pressed his mistress to take 'bearsfoot and savon boiled, and drink it in milk, and likewise, hay madder chopt, and boiled in beer', while another poor girl in Colchester drank mercury, oil and 'steel filings in a bottle'.

Mother Midnight may have been offering to procure and administer one of these remedies. However, as Moll was several months pregnant, she was probably suggesting a stronger intervention. Poison was more effective when it was injected directly into the womb, and if this did not work, the abortionist inserted a sharp implement to dislodge the foetus and cause an early stillbirth. Either of these methods was desperately unsafe, threatening the life of the mother as well as that of the unborn child.'[10] Moll, in any case, rejects any suggestion of abortion, and so Mother Midnight turns to discussion of the other service she provides.

> This grave matron had several sorts of practise, and this was one partic-
> ular, that if a child was born, tho' not in her house (for she had the

---

[10] Just before the Abortion Act was passed in England in 1967, it was estimated that 20 per cent of gynaecological admissions to the NHS were the result of back-street abortions gone wrong.

occasion to be call'd to many private labours), she had people at hand, who for a peice of money would take the child off their hands, and off from the hands of the parish too; and those children, as she said were honestly provided for, and taken care of.

She was proposing a private version of the fostering system used by parish authorities and paid for from public funds. London parishes often sent their bastards and foundlings out to healthier parishes in the country, where women like Moll's old Colchester dame took them in for a fee. A parish officer was supposed to visit these farmed-out children once a year and make sure the money paid for their maintenance was being properly spent. There were regular abuses of this system, however. Horror stories abounded of bad nurses taking in more children than they could care for, or spending parish funds on themselves and neglecting their charges. The starvation and abuse of fostered orphans was still a scandal in the 1720s: 'those who cannot be so hard-hearted to murder their own offspring themselves,' Defoe wrote in his *Augusta Triumphans* of 1728, 'take a slower, tho' as sure a way, and get it done by others, by dropping their children, and leaving them to be starved by parish nurses'.

A fostered child could face graver danger than a neglectful or cruel nurse. There had long been a trade in small girls and boys sold as aids to begging. Disabled – particularly blind – children fetched a premium. The seventeenth century also saw the growth of a new version of people-trafficking, known as spiriting. Labour was sought in the colonies, where employers were prepared to pay well for it and ask few questions as to whence it came. Although some men worked in this nasty but profitable business, spiriting was a crime actively taken up by women, some of whom seem to have specialised in the trafficking of children. There is little direct evidence to illuminate their networks or the experiences of the individuals sold, but it is probable that many of these children were the unwanted issue of destitute or desperate mothers or the wards of parish officials who failed to check on their welfare. In a time when people moved frequently and there was high infant mortality, children could easily slip from view.

Take the case of an infant in the Pepys family, a relatively wealthy and visible clan. Samuel Pepys, whose childlessness was a sorrow to him and his wife Elizabeth, dealt brutally with his dead brother's only offspring, following the pattern set by the girl's own father before his death. The infant was illegitimate, the product of Tom Pepys' fornication with a maidservant, an 'ugly jade' called Margaret. Margaret was 'brought to bed in St Sepulchre's parish of two children; one is dead, the other is alive; her name Elizabeth, and goes by the name of Taylor, daughter to John Taylor', presumably an alias used by Tom Pepys. Tom had refused to provide for the pregnant woman, and the baby was born a parish pauper. Forced subsequently to acknowledge paternity, he tried various ways to rid himself of his daughter. Samuel learnt of the girl's existence only after Tom's death in March 1664, when John Noble, an old manservant who had known of the affair, asked Samuel and his father for money to support the babe. His brother's 'first plott', Samuel learnt on 6 April 1664, had been

> to go on the other side the water [across the Thames] and give a beggar woman something to take the child. They did once go, but did nothing, J Noble saying that seven years hence the mother might come to demand the child and force him to produce it, or to be suspected of murder. Then I think it was that they consulted, and got one Cave, a poor pensioner in St Bride's parish to take it, giving him L5, he thereby promising to keepe it for ever without more charge to them.

The plan misfired. Cave had immediately presented the child to the parish in order to receive extra poor relief, been denounced and bound over for trial. When Tom Pepys hastily intervened and secured his release before the full embarrassing details came out in court, Cave 'demand[ed] L5 more to secure my brother for ever against the child; and he was forced to give it to him and took bond of Cave in L100, made at a scrivener's . . . to secure John Taylor [Tom Pepys] and his assigns, &c. (in consideration of L10 paid him), from all trouble, or charge of meat, drink, clothes, and breeding of Elizabeth Taylor'. Tom had also promised to pay Cave a further twenty shillings 'this next Easter Monday', and this was what John Noble had come to Samuel to procure. Samuel refused to pay it from his own pocket, although he did promise reluctantly that he would do his best to see the sum was paid from Tom's estate, and the poor little girl disappeared from his diary, dead, sold or simply abandoned.

Plenty of child-merchants appeared in the 1650s. One Anne Shaddocke, 'wife of Robert Shaddocke of Christopher's Island [St Kitts] in the partes of America', was accused in 1655 of being 'one that taketh up children to transport them' thither. Katherine Danvers was accused of 'having a girle or young mayd . . . which she profferred to sell demaunding a hundred pound for her, and afterwards would have taken fiftene shillings for her, and for suspition of being such a person that doth take up children and sell and convey them beyond sea'. Sarah Weaver alias Floyd was commonly thought to make her living 'taking up children and selling them'. By the last years of the decade, spiriting had become so well known and detested a crime that those suspected of it were liable to be lynched. Katherine Wall was viciously attacked by a woman in May 1657 who believed she was 'a common taker up of children, and a setter to betray young men and maydens to be conveyed into shipps' and was ready to swear in court that Katherine had confessed 'that she hath at this time fower persons aboard a ship whereof one is a child about eleven years of age, all to be transported to forrain parts as the Barbadoes and Virginia'.

Moll cannot but know of the terrible things that happen to unwanted children. She has personal knowledge of the parish system and of labour auctions on colonial wharves. Lying in Mother Midnight's house, waiting, she turns her possible courses of action about and about in her head. In May she gives birth to a 'brave boy' and is nursing the infant, still undecided, when another letter from her suitor arrives. His estranged wife has committed suicide, he announces with joy, and there can therefore be no possible legal obstacle to his remarriage. 'Exceedingly surpriz'd' at this news, Moll reflects on 'the inexpressible misfortune it was to me to have a child upon my hands, and what to do in it I knew not'. Her mind a-whirl, she confides her whole situation to Mother Midnight, whom she has now taken to calling her governess, and even, sometimes, mother, in recognition of the older woman's wisdom. Explaining why her married life with Jemmy cannot be resumed, she asks plaintively what she should do. The governess brushes aside any reservations over marrying again, telling her the marriage to Jemmy 'was no marriage, but a cheat on both sides, and that as we were parted by mutual consent, the nature of the contract was destroy'd'. Next they turn to the subject of the child in Moll's arms, and the governess returns to the topic of fostering.

I had many times discourses upon that subject with her; but she was full of this argument, that she sav'd the life of many an innocent lamb, as she call'd them, which would otherwise perhaps have been murder'd; and of many a woman, who made desperate by the misfortune, would otherwise be tempted to destroy their children, and bring themselves to the gallows: I granted her that this was true, and a very commendable thing, provided the poor children fell into good hands afterwards, and were not abus'd, starv'd, and neglected by the nurses that bred them up; she answer'd, that she always took care of that, and had no nurses in her business, but what were very good honest people, and such as might be depended upon.

It is the most difficult decision Moll the mother has yet had to take. Here, on the one hand, is the banker, offering perhaps her last chance to attain security and respectability; there, on the other, is an infant at her breast, and one whose father was her last love. At heart, however, she has always known she cannot keep him. She is tormented by the thought that the child may be badly looked after until the governess brings a healthy Hertfordshire countrywoman to meet Moll. She finds her a 'very wholesome look'd likely woman, a cottager's wife, but she had very good cloaths and linen, and every thing well about her'. For ten pounds up front, the woman would never 'return the child back to me, or . . . claim anything more for its keeping or bringing up'; for a further five pounds per year, she will undertake to bring the child as often as requested to the governess's house 'or we should come down and look at it, and see how well she us'd it'. And so the baby boy is taken away to his new country life.

Is this the heartless business it seems? The banker would not take her with this child and all its conception implied, and if the banker does not take her, life will be miserable for both mother and infant. One of the questions to which historians of family life return again and again is whether people living in past centuries felt the same affection for their offspring as modern parents are assumed to do. Was something necessarily held back when the expectation was that a child would not survive? Was an investment in love consciously reduced so as not to wreck the investor when the business failed? It is a question that will never be resolved. Anecdotes can always be found which suggest different answers, and affection or its lack cannot always be disentangled from other needs and emotions when analysing why parents or guardians behaved as they did.

Moll has resolved the matter of her child 'after a manner, which tho' it did not at all satisfie my mind, yet was the most convenient for me, as my affairs then stood' and is able to turn, unencumbered, towards her banker. Her fifth marriage is a tranquil, uneventful, perfunctory business: a 'safe harbour', she calls it, 'after the stormy voyage of life past'. Two children are born but 'no more, for, to tell the truth, it began to be time for me to leave bearing children, for I was now eight-and-forty'. Her husband keeps her in 'ease and content' and Moll settles once again into the role of virtuous wife and mother.

There is perhaps a moment when her wifely resolve wobbles. Three letters arrive, addressed in the familiar hand of Jemmy, the beloved Lancashire husband whom she thought she would never hear from again. He has money, he writes. (She does not know it – and would have cared little if she did – but the money comes from holding up coaches in Nottinghamshire and robbing farmers in Wiltshire.) Now, writes Jemmy, he can take up her 'proposal of going with me to *Virginia*; or [to settle] in a plantation, on some other parts of the *English* colonies in *America*'. But the letters have come too late. As she later recalls, she 'could do nothing in it'. If she contacted Jemmy, the story of the child he fathered must be told, along with all the uncomfortable facts of her remarriage to a man whom she had met before she travelled to Lancashire. The thing was impossible. She 'therefore chose to give no answer, that so he might rather believe they had miscarried'.

It seems the final veil has been drawn over Moll's marital history, while outside the couple's quiet London house the revolution sputtered and then failed. Oliver Cromwell died in 1658, his ineffectual son Richard failed to inspire confidence, and Charles II, son of the executed King, was invited back from his European exile. The great experiment was over. In April 1661 Charles was crowned at Westminster Abbey and triumphal arches were erected in streets whose conduits literally ran with wine. Cromwell's corpse was exhumed, and his head cut off and displayed on a pike on London Bridge. England and Wales, Scotland and Ireland, so briefly under republican rule, once more had a king. Yet Moll, ever perverse, has no truck with the giddy joy of the Restoration. Just as she quietly flouted Puritan strictures within her own walls, she now turns her back on the riotous return to colour, dancing, music, the celebration of Mayday and Christmas, poetry, theatre and consumption. As Charles II ostentatiously rejects the Puritans' idea of the godly life, installing his mistresses at court and fathering a string of illegitimate children, Moll settles into the life of a godly spouse, living 'retir'd, frugal, and within our selves. I kept no company, made no visits; minded my family, and oblig'd my husband; and this kind of life became a pleasure to me.'

10

Moll and the Devil, 1663–5

Moll may not be given to spiritual exploration, but she is as certain as anyone else in pre-Enlightenment England that God and the Devil take a personal interest in her life. Satan has been paying her occasional visits, she knows, ever since her early days in Colchester, whispering encouragement in her ear whenever she is tempted to sin. He was there when she failed to discourage the young master's seduction: who else allowed him the opportunity of passing the fatal invitation to a coach ride? 'As the devil is an unwearied tempter, so he never fails to find opportunity for that wickedness he invites to': he was with them in the Colchester garden where they made their assignation! Satan also came to find her in Hammersmith when her lover cast her off, leaving her 'exposed to the temptations which the devil never fails to excite us to from the frightful prospect of poverty and distress'. Only a second bill for fifty pounds and a swift trip to Liverpool had held him off then. He flirted constantly around her head, buzzing in and out of her mind at Mother Midnight's house when wicked possibilities were considered, but she had not given in.

He re-enters Moll's tranquil life in the early 1660s, when, she tells us, a 'sudden blow from an almost invisible hand, blasted all my happiness, and turn'd me out into the world in a condition the reverse of all that had been before it'. Overnight, Moll's husband is ruined: 'having trusted one of his fellow clarks with a sum of money too much for our fortunes to bear the loss of, the clark fail'd [went bankrupt]'. Every-

thing they own is lost in the wreck and the husband grows 'melan-
choly, and disconsolate, and from thence lethargic, and died'. The whole
marriage takes up less than two pages. Once more Moll is left with no
income to support herself and a small child – the other child of the
marriage seems to have died, for no further mention is made of it. It
was, as she says, 'a dismal and disconsolate case indeed'.

> I was left perfectly friendless and helpless, and the loss my husband
> had sustain'd had reduc'd his circumstances so low, that tho' indeed I
> was not in debt, yet I could easily foresee that what was left would not
> support me long; that while it wasted daily for subsistence, I had no
> way to encrease it one shilling, so that it would be soon all spent, and
> then I saw nothing before me but the utmost distress, and this repre-
> sented it self so lively to my thoughts, that it seem'd as if it was come,
> before it was really very near; also my very apprehensions doubl'd the
> misery, for I fancied every sixpence that I paid but for a loaf of bread,
> was the last that I had in the world, and that to-morrow I was to fast,
> and be starv'd to death.

For two years Moll and the child live as cheaply as they can. She leaves
her comfortable house and goes into shabby lodgings, sells her goods
to raise a little money, 'spending very sparingly and eking things out
to the utmost'. A few years ago her little boy might have gone into
an orphanage for, with all its failings, Cromwell's administration had
had some concern for the welfare of the poorest in the Commonwealth. In 1649 Parliament had taken over royal property in Blackfriars
and turned it into a home where destitute children such as Moll's little
son might be trained in some trade. With the return of King Charles
II, the infants were returned to the streets. The building was required
for the new Master of the Wardrobe, Lord Montagu. Montagu took
Samuel Pepys to see his splendid new premises, where, Pepys recalled
on 21 June 1660, 'Mr Townsend brought us to the governor of some
poor children in tawny clothes; who had been maintained there these
eleven years, which put my Lord to a stand how to dispose of them,
that he may have the house for his use. The children did sing finely,
and my Lord did bid me give them five pieces in gold at his going
away.' Soon after, he closed the orphanage.

What is Moll to do? If she goes upon the parish, the child will be taken from her anyway, and she will be set to one of the dismal tasks of her earliest youth: carding, spinning, beating hemp in return for the most basic of diets, a dormitory bed and all the daily humiliations of the poor. She can sell her body for the few pence that aging commodity will bring or she can steal. Satan, seeing her alone on the brink of a chasm, seizes his moment and gives her a little push. Or so Moll, at least, believes, for she is adamant that two things drove her to crime. 'The devil,' she said, 'began, by the help of an irresistible poverty, to push me into this wickedness.'

Moll's claim is not just a refusal to accept responsibility for her own actions, for the Devil is acknowledged by all but a very avant-garde and sceptical few to play a decisive role in human affairs, criminal as well as moral, national as much as personal. Satan was, to the vast majority of people, a real presence, a physical entity who might be walking among them on the streets and fields where they lived. Although belief in satanic apparition began to wane around the turn of the century, Defoe remained convinced of its reality. Five years after *Moll Flanders* was published, he completed his *Political History of the Devil, as well Ancient as Modern*, contesting that the Devil 'most certainly has a Power and Liberty of moving about in this World, after *some manner or another*'. ''Tis not [Satan's] Business,' he wrote, 'to be public, or to walk up and down in the World visibly, and in his own Shape; his affairs require a quite different Management.' Where women were concerned, that 'different Management' in the seventeenth century generally came in the guise of witchcraft.

While Moll was taking the waters in Bath a decade earlier, a man who had awarded himself the title of witchfinder-general had been terrorising East Anglia. Matthew Hopkins, son of a Puritan cleric, began his witch-finding career in 1644 when he was living in Colchester, Moll's old home and a Puritan stronghold. He had, he claimed, overheard a group of women discussing their meetings with Satan. Thus started a three-year reign of terror during which Hopkins and his assistants travelled the eastern counties of England and imprisoned women in Colchester Castle for interrogation. There were women everywhere, Hopkins believed, in league with Satan, and it was his mission to root them out. Pet cat or dog? This was the woman's 'familiar', an instrument of Satan which sucked her blood. Skin flap, mole, birthmark or boil? That was the Devil's mark. Did she swim or float when thrown into blessed water? If she swam, the water had rejected her and so she was a witch; if she sank, she was innocent and, if pulled out in time, could continue her life. Nineteen women were hanged as a result of Hopkins' activities, and four more died in prison. The last women in England to be executed as witches were hanged in 1684, the year after Moll ostensibly wrote her memoir. The most famous case of the century, in Salem, Massachusetts, came eight years after that.

Many poor women imprisoned, and hanged for Witches.
A. *Hangman.* **B.** *Belman.* **C.** *Two Sergeants.* **D.** *Witch-finder taking his money for his work.*

(A) **I** Ob. *Wheeler* of *London,* upon his Oath said, that in or a-

The execution of poor women convicted of witchcraft in the early 17th century

Witchcraft and poltergeistery were the extreme end of Satan's reach, but he also meddled with ordinary people going about their ordinary business. He comes to Moll in Leadenhall Street. Being brought 'to the last gasp, I think I may truly say I was distracted and raving, when prompted by I know not what spirit', she leaves her house one evening and wanders into the City. She is passing an apothecary's shop and sees a bundle lying on a stool by the counter. Maidservant and apprentice are engaged elsewhere and there is no one else in the shop.

This was the bait; and the devil, who . . . laid the snare, as readily
prompted me as if he had spoke, for I remember, and shall never forget
it, 'twas like a voice spoken to me over my shoulder, 'Take the bundle;
be quick; do it this moment.' It was no sooner said but I stepped into
the shop and with my back to the wench, as if I had stood up for a
cart that was going by, I put my hand behind me and took the bundle,
and went off with it.

She stumbles from the shop, horrified by what she has just done, her
blood 'all in a fire' and unable to think coherently. She takes this
turning, then that, scarcely aware of where she is, or where she is
heading. As night falls, she comes to her senses and makes for her
lodgings, where she opens the stolen bundle on the bed and exam-
ines it. Weeping, and 'under such dreadful impressions of fear, and in
such terror of mind, though I was perfectly safe', she finds baby clothes,
silver and cash.

I sat me down and cried most vehemently; 'Lord,' *said I*, 'what am I
now? A thief? Why, I shall be taken next time, and be carry'd to *Newgate*
and be tried for my life!' And with that I cry'd again a long time, and,
I am sure, as poor as I was, if I had durst for fear [if I had not been
too frightened], I would certainly have carried the things back again;
but that went off after a while.

She cannot sleep that night, wondering if perhaps she has robbed a
poor widow like herself, 'that had pack'd up these goods to go and
sell them for a little bread for herself and a poor child, and are now
starving and breaking their hearts for want of that little they would
have fetch'd'. Three or four days are spent in fear and penitence. She
prays constantly but receives no answer which will help her out of
her immediate distress, and assuage her constant fear of poverty.
Instead, 'I had an evil counsellor within, and he was continually
prompting me to relieve myself by the worst means; so one evening
he tempted me again, by the same wicked impulse that had said *Take
that bundle*, to go out again and seek for what might happen.'

Most people believed that, even if Satan did not literally appear, he
meddled with the minds of his victims in less tangible ways. Pamphleteers, broadsheet writers and members of the court as well as offenders

had recourse to the Devil in explaining motivation for crime. This was particularly true in cases which provoked horror, such as infanticide, rape or sodomy ('a crime grievous in the sight of God'). The notion of demonic temptation was built into the description of crimes: the phrase 'for that he/she not having the fear of God before her/his eyes' preceded many arraignments, as did such phrases as 'moved and seduced by the instigation of the Devil'. Convicts sentenced to death and making their last confessions frequently cited the Devil as instrumental in their descent into crime: 'the Devil was very busie with me, to tempt me into Sin'; 'I was tempted by the Devil to rob my Master'; 'the devil put it into my head, and I could not rest till I had done it'.

In 1674 a woman called Rose Goodman was sentenced to death at the Old Bailey 'for the Felonious taking away of Cloaths from the persons of two children'. It was her practice 'to intice little children that she found in the Streets, to go along with her, and having got them in some private place remote from their dwellings, and there strip them of their cloaths, and after sold them, leaving the poor children in that pitiful condition to shift for themselves'. The Old Bailey Sessions Papers do not record her defence, but doubtless she (and everyone else in court), was sure that the Devil had been urging her on. Neither will he leave Moll alone, and his next intervention is to push her down the same vicious path as Rose Goodman. She is walking in Aldersgate a few days after her first theft when she comes across a pretty little child on her way to dancing school, a necklace of gold beads around her neck. This time the Devil's snare, says Moll, is 'of a dreadful nature indeed'. Inveigling the little girl into an alley, 'I stooped, pretending to mend the child's clog that was loose, and took off her necklace, and the child never felt it, and so led the child on again. Here, I saw, the devil put me upon killing the child in the dark alley, that it might not cry, but the very thought frighted me so that I was ready to drop down; but I turned the child about and bade it go back again.'

For a modern reader this is Moll's dark night of the soul; not her seduction as a teenager, her bigamous marriages or unwitting incest; not the turning to theft to relieve hunger or even putting her children out to nurse. It is the chilling vertiginous moment when she contemplates, however briefly, killing a small child to cover up a petty theft. And although Defoe allows her a few lines to give her conscience a cursory examination and absolution – she has not harmed the child, she reasons, nor even frightened it; anyway, it is the mother's fault for giving her an expensive necklace; that will teach the parents not to let the 'poor baby' wander alone – it appears that her heart has been irredeemably hardened by the twin spectres of old age and destitution. 'My own necessities,' as she says grimly, 'made me regardless of anything.' The Devil defeats all her attempts to repent and reform. 'Let none read this part without seriously reflecting on the circumstances of a desolate state, and how they would grapple with mere want of friends and want of bread . . . let them remember that a time of distress is a time of dreadful temptation, and all the strength to resist is taken away; poverty presses, the soul is made desperate by distress, and what can be done?'

It was a subject which fascinated Defoe. He was writing at a time when character rather than circumstances was generally thought to determine the descent of an individual into crime and, against this background, he can seem almost modern in his insistence that circumstances can and do influence choices. However, this stems less from any desire for social reform than from his obstinate convictions over satanic intervention. For Defoe circumstances do not oblige a person to turn to crime; rather, they open that person's mind to the Devil. He has no doubt that Moll is correct to blame her descent into crime on poverty, for poverty was one of the doors through which Satan was most adept at slipping.

Moll's next thefts are carried out almost in a trance: she cannot yet identify herself as a committed active thief. A man being chased by constables shoves a parcel of stolen goods into her hands, shouting, 'God bless you mistress, let it lie there a little,' and in the confusion of his arrest she walks away with the bundle. She lifts a few things here, takes a few there. She wanders the streets, wondering what she is doing and how her life came to this. She resolves to reform, but 'the prospect of my starving, which grew every day more frightful to me, hardened my heart by degrees'. Occasionally she feels remorse: tearful prayers and vows of repentance alternate with resignation to her new wickedness and a realisation there is no going back. Or, as Moll sees it, 'the diligent devil, who resolved I should continue in his service, continually prompted me to go out and take a walk, that is to say, to see if anything would offer'. One distracted evening, having 'blindly obeyed his summons', she smashes a window to grab three rings left temptingly visible just inside. This is housebreaking, and she could hang for it. The same offence leads her into organised crime, for she has run up against the difficulty of any small-time thief. 'I was now at a loss for a market for my goods . . . I was very loth to dispose of them for a trifle, as the poor unhappy theives in general do, who, after they have ventured their lives for perhaps a thing of value, are fain to sell it for a song when they have done . . . At last, I resolv'd to go to my old governess and acquaint myself with her again.'

It is five or six years since Moll last met Mother Midnight, her governess, but she believes that the older woman may again be able to help her out of her difficulties. Moll can no longer afford to send money to the Hertfordshire cottager's wife who took Jemmy's son off her hands a few years ago. She therefore writes to her old adviser, telling her 'my circumstances were reduc'd very low; that I had lost my husband' and that although she 'had punctually supplied the £5 per year to her for my little boy as long as I was able' she could do so no more, begging 'the poor child might not suffer too much for its mother's misfortunes'.

When Mother Midnight receives the letter, she invites Moll to call. Moll finds the other woman 'not in such flourishing circumstances as before'. She has been incautious in the child-trafficking side of her business and 'sued by a certain gentleman who had had his daughter stolen from him, and who, it seems, she had helped to convey away; and it was very narrowly that she escap'd the gallows'. The governess has turned to pawnbroking to make ends meet after that little misadventure, although it soon becomes clear that this is only a cover for receiving. The first practical steps she takes to help Moll are therefore to tell the Hertfordshire woman that no more money will be coming, and to exchange her stolen goods for cash. A string of gold beads, two parcels of silk and a diamond ring are all immediately pawned for good prices. Moll's spirits are raised by the clink of coins in her pocket and she tentatively suggests that her governess might help her find enough needlework to make a living. That timid suggestion is quashed and she is given to understand that 'honest business did not come within her reach'. A second possible livelihood is also dismissed: 'had I been younger,' Moll recalls, 'she might have helped me to a spark' – pimped her – 'but my thoughts were off that kind of livelihood, as being quite out of the way after fifty, which was my case, and so I told her'. Instead, the kind governess invites Moll to come and stay until they can devise some way for her to make a living.

Veiled negotiations go on between guest and hostess as to how each might best help the other. It becomes clear that one principal obstacle remains to Moll's return to prosperity. 'Now living a little easier, I enter'd into some measures to have my little son by my last husband taken off [taken care of].' This her governess 'made easie too, reserving a payment only of 5 *l.* a year, if I could pay it'. And so Moll severs her ties with her last surviving child, who also goes into foster-care, and turns unencumbered to whatever her new life might bring.

II

Moll's governess, 1665

In the introduction to the first edition of *Moll Flanders* Defoe indicated he would follow up with 'histories' of both Mother Midnight, now known as Moll's governess, and of Jemmy the highwayman. He never did.

What we know of the governess must be pieced together from Moll's scattered reminiscences. She had been, Moll was given to understand, 'born a pick-pocket' and had 'run thro' all the several degrees of that art'. So skilled was she that she had only once been taken in the act, but that had been enough for her to be sentenced to transport herself out of the kingdom. She had boarded her ship for America, but 'being a woman of a rare tongue and withal having money in her pocket; she found means, the ship putting into Ireland for provisions, to get on shore there, where she liv'd and practis'd her old trade for some years'. It was also in Ireland that she had learnt the criminal arts of abortion and brothel-keeping. She had returned to England when she became rather too well known in Dublin. As the term of her transportation had not yet expired, however, she could not return to thieving, for if she were arrested 'she was sure to have gone to wreck': the fact of her previous sentence of transportation would emerge and she would hang for 'returning before her time'. Instead she concentrated on midwifery, abortion and procuring, and had done well until embroiling herself in the scandal of the little girl's disappearance. Since then she had worked principally as a pawnbroker, and, behind that already none-too-respectable facade, a receiver and general facilitator for those seeking assistance and guidance through London's criminal underworld.

Receiving, pawnbroking, moneylending, dealing in second-hand goods: all these went together in a tangle of licit and illicit business. London's trades were regulated by guilds, male-only institutions established in medieval times to protect common interests and uphold standards. Behind the guilds lay a parallel, shadowy, unlicensed world of people trading and making whatever they could, wherever was available and whenever was possible. Most women in business or trade inhabited this world by default. They might become dealers in second-hand clothes and fabric, peddlers or hawkers, flower sellers or victuallers. They might run a food stall in the street or sell home-made pies, bread and cakes on a round. They might run an endless series of errands: fabric from warehouse to shop, from shop to tailor, from tailor to customer, from customer back to tailor, in return for the remnants of material to pawn, make up or sell on their own account. London was full of women scurrying about with bundles on their heads, or cradling piles of laundry, clothes, fabric, stacks of hats or small livestock in their aprons.

Better-off women – often tradesmen's widows – might run shops or lodging houses, and conduct a variety of linked trades from their premises, typically small-scale moneylending, pawning and dealing. If a pawnbroker dabbled in receiving, she often employed other women to disguise the stolen goods. In an age which did not know mass production, each item bore marks left by the craftsman, the retailer or the owner that made it easily identifiable. These could be initials, a monogram, an inscription, the shop mark left on cloth by drapers, or a jeweller's engraving. Women who knew their way around fabric could be casually employed to render clothes and lengths of fabric unidentifiable; those who had worked for jewellers might help melt down or deface items of metal. This is the dim half-hidden world in which Moll's governess now operates. It was also the home of Mary Frith, who like the governess made a successful career in thieving, receiving and procuring. Mary Frith, however, took her receiving business to a height which Moll's governess never attained.

Better known to her contemporaries as Moll Cutpurse,[11] Mary Frith had been one of London's 'Roaring Girls' fifty years ago, a small but

---

11 To avoid confusion, I will now refer to Moll Cutpurse as Mary Frith to differentiate her from Moll Flanders.

scandalous group of women who insisted on behaving like men. She frequented taverns, fought, swore, appeared illegally on stage in men's apparel to tell dirty jokes and sing suggestive songs, and was finally ordered to do a humiliating public penance in St Paul's church in 1611, wrapped in a white sheet. It was too much for her family, who arranged for her to be kidnapped and sent aboard a ship bound for Virginia where, Frith would write, 'the necessity of Women be they what they would, could not but commend me to some Jack as good as myself, whose Dominion over me might subdue that violence of my spirit, or else I should be so broke by hard labor, that I would of my own accord return to a womanly and civil behaviour'. She might have ended up Moll's mother's neighbour; instead, she bribed the ship's coxswain and escaped.

Knowing her family were stronger than she was, Frith lay low for some time. When she emerged from obscurity in the late 1610s, she began casting about for what she might do to earn her living and strengthen her position. She had, as she said, 'but very little choice' and so 'listed myself of another Colony or Plantation (but who neither sow nor reap) of the Divers or File-clerks. A cunning Nation being a kind of Land Pirates, trading altogether in other men's Bottoms, for no other Merchandizes then Bullion and ready Coin, and keep most of the great Fairs and Marts of the world.'

Decoded from seventeenth-century slang, she joined London's criminal underworld, where divers and file-clerks were pickpockets and thieves. Land pirates – street criminals – traded in 'other men's bottoms' not because that was where the back pocket and the wallet lay but because trading vessels were referred to as bottoms in commercial language. Frith dealt, as she jested, in gold and coin rather than in the cloth or liquor of reputable dealers, but her activity was the same. Likewise, wherever a great fair or market was to be found for commercial activity, alongside those who came to buy and sell were those who came to steal. With this rather laboured metaphor, Frith's biographer placed her within the business world of her time, alongside merchants, investors, consumers and adventurers.[12]

---

12 *The Life of Mrs Mary Frith* was a sensationalised version of her life, published two or three years after her death. Although written in the first person, it is not known how much Mary Frith actually dictated or approved its contents and cannot therefore always be assumed to be accurate.

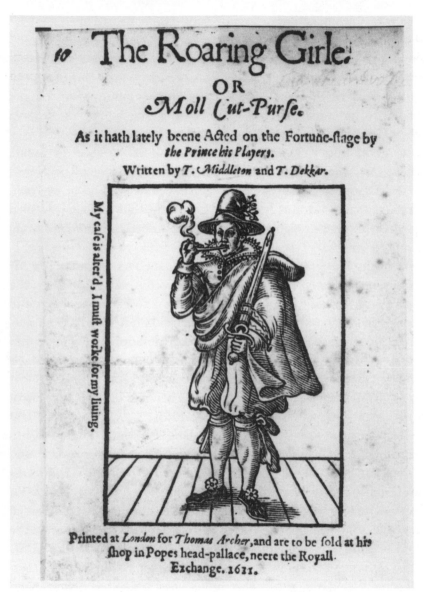

The frontispiece to 'The Roaring Girle' or 'Moll Cut-Purse', a play by Thomas Middleton and Thomas Dekker in which Mary Frith played the leading role

Although Frith's 1662 biography did not give details (perhaps because some of her colleagues were still alive), it provided a tantalising glimpse of her entering an ordered and regulated community, one running parallel to the legitimate world it lived from and beneath. It seems she was able to contact criminal acquaintances, presumably made during her years in taverns and theatres, where the two worlds collided, and was accepted in a semi-official capacity into a structured organisation. She did not fall clumsily into crime; she entered it as an apprentice joined a master, or a master a guild. At her 'admission'

> I was examined to several questions, relating to my fitness and capacity of being a Member; to which I gave such satisfactory answers, as rendered me very acceptable to be one of their Community. I remember they viewed my Hands, not only to see whether I had not been manumitted [i.e. branded] at Sessions, but if they were not naturally fitted and made convenient for the Exercise of the Trade, being indeed the neatest Manufacture of the world. The best Signs and Marks of a happy and industrious hand, is a long middle Finger, equally suited with that they call the fools or first Finger; nor can any Surgeon or Doctor of Physic read a learneder Anatomy Lecture of the Nerves, Fibre, and Arteries of the same; then these secant and cutting Empirics.

Once upon a time Frith could have met these requirements. She had gone by the nickname Cutpurse in 1611 because she was a convicted thief. Men's pockets, or purses, were sewn into the linings of their coats, waistcoats and breeches, and were easily accessible in an embrace or the crush of a crowd. Women's, equally vulnerable, were drawstring bags hanging from hoops around the waist or a ribbon round the thigh, accessed through slits cut in the seams of their skirts. Inserting a delicate hand to slash the string was easy enough for a practised cutter. Natasha Korda, researching her book *The Case of Moll Frith: Women's Work and the All-Male Stage* in 2004, discovered an early conviction for theft. In 1602 Mary Frith and two other women were charged with 'cutting' a man's purse in Clerkenwell. They were acquitted on that occasion, but Frith's notoriety by the time of her appearance on stage in 1611 suggests she had continued her criminal career. After too much clutching of swords and slamming her fist on tavern tables, however, Frith's hands were no longer small and supple. Instead, she was 'judged by these Palmisters from the hardness and largeness of the Table of my Hand, to be very well qualified for a receiver and entertainer of their fortunate Achievements, and was thereupon with the usual Customs and Ceremonies admitted.'

Mary Frith worked for a year as a 'company' receiver, but did so in constant fear, for she 'could not but foresee the danger'. An apprenticeship was necessary for her to learn the trade, earn respect and goodwill, and make a wide acquaintance, but she set up her own operation as soon as she could, resolving 'to run no longer the desperate hazard of these Courses (which I see so many of my Comrades monthly expiate with their Lives, &c. at least by whipping and the satisfaction of Bridewell Work-house)'. Frith's plan was 'a very fair expedient, whereby I might live, if not Honestly, yet Safely; a mean betwixt the strokes of Justice, and the Torments of Poverty'. The operation she had in mind would allow her to continue working with her criminal clients but would keep her, personally, on the right side of the law. In or around 1620 she rented rooms 'within 2 doors of the Globe Tavern in Fleet Street' and set up within them what she called 'an Exchange'. It was

a kind of brokery for Jewels, Rings and Watches, which had been pinched or stolen any manner of way, at never so great distances from any person; I might properly enough call it the Insurance Office for such Merchandize, for the Losers were sure upon Composition [i.e. negotiation of a fee] to recover their Goods again, and the Pirates were as sure to have good ransom, and I so much in the Grosse for Brokage without any more danger; the Hue and Cry being always directed to me for the Discovery of the Goods not the Takers.

This may be where she was working when we get our next glimpse of her. In 1621 Henry Killigrew, gentleman, suffered the common indignity of having his purse pinched while 'in private familiarity' with a prostitute. Having heard, he informed the court, that 'many that had had theire purses Cutt or goods stolen, had beene helped to theire goods againe and diuers of the offenders taken or discouered' by Mary Frith, he called at her premises. She led him to Margaret Dell, who was duly prosecuted. Mr Killigrew got his purse back, and Mary Frith pocketed both a fee from Killigrew and the bounty due to her as thief-taker, or private detective.

Mary Frith's enterprise succeeded because she presented herself as an intermediary, not as a receiver. Ostensibly, she was not selling stolen goods but merely detecting their whereabouts and reuniting them with their owners. Her profit was presented not as payment for those goods, but as recompense for the time and expenses incurred in finding them, and her operation soon became more sophisticated than that of the normal thief-taker. Frith hit on two methods of getting stolen goods more easily to her: first, she commissioned thieves to do the thieving; second, she contacted those who were working independently but whose thefts had been reported to her, and suggested she get in touch with their victims and arrange a profitable redemption. She ensured the loyalty of her criminal associates by always dealing honestly with them, or so at least she would claim. Quid pro quo was their silence: 'among all the Thieveries they did, my name was never heard of; for they made it the chiefest of their Religion to Conceal me and to Conceal nothing of their designs from me'.

When goods were stolen, Frith was the first to know. Her informers and casual employees advised her constantly of who had been working where and what the booty was. Nor did she stop at jewels and watches; she spotted a lucrative trade in items which had no street value but which were essential to the owner. These were stolen by 'a new sort of Thieves called the Heavers', whose speciality was to take 'Shop Books' left unattended: records of sales, orders, names and receipts, whose loss would throw a business into confusion and were pinched 'with an intent only of some redemptory Money upon [their] Delivery, for which they had the Convenience of my Mediation'.

If some suspected that Mary Frith's methods and objectives did not tend to the greater good, they had also to acknowledge that she and her ilk were supremely useful in a city which was riddled with crime and corruption but had only rudimentary mechanisms to keep order. Criminal cases were not yet brought by the Crown with the vast state-funded apparatus of detection and pressure which it has since built up. Each case had to be brought by the prosecutor – the victim – personally. Constables and magistrates might help, depending on the time at their disposal and how seriously they took their duties, but the victim was the principal detective, and often had to find his own witnesses and call on experts to assess values and the damages he had suffered. An adviser like Mary Frith was frequently needed, not only to find the stolen goods but because she made it her business to know the names, associates and specialities of London's criminals.

Over two decades Mary Frith spread her net far. 'I could have told,' she would boast, 'in what quarter of the Town a Robbery was done the Evening before by very early day next morning, and had a perfect Inventory of what they had taken as soon as it came to the Dividend.' Her Fleet Street exchange became well known as the first place for victims of theft to go, and in Frith's eyes, at least, she was doing everyone a service. Her way of working was, she claimed, 'more advantageous by far to the injured, then the Courts of Justice and benefits of the Law'. Thief-takers and parish officials were notorious for violence, perjury and their fondness for bribes, whereas she dealt honestly with both thieves and victims. As a result, during her 'Mistress-ship and government' of the business robberies were neither 'so frequent nor so grievous as when my Discipline was cast off, and this sort of Cattle left to themselves'.

Recalling this period of her life, Frith attempted to give the impression of a warm motherly sort of woman who spread her arms around her brood of thieving chicks with a loving reproof here and a soothing pat there. However, other anecdotes in the biography suggest she was also vain, thuggish and proud, and that her hold over her confederates was gained by fear as much as respect, let alone affection. There are casual stories of humiliating this person, or setting a gang on that to have her 'soundly kicked' for some impudence or attempted betrayal. She took vicious revenge on those who objected to her general way of life, for she still wore men's clothes, drank lustily in taverns, presided over bull baiting and smoked, the last in particular considered a vile thing for a woman to do. With London's thugs ready to do her bidding, she no longer had anything to fear from her family, but the Bishop of London still dogged her heels. When someone denounced her for wearing man's apparel, she was dragged back to St Paul's to stand again in the white sheet of a penitent. This time she took her revenge by setting loose an army of deft little pickpockets on the congregation – not to steal but to cut holes in 'their Cloaks and Gowns, and [send] them home as naked behind as an Ape's Tail'.

In the 1630s Frith found another way to make money. She became, she claimed, an intimate friend of Bess Holland, madam of the Paris Garden brothel next to the Mint in Southwark. Seeing how much money Holland was making, Frith decided to set up her own operation. Although the Paris Garden only offered female flesh, Frith knew there was an equal but unorganised market in the male variety. The brokery of stolen goods was reconfigured as a brokery of introductions, and men flocked to her for work. These were mainly soldiers – wages were notoriously paid late in both Royalist and Parliamentary armies – whom she pimped to ladies. Having given the reader a tantalising glimpse of this operation, however, Frith cuts herself hypocritically short: she only confessed to running a male brothel, she said,

> to unburden my conscience, and shame the private practices of some great Women; who to this very purpose keep Emissaries and Agents to procure Stallions to satiate their desires, as confidently as they entertain Grooms and Laundries. I will stir this Puddle no longer, nor dive into the depth of it any further, least I pollute and inquinate the Reader with the Filth hereof.

Mary Frith flourished for twenty years, changing her way of living only because of the calamity, as she saw it, of the revolt against the King. She retired sadly from business in the 1640s, converting her brothel into a lodging house where she lived quietly during the Civil War. When the Rump, then Cromwell, restored some kind of order to London, she did not resume trading, too fearful of the new morality laws. The Adultery Act of May 1650 had spawned what she called trepanners, a kind of venal morality police. Men fearful of blackmail would no longer seek mistresses or consort with prostitutes in case the trepanners found them and threatened them with prosecution or a heavy bribe in its stead. For Frith the 1650s were a dreary twilight. Her money was going, many of her friends were gone and the good times were over. When she began to suffer from dropsy and was forced to discard her uncomfortably constraining doublet and hose, she retired from society, living in the company only of three maidservants and a menagerie of dogs, squirrels and birds. She died in July 1659, just too early to see the son of her beloved King Charles back on the throne, and three or so years before Moll Flanders returns to her own governess.

Mary Frith, then, is an obvious model for the woman in whose house Moll, newly childless, takes refuge in the early 1660s. At first Moll attempts to earn her living there quietly and decently, taking in 'quilting-work for ladies beds, petticoats, and the like'. However, Satan and the governess have other plans: 'the diligent Devil who resolv'd I should continue in his service, continually prompted me to go out and take a walk, that is to say, to see if any thing would offer in the old way'. Passing an inn one evening, she peeps into a booth and sees a silver tankard standing unattended on the table. With Satan on her shoulder, she takes it and hurries away. When she reveals her theft to her governess, that lady is delighted and pushes aside Moll's repentant suggestion that perhaps she should return the tankard to the tavern. 'Don't you want it more than they do?' she says. 'I wish you cou'd light of such a bargain once a week.' The tankard goes into the weekly meltdown of stolen silver and Moll gets her share. And when, a few days later, Moll bemoans the fact that her virtuous piecework is bringing in too little money to live, the governess is brisk and efficient in pushing her further down the path of vice, encouraging her to go out and steal. Moll demurs.

> O, mother! *says I*, that is a trade I have no skill in, and if I should be taken I am undone at once; *says she*, I cou'd help you to a schoolmistress that shall make you as dexterous as her self. I trembled at that proposal for hitherto I had had no confederates, nor any acquaintance among that tribe; but she conquer'd all my modesty, and all my fears; and in a little time, by the help of this confederate I grew as impudent a thief, and as dexterous as ever *Moll Cut-purse* was.

12

Moll the London thief, 1665–73

Seventeenth-and-eighteenth-century criminality created colourful dialects: secret linguistic codes used by thieves, Gypsies, vagabonds and beggars to disguise their lives and purposes from the rest of society. The most famous of these, known as thieves' cant, was primarily a lexicon of crime, minutely particularising each variation of each offence. Its existence was first noted in late Elizabethan times, and it continued to fascinate and bamboozle outsiders for the next two centuries.

Nathan Bailey's *Dictionary of Thieving Slang*, compiled in 1737, lists hundreds of terms. We still use several of them: a dab, for example (as in dab hand), was 'a very dextrous Fellow at Thieving, Cheating, Sharping &c'; and a sharper (as in card sharp and sharp practice) was defined as 'a Cheat, one that lives by his Wits'. Have you ever saved someone's bacon? You are using cant: 'it is commonly used,' explains Bailey, 'for any narrow Escape'. The corrupt still receive a bung for their dirty work: this was the thieves' term for 'a purse, or pocket'. Do you have kids? You've taken the word from seventeenth-century London. A magistrate is still a beak. Did the producers of the *Die Hard* film series know they had taken their title from cant? In those days to die hard meant 'to show no fear or remorse at the gallows'. Did you go through a punk period? You were borrowing the Eliza-bethan term for a rough prostitute. Ever been shoplifting? Your crim-inal forebears coined the term 400 years ago.

Illegal sex had its own rich vocabulary. Popping into a bawdy house (also known as a fencing school, a nunnery, an academy and a snoozing ken), the seventeenth-century man about town would meet first the aunt or abbess before being introduced to the women variously known as bawds, tails, cattle, laced mutton or public ledgers. If his tastes were specialised, the abbess might offer him dells: 'young bucksome Wenches, ripe and prone to Venery, but who have not lost their Virginity, which the Upright Man pretends to, and seizes'; or mollies, male prostitutes; or posture-girls, who created tableaux of erotic poses. A man with less money in his pocket could find a cheaper mort – woman – on the street outside, but had to be careful. She could be a buttock and file – one who picked her customer's pocket as he laboured – or even more dangerous, a 'queer mort', a woman diseased.

Every night saw a selection of canary-birds – 'Rogues or Whores taken and clapp'd into the Cage or Round-house' – in the London lock-ups (naskins, as the thieves knew them), waiting their turn before the magistrate. Among them would be bung-nippers, also known as files: those who 'cut purses, with a short sharp Knife, and a horn Thumb'. With them (unless they got away) were their bulkers, 'whose Business 'tis to jostle the person against the Wall, while the File picks his Pocket; and generally gives it to an Adam-tiler, who scowers off with it'. Perhaps there was a kate or two, who had been out picking locks for her mates to bite the ken (rob the house). There might be one of the kidlays, 'an Order of Rogues, who meeting a Youth with a Bundle or Parcel of Goods, wheedle him by fair Words, and whipping Six-pence into his Hand, to step on a short and sham Errand, in the mean Time run away with the Goods'. There would be any number of priggers and nappers (or nabbers); priggers of prancers, who stole horses; priggers of cacklers, or poultry thieves; nappers of naps, who took sheep; bufe nappers, or stealers of dogs.

Some of London's thousands of thieves committed their offences casually and opportunistically, such as the clank nappers, who snatched unattended tankards and the strum nappers, who took wigs left in a barber's open window. More professional systematic thieves, however, tended to have a few lays, or specific operations, at which they had become expert. Filchers and anglers, for example, were those 'who go armed with a Staff, with a Hole thro' and a Spike at the Bottom, to pluck Cloaths from a Hedge or any thing out of a Casement'.

Curtails specialised in cutting off pieces of cloth from the train of a woman's dress, a dangling scarf or hood, or a length of fabric hanging out of a shop window. Heavers (whom Mary Frith had encountered some decades before) stole only tradesmen's account books.

Academy had another meaning in cant. It was not only a brothel, but also 'a receptacle for all sorts of Villains, where the Young Ones are initiated in the *Canting* Language, and all manners of Cheats and Impostures, and sorted into Tribes and Bands, according to their several Capacities for Mischief'. The academy staff – the schoolmistress and schoolmaster – were familiar figures in the literature of those 'bred up to crime', children who received semi-formal tuition in the arts of thieving from their families or surrogate families. They occasionally popped up in court, as in December 1678, when an irate Old Bailey judge addressed a group of women he would have liked to hang but could not.

> You the Prisoners at the Bar, I have observed in the time that I have attended here, that you Pick-pockets, Shop-lifters, and you other Artists, which I am not so well acquainted with, which fill up this place, throng it most with Women, and generally such as she there, Mary Hipkins, with whom no admonitions will prevail. They are such, whose happiness is placed in being thought able to teach others to be cunning in their wickedness, and their Pride is to be thought more flie [fly, or cunning] than the rest.

One such Mary Hipkins is the schoolmistress to whom Moll Flanders is introduced by her governess. She is particularly skilled, Moll tells us, 'in three sorts of craft: shoplifting, stealing of shop-books, and pocket-books, and taking off gold watches from the ladies sides; and this last she did so dexterously that no woman ever arriv'd to the perfection of that art, so as to do it like her.'

Although Moll is taking her lessons late in life, she is a quick learner. For some time, she attends her schoolmistress 'in the practice, just as a deputy attends a midwife, without any pay'. The day comes when the pupil is sent on to the street to put what she has learnt into practice. Their first victim is a 'lady big with child, who had a charming watch', and 'the thing was to be done as she came out of church'. The schoolmistress, acting as the bulker, 'goes on one side of the lady, and pretends, just as she came to the steps, to fall, and fell against the lady with so much violence as put her into a great fright, and both cried out terribly. In the very moment that she jostled the lady' Moll 'had hold of the watch, and holding it the right way, the start she gave drew the hook out, and she never felt it.' Moll then melts away, and when the lady, recovered, finds she had lost her watch, the other woman is ready with an explanation: 'It was those rogues that thrust me down, I warrant ye.' The governess gives Moll and the schoolmistress ten pounds each for the watch 'and thus,' Moll says, 'I was entered a complete thief'. More precisely, she has become an autem diver, a pickpocket who specialises in robbing churchgoers.

Moll discovers how much more profitable is a life of crime than the life of a seamstress when, only a few months and a few picked pockets later, she finds she has amassed £200. No longer threatened by destitution, she contemplates walking away from crime: 'why should I not now leave off, as they say, while I was well; that I could not expect to go always free; and if I was once surpris'd, and miscarry'd, I was undone'. One mishandled theft would be enough to land her in Newgate, and Tyburn is the next step down that road. But Satan still has her in his insatiable toils: 'the busy devil that so industriously drew me in had too fast hold of me to let me go back'. Indeed, with each crime committed Moll is now hungry to commit a greater one: 'I must get still farther, and more, and the avarice joined so with the success, that I had no more thoughts of coming to a timely alteration of life.'

This section of Moll's memoir is rendered in a curiously deadpan tone, almost with the sing-song intonation of a person reciting some well-worn folk tale or ballad from which the reciter herself is removed. There is a monotonous sameness of crime, place and name; a routine of drifting about the streets, seizing an opportunity in a burst of adrenalin then coming home and picking over the illicit bundle on the bed; the occasional death of comrades, briefly mourned, then pushed to the back of the mind; the same expectation that one day their fate must be hers – but not yet, not yet, not until the next pocket is picked, the next stolen bundle gloated over.

Several years are spent in partnership with her governess, and once again Moll's personal world is so absorbing that great events occur unnoticed around her. In the mid-1660s England and the Netherlands went to war: the friendship between Charles II and the Princes of Orange, hereditary rulers of the Dutch republic, was not enough to overcome vicious Anglo-Dutch competition for trade in expanding colonial markets. At first the war was popular in Britain, for it was expected that rapid victory would be followed by opportunities for rapid profit. In West Africa English forces evicted the Dutch from their slaving factories; in America, in 1664, they invaded New Amsterdam and renamed it New York. However, England had reckoned without recent improvements in the Dutch navy and without French support for the Netherlands, which would disastrously alter the balance of power between the combatants. As Charles II's ambassadors scrambled to placate Louis XIV of France, the Dutch fleet sailed audaciously into the River Medway at the mouth of the River Thames in 1667, blew up Royal Navy ships, seized the flagship and set off an invasion scare.

Defeat by the Dutch was matched by domestic disasters. In 1665 an outbreak of plague killed perhaps 100,000 people in London, 20 per cent of its population. The disease was thought to have arrived from Amsterdam, which had suffered an earlier epidemic, and it swept across the city from the docks in the east. At the height of the epidemic 7,000 people were dying each week. The court, government and royal family decamped to Oxfordshire, but most City administrators stayed courageously in their places. On 2 September 1666 a second catastrophe hit the capital as the Great Fire roared from the Tower to Ludgate Hill. Most of Tudor London was reduced to smoking ruins. The great church of St Paul's collapsed and its charred timbers smoked for days. The old Royal Exchange was burnt to the ground and Newgate gaol was a roofless shell. After the shock came the reaction: building sites were everywhere, the City full of dust, scaffolding, dray horses heaving stone from country quarries, brick piles and the clink of hammers. Around Moll, the face of London began to change from a Stuart shambles to a recognisable version of the city it is today. But Moll ignores the sudden gaping spaces where packed tenements used to be, the disappearance of ancient reference points, the mass graves and silent streets of 1665, the building sites and homeless families of 1666. She is not interested in the new metropolis slowly rising around her. Her eyes are fixed on ledges, shop windows, the curve of a walker's hip or a woman's apron, the glint of a man's watch, the shadow beyond a doorway.

With the governess's devoted guidance and her schoolmistress's expert tuition, Moll has become one of the most successful pickpockets in London. The thought that she might now retire from crime continues occasionally to flit through her mind, but it is always brushed away. It is not provoked by qualms about the immorality of what she is doing, but solely by fear of punishment. Each time a comrade goes to the nubbing cheat, the three-legged mare, the deadly nevergreen, to take the morning drop, Moll shivers. Hanging is a dreadful death, and if she is convicted of a non-capital crime, she will still be char-actered – branded on the hand or cheek with a red-hot iron – or receive a vicious beating. 'Your Sentence is this,' the judge told Mary Hipkins and her comrades with relish: 'that you be carried from hence to the place whence you came, and from thence be dragg'd ti'd to a Carts-rail through the streets, your Bodies being stript from the Girdle upwards, and be Whipt till your Bodies bleed.' The prospect of such publicly inflicted violence is sometimes enough to scare Moll into staying indoors; occasionally, she even leaves London for a few days to calm her nerves and rest.

Even the schoolmistress to whom Moll's governess introduced her at the beginning of her career is caught in the late 1660s. She and a friend 'made an attempt upon a linen-draper in Cheapside, but were snap'd by a hawks-ey'd journeyman, and seiz'd with two pieces of cambrick'. 'Take notice of it,' the judge had warned Mary Hipkins as he sentenced her to be whipped. 'You that will take no warning, I pass my word for it, if e'er I catch you here again, I will take care you shall not easily escape.' All the governess's threats and bribes cannot save Moll's schoolmistress, for she too is an old offender and habituée of the Sessions Yard. She is executed.

One August a client of a different kind stumbles across Moll's path at Bartholomew Fair. The Fair, held at Smithfield, was an annual two-week revelry, ostensibly for the sale of cloth but in fact a bacchanalia of gambling, vulgar entertainment, freak shows, prostitution and thievery. Moll takes a stroll about to see what offers and looks into a gambling booth. It was the custom here that if a gentleman playing at dice won, he gave his prize to whatever lady happened to be standing next to him. Moll finds herself presented with a feather muff by a rather attractive gentleman who then suggests they take a turn together about the fair. Slightly drunk and extremely flirtatious, the gentleman begins a gentle propositioning: would she trust herself in a coach with him? He is, he swears, a man of honour. She agrees to go with him to Knightsbridge, still a village, 'where we walk'd in the gardens' – pleasure gardens on the site of what is now Lowndes Square – and, Moll says, 'he treated me very handsomely'. The hour grows late, the summer light fades and inevitably they end up at a house well known to Moll's new friend. She is invited to walk into a bedchamber where, he protests with a hiccup, he would not dream of touching her. She prosaically accepts what is coming, 'being indeed willing to see the end of it, and in hopes to make something of it at last; as for the bed &c. I was not much concern'd about that part'.

With these rather tired words begins the anecdote in Moll's memoir which has become the basis of her posthumous reputation. 'He did what he pleas'd with me, I need say no more,' and then they get back in the coach and the man nods off. Moll relieves him of 'a gold watch, with a silk purse of gold, his fine full bottom perriwig, and silver fring'd gloves, his sword, and fine snuff-box', and lets herself quietly out.

When the governess hears of the affair, she realises she knows who this gentleman is and how she can improve upon the situation. Her technique is a gentle blend of invitation and blackmail. Clearly the man finds Moll attractive and Moll has been wavering in her commitment to crime. If the man can be tracked down and brought home, he would serve very well as a keeping-cully: 'one that maintains a Mistress, and parts with his Money very generously to her'. Going to visit the gentleman on some pretext, the governess quietly lets him know that she knows he was not really robbed on Hampstead Heath, as he has told his friends and family, but coming back from Knightsbridge in company with a lady who was not his wife. The gentleman is keen to humour this woman with her dangerous knowledge, and, at least in Moll's telling, equally keen to see again the pick-up who caused him all this trouble. When he calls upon her, Moll makes routine protestations that it was the first time she ever did such a thing; she would not have done it had her circumstances not been dire and so on and so forth. She then allows herself to be led to a bedchamber and an arrangement of sorts is arrived at. It is never a very satisfactory one: 'he never came into a settled way of maintenance, which is what I would have been best pleas'd

with'. Nonetheless, for a time he makes her handsome enough presents that she can take a little holiday from thieving.

The careers of Moll Flanders and Mary Carleton cross again during
this period of Moll's life, for the German Princess too kept herself
afloat during the 1660s by a combination of crime and keeping-cullies.
Indeed, the Newgate Ordinary's account of Mary Carleton's life as a
criminal comes much closer to the popular idea of Moll Flanders'
activities than anything Moll herself recounts. After their illegal
wedding in 1663 John Carleton had disowned his bride but refused to
return any of her property. Mary therefore had to make her own
living. She did so, again, in some style, becoming one of the first
generation of female players to legitimately appear in English theatres:
'she got,' said the Newgate Ordinary, 'a great deal of applause in her
dramatical capacity, by the several characters she performed, which
were generally jilt, coquette, or chambermaid'. Her greatest success,
however, was in a play written specifically for her and called *The German
Princess*. Samuel Pepys went to see it in April 1664, but did not think
much of it: 'with my wife by coach to the Duke's house, and there
saw "The German Princess" acted, by the woman herself; but never
was any thing so well done in earnest, worse performed in jest upon
the stage'. Soon the public moved on from the pretty bigamist to some
other sensation or scandal. No longer offered parts in the playhouse,
Mary Carleton was left to find some other way to support herself.

Her appearances on stage earned her 'a considerable number of
adorers', who paid her way for some time. First came two rich young
'bullies': in thieves' cant prostitutes' minders and in more general usage
hired thugs, or simply rather stupid and brutish young men. These two
were encouraged 'till she had drained about three hundred pounds apiece
out of them, and then, finding their stock pretty well exhausted, she
turned them both off, telling them she wondered how they could have
the impudence to pretend love to a princess'. Next an 'elderly gentleman'
(fifty years of age) persuaded Mary, by means of many costly gifts, to
live with him. The gifts continued after they moved in together, the aging
lover ever more infatuated with his mistress. She received them 'with an
appearance of being ashamed he should bear so many obligations on
her, telling him continually that she was not worthy of so many favours',
until, presumably unable to stand it any longer, she picked a night when
he got drunk, stole 'twenty pieces of old gold, a gold watch, a gold seal,

an old silver watch, and several pieces of plate, with other valuable movables, to the value in all of one hundred and fifty pounds' and left to seek out her next victim and begin the game again. 'It would be impossible,' wrote the Ordinary, 'to relate half the tricks which she played.'

Moll Flanders, on the other hand, sticks to her one man, and deals with him honestly. The relationship is never serious, however, and is brought to an end not by her robbing and leaving him, but because he loses interest. 'After about a year,' she writes, 'I found that he did not come so often as usual, and at last he left it off altogether, without any dislike [hostility], or bidding adieu; and so there was an end of that short scene of life, which added no great store to me, only to make more work for repentance.' The money he has given her does not last long, and as her governess becomes restive about her idleness and lack of funds, Moll finds she must 'think of my old trade, and to look abroad into the street again'. Rather than return to the diving and shoplifting of previously, however, she now embarks on a series of more sophisticated crimes. By means of dressing up and giving a plausible story, she begins working a variety of bilking lays, or frauds.

Again, she is treading in the Princess's footsteps. Gradually, perhaps as Mary Carleton's looks began to fade or she became fed up with male demands, she abandoned keeping-cullies and turned to crime. Working the bilking lay required intelligence, nerve and the ability to inhabit a persona, and Mary Carleton had all these gifts. She was particularly skilled at persuading shopkeepers to part with their goods on approval. Visiting a Cheapside draper one day with her pretended maid, for example, she found she did not have coins small enough for the silk she wanted to buy, and so one of the draper's men accompanied her home, carrying the parcel of fabric.

When they came to the Royal Exchange, madam ordered the coachman to set her down, pretending to the mercer that she wanted to buy some ribbons suitable to the silk; upon which he suffered the maid, without any scruple, to take the goods along with her, staying in the coach for their return. But he might have stayed long enough if he had attended till they came again, for they found means to get off into Threadneedle Street, and the young man having waited till he was quite weary made the best of his way home to rehearse his misfortune to his master.

A seventeenth-century lace shop

She did the same thing in Spitalfields, persuading a French weaver to deliver a parcel of expensive cloth to her lodgings. When the weaver's man brought it, she explained that half was for her niece, who lodged next door, took it for that young lady to view and never came back. And she did it again in the New Exchange in the Strand, another fashionable shopping galleria, where another pretended maid ordered armfuls of mourning – 'hoods, knots, scarves, aprons, cuffs and other mourning accoutrements' – be delivered to the new widow's house. When 'madam milliner' obligingly presented herself, she was told her bereaved client was indisposed and asked to leave the goods on approval and call again. When she did so, she was told 'to her great mortification, that [the lady] was gone out, they could not tell whither, and that they believed she would never return again; for she had found means, before her departure, to convey away several of the most valuable parts of furniture in the room which she had hired'.

These frauds are more to Moll's liking now than the old, risky snatching of goods here, and running away with them there. Her first schoolmistress is dead, but there are plenty of other women in her governess's circle who can hand on cheating tips. One fraud, she recalls, 'was given me by one that had practis'd it with success, and my governess lik'd it extreamly'. It is simple but effective. Dressing up as a maidservant 'in a very mean habit', Moll hangs about the inns where stagecoaches arrive. 'People come frequently with bundles and small parcels to those inns, and call for such carriers, or coaches as they want, to carry them into the country; and there generally attends women, porters wives, or daughters, ready to take in [look after] such things for their respective people that employ them.'

Having promised to look after travellers' belongings while they take refreshment in the inn, Moll slips away with whatever she can carry. She practises a cleverer fraud at the riverside warehouses which serve the busy coastal trade from Scotland and the north-east. When a young man comes to claim goods sent down from Newcastle, she asks for the letter giving the mark by which the box is to be identified and itemising its contents. Bidding the man 'come in the morning, for that the warehouse keeper, would not be there any more than night' she then copies the salient details into a new letter, this one addressed to Mr Jemey Cole of London. Returning to the warehouse, she innocently finds the keeper, presents herself as Mr Cole's housekeeper and receives the box.

She keeps her hand in with shoplifting when nothing better offers, assuming a variety of disguises. She visits the new Royal Exchange, finely dressed to deflect attention. Shoppers and shopkeepers alike are caught up in a sudden bustle when a 'great dutchess' is said to have just entered, with the rumour that the queen is just behind, and Moll takes advantage of the moment to

> set myself close up to a shopside with my back to the compter [counter], as if to let the crowd pass by, when keeping my eye upon a parcel of lace, which the shop-keeper and her maid were so taken up with looking to see who was coming . . . that I found means to slip a paper of lace into my pocket, and come clear off with it . . . I went off from the shop, as if driven along by the throng, and mingling myself with the crowd, went out at the other door of the Exchange.'

She has become a chameleon, a mistress of disguise, escape and opportunity. As she recalls rather wearily, 'I could fill up this whole discourse with the variety of such adventures which daily invention directed to, and which I manag'd with the utmost dexterity.' Each day she sets out anew from her governess's house to see what the credulous world is offering, deferring again and again the moment when she must retire into a life of virtuous but banal leisure. With longevity, however, comes notoriety, and that is dangerous for a woman whose success depends on drifting anonymously through the crowds. 'One of the greatest dangers I was now in, was that I was too well known among the trade, and some of them whose hatred was owing rather to envy, than any injury I had done them began to be angry, that I should always escape when they were always catch'd and hurried to Newgate. These they were that gave me the name of *Moll Flanders*.'

There is a knowingness to the name which both Defoe's readers and Moll's acquaintances appreciated. Moll was not just the diminutive of Mary; it also carried connotations of sex – moll was one of many terms for prostitute in thieves' cant – and of crime, as in the phrase which has come down to us, gangster's moll. The name Flanders too was not arrived at by chance. Lace from Flanders was prohibited in order to aid the domestic weaving industry and had therefore become highly prized by thieves, receivers and society ladies, who bought it on the black market. It is the second time Moll has gone by the name. Once, as a young 'widow' in the Mint, she adopted it herself. Now it is given her by London's thievery as a half-admiring, half-angry homage, even though many who tell tales of 'Moll Flanders' are not sure if they know who she actually is.

There are crimes she will not commit, either because they are outside her expertise or because they carry too fearful a punishment. On one occasion she bizarrely prigs a prancer – takes a horse – but when she brings it home to her governess, they agree she must take it away again, for neither knows what to do with it. Nor would she join, when invited, one of the many roaming gangs of housebreakers, or ken millers, for she is always wary of working with too many people. Companions are potential informers. On another occasion she is approached by a gang of coiners – queer cole makers – but this is a very dangerous trade. It is not only a capital crime, but the sentence would be the archaic, terrible one of burning at the stake, which prospect, says Moll, 'struck terror into my very soul, chill'd my blood, and gave me the vapours to such a degree as I could no think of it without trembling'. Nor was the sentence a mere left-over form of words; burnings happened.

The age in which Moll lived was still one of routine violence from the state. Regicides and traitors were hanged, drawn and quartered, but those guilty of far less threatening crimes were also put to dreadful deaths. Elderly widow Ann Petty was sentenced to be 'drawn on a hurdle or sled to Smithfield and there to be burned to Death' for the 'clipping of money' – cutting tiny pieces off legal tender and making new coins with the scraps. In 1675 Elizabeth Lillyman, for the crime of petty treason in murdering her husband, was also sentenced to be 'burned to ashes'. In 1676 a male housebreaker and two women who refused to enter pleas for their separate crimes were ordered to be 'pres't to death'. It was only through the intercession of the sheriff and when the housebreaker went down on his knees and begged 'very importunately', that the court agreed he could enter a belated plea and stand trial. The women refused to beg and were presumably killed as the sentence prescribed.

Despite her fears of punishment, Moll is still caught fast in the Devil's net, pushing away any thoughts of frugal but honest retirement. She guards her identity ever more closely: 'I took up new figures,' she says, 'and contriv'd to appear in new shapes every time I went abroad.' Now she goes thieving dressed as a man, now as a beggar-woman; sometimes in the black dress of a widow – an ace of spades – and sometimes 'equipt', or richly dressed, with a purse of gold and a maidservant following obediently behind. Each disguise presents its own opportunities. There are, however, only two ways in which a criminal career ends, and by refusing to retire, she lays herself open to the other.

She is wandering, well-dressed, one day when she sees an open door, no one within and lengths of brocaded silk unattended. It is that day's opportunity, and she takes it. Disaster finally strikes. Leaving, she is 'attacked by two wenches that came open-mouthed at me just as I was going out at the door, and one of them pulled me back into the room, while the other shut the door upon me. I would have given them good words, but there was no room for it, two fiery dragons could not have been more furious than they were.'

The constable comes, and although the owner of the warehouse and his wife would have given in to Moll's protestations that she had never done anything the like and never would again, here was two shillings in recompense and so on and so forth, the constable is obliged to take her before the magistrate, who sends her to Newgate to await trial at the Old Bailey.

That horrid place! My very blood chills at the mention of its name; the place, where so many of my comrades had been lock'd up, and from whence they went to the fatal tree; the place where my mother suffered so deeply, where I was brought into the world, and from whence I expected no redemption, but by an infamous death; to conclude, the place that had so long expected me, and which with so much art and success I had so long avoided.

She is back where she started. Almost.

13

Moll the Newgate-bird, 1673–4

The Great Fire of London reached Newgate Gaol on its third day. By the fifth, the building had burnt to the ground, the stones of the press yard wall exploding into the street outside as the heat built inside them. Just in time the gaol's inmates had been marched across the river to Southwark and housed temporarily in the Clink, the debtors' prison next to Moll's old refuge. Rebuilding Newgate took six years. In 1672 it was again ready for its inhabitants and Moll Flanders is imprisoned behind its grand new facade.

A new gatehouse and towers fronted onto Newgate Street. Statues of Justice, Mercy and Truth looked east, and Liberty, Peace, Plenty and Concord looked west. Some £10,000 of City funds had been spent on the reconstruction, but most of that sum had been dedicated to the decoration of its external walls. What the old overcrowded Newgate had most needed was an increase in capacity. The new design did not supply it: scarcely was the building opened to the manacled crowds brought back from Southwark than all the gruesome sights, smells and sounds of too many people in too little space reappeared.

Newgate's management was as ripe for reform as its layout, but that opportunity too was lost. Money had always talked in gaol, just as it did in the outside world. Prisons were not institutes of correction, but glorified versions of the sponging-house, where prisoners were milked for all they were worth before judges put an end to the moneymaking by punishing or releasing them. A prison was run as a private concern, with its keepership bought by the highest bidder. That price had to be recouped as swiftly as possible and then whatever profit the keeper could extort from those in his custody was his. This culture trickled down the hierarchy of prison staff. Imagination and ingenuity were expended on the creation of tariffs and penalties which touched every part of prison life: easement of fetters (replacing heavy irons with lighter ones), food, the admission of visitors, the provision of a Newgate Wag or prostitute, clean clothes, a mattress, a blanket, receipt or delivery of letters. Some prison staff, more daringly, even went into partnership with those in their custody. Moll knew one of these night-flyers in Newgate, a man who 'by connivance was admitted to go abroad every evening, when he play'd his pranks', bringing back his booty and sharing it with the gaoler.

But not quite everyone in Moll's world is swayed by the laws of the market. An unfortunate and stubborn honesty possesses the two shop girls who caught her stealing. Moll has swiftly informed her governess of her arrest and imprisonment, and that lady 'immediately applied her self to all the proper methods to prevent the effects of it'. Finding the shop girls, she 'tamper'd with them, persuad'd them, offer'd them money, and in a word, try'd all imaginable ways to prevent a prosecution; she offer'd one of the wenches 100 *l.* to go away from her mistress, and not to appear against me'. Nothing works. The 'jades' are adamant. Nor are their employers any more malleable: the woman shows some trace of sympathy, but the man has put up a forty-pound bond to the court committing himself to appear there against Moll, and is reluctant to forgo it. Among the governess's network are insiders who, she promises, could make the relevant paperwork disappear, but he still refuses. As each attempt by her governess to save her fails, Moll sinks into terror. 'I liv'd many days here under the utmost horror of soul; I had death as it were in view, and thought of nothing night and day, but of gibbets and halters, evil spirits and devils; it is not to be express'd by words how I was harrass'd, between the dreadful apprehensions of death, and the terror of my conscience reproaching me with my past horrible life.'

The Ordinary comes to see her, but she finds him ineffectual and is nauseated by his drunkenness and his practice of writing up the confessions of executed criminals and selling them in twopenny pamphlets. The 'indefatigable application' of her governess means her case is postponed for a month, but this is a mixed blessing, for there are terrible sights and sounds all around her and Moll feels herself succumbing to the corrosive moral influence of her surroundings. On the 'Master's side' of Newgate those who have money may rent private apartments, and perhaps Moll lodges here, in what is facetiously known as My Lady's Hold: a small and windowless cell furnished with two beds. Despite this touch of relative luxury, Moll cannot block out all sight or sound of the other prisoners. They are all around her, and their cries and shrieks fill the gaol. It was commonly said that women were the worst, the loudest, the dirtiest and dirtiest-minded of the prisoners in Newgate, and if some of that observation was routine misogyny, another part was rooted in fact. Hardened female criminals, wrote one male gaol-visitor in his poem *A Glimpse of Hell*, 1715, were beings

> Who neither have fear nor have regard
> To God or Man or Moral Laws
> But plague the World without a Cause
> . . .
> I've seen a well-fill'd Chamber Pot
> Like Lightning toss'd from hand to hand
> Till tyr'd with Stink, they Breathless stand.
> But Silence for a Minute's pain.
> Old B——ch, damn'd B——d one cries again
> I'll rup you up, and split your Scull
> You curst confounded dirty Trull.
> The Matron, much enraged, cry's
> You nasty B——ch, pray cease your noise,
> You Copper C—t—ed Pocky W——e
> I ne'r was burn i'th'Cheek, as you're

At first Moll regards these women with horror, but as her time among them wears on, she begins to find that 'conversing with such a crew of hell-hounds as I was with' brings her into the same state of grim gaiety which possesses them. She hardens and degenerates: 'a certain lethargy of soul' takes hold of her, and although there is 'an infamous death just at the door . . . yet I had no sense of my condition, no thought of Heaven or Hell at least, that went farther than a bare flying touch . . . I neither had a heart to ask God's mercy, or indeed to think of it, and in this I think I have given a brief description of the compleatest misery on earth'.

For a person of faith, the feeling of being shut out of the Lord's presence is despair, and any reader of Moll's (or Defoe's) generation would understand this passage to mean that she has reached her lowest state. It is not prayer, Bible study, the exhortations of the chaplain or any other extension of divine mercy which calls her back from this petrified state of indifference, however, but news that three high-waymen are about to be brought into the gaol. They have robbed a coach on the road to Windsor, been pursued to Uxbridge and taken there 'after a gallant resistance'. Highwaymen were the glamour boys of the criminal world, and it was not, as Moll said, 'to be wondered that we prisoners [especially the women] were all desirous enough to see these brave, topping gentlemen'. Perking up a little, Moll lines up with the rest of her unholy crew, waits to see the three walk by and is amazed – 'struck dumb at the sight' – of the first to appear. It is none other than her beloved Jemmy, the 'Lancashire husband' she has not seen for years. She reels in shock and the prison buzzes with gossip about the new inmates. They are old offenders, it seems, and Jemmy is their leader. He has committed so many robberies, the whisperers are saying 'that *Hind*, or *Whitney*, or the *Golden Farmer* were fools to him'.

If, as he indicated in the first edition, Daniel Defoe sincerely intended to follow up *Moll Flanders* with histories of both the governess and the Lancashire husband, he probably had tucked away a clutch of pamphlet biographies of highwaymen, just as he had his 'Lives' of Mary Frith and Mary Carleton. James Hind, James Whitney and William Davis, the 'Golden Farmer,' three of the seventeenth century's most notorious highwaymen, were obvious models for his hero, Jemmy, and all spawned a small library of memoirs after their deaths.

'Captain' James Hind of Oxfordshire was hanged in 1652, when Moll was still happily living in Hammersmith. Born to a decent working family, he had been educated well and placed by parents attentive to his welfare as apprentice to a butcher. Liking neither the work nor the master, however, he ran away to London and fell into wicked ways. Among his new acquaintance in the capital was Thomas Allen, already a well-known highwayman, who acted as Hind's own 'schoolmaster', taking the young man out on the road for a few first forays. It was the execution of Charles I, however, which really spurred Hind on. As a devoted Royalist, he said, he made it his mission to stop and rob as many Roundheads as he could, including Oliver Cromwell among his victims. In 1651 he joined Charles II's army, which invaded from Scotland and was stopped at Worcester by the New Model Army. Charles II escaped and famously hid in an oak tree, but 10,000 Royalists were taken prisoner and around 8,000 Scots transported to the Americas. James Hind made it back to London, only to be turned in to the magistrates by 'a very intimate acquaintance'. The informer's reasons – political, personal, professional – are unknown. Convicted of not only robbery and murder but also high treason, Hind was hanged, drawn and quartered. His head and limbs were affixed to posts on the bridge across the River Severn where it runs through Worcester.

William Davis, the 'Golden Farmer', was less interested in politics. Under cover of farming his comfortable Surrey acres, Davis took to the road for adventure in 1649, when he was twenty-three years old. His charm and respectable persona allowed him to gain vital information about the movements of wealthy persons and richly laden coaches, which he acted on in clever disguises. Even his own landlord did not recognise the man who held him up and took back the rent he had just collected from Davis's farm. In time, Davis gathered a gang around him and roamed the coach roads as far west as Gloucester. On one famous occasion he held up the Duchess of Albemarle on Salisbury Plain and taxed her with immoral use of cosmetics while ripping three diamond rings from her fingers. Prudently, he retired in middle age, but was tempted back to the road one last time to finance the purchase of land adjacent to his farm. He had lost his touch, however, and was recognised. Hunted down in Fleet Street shortly afterwards, he shot one of his pursuers. He was executed in December 1689 and 'kept an ironmonger's shop', as his comrades left behind would have said, when his body was hung in chains on Bagshot Heath, scene of some of his robberies.

James Whitney was another butcher manqué who left the provinces for London, learned to dress like a gentleman and started to make his illicit fortune. Petty theft gave way to fraud, and fraud to hold-ups on the King's highway. Like the best highwaymen of fiction, Whitney had a reputation for wit and gallantry. 'Meeting one day with a gentleman on Newmarket Heath,' the Newgate Ordinary recorded at his death in 1684,

> whose name was Long, and having robbed him of a hundred pounds in silver, which was in his portmanteau tied up in a great bag, the gentleman told him that he had a great way to go, and as he was unknown upon the road should meet with many difficulties if he did not restore as much as would bear his expenses. Whitney upon this opened the mouth of the bag, and held it out to Mr Long. 'Here,' says he, 'take what you have occasion for.' Mr Long put in his hand and took out as much as he could hold. To which Whitney made no opposition, but only said with a smile: 'I thought you would have had more conscience, sir.'

Twelve years before he met Moll, Jemmy too had 'taken to the road' as one of a gang of highwaymen. They depended for their information on a network of spies, and the woman who befriended Moll in London and invited her to Lancashire was one of these, as well as being Jemmy's mistress. By then Jemmy was growing tired of the profession and of constantly watching over his shoulder for a constable or a comrade turned informer. When Moll's false friend reported this different kind of booty, he seized the opportunity to 'leave off the road and live a retired, sober life'. Moll had not known his true identity then, but as she learns it now she realises that Jemmy, like her, will almost certainly be sentenced to death.

> I was overwhelmed with grief for him; my own case gave me no disturbance compar'd to this, and I loaded my self with reproaches on his account; I bewailed his misfortunes, and the ruin he was now come to, at such a rate, that I relish'd nothing now, as I did before, and the first reflections I made upon the horrid detestable life I had liv'd began to return upon me, and as these things return'd my abhorrance of the place I was in, and of the way of living in it, return'd also; in a word, I was perfectly chang'd, and become another body.

It is the wrong moment for sensitivity to return. Just after Jemmy's arrival, Moll hears that her own case will be heard at the next Old

Bailey Sessions. Her governess visits and together they rack their brains for some way out. But the members of the jury whom her governess approaches will not be bribed, and the shop girls remain immoveable. The court hearing is two days away, and it seems Moll has left to her a fortnight of life at most. Utterly terrified, she even begs one of the gaolkeepers for advice: 'Lord! Mr —— what must I do? Do, *says he*, send for the Ordinary, send for a minister and talk to him, indeed, Mrs Flanders, unless you have very good friends, you are no woman for this world.'

The trial goes off as all have predicted: the indictment read, the plea requested and given – 'Not guilty' – the witnesses sworn and examined, the guilty verdict pronounced and sentence of death passed. The next hanging day is in two weeks' time, and the governess performs what she thinks will be her final service to her old friend: sending in a minister to bring Moll to a state of true repentance. This good man achieves what the drunken Ordinary did not: he 'unlock'd,' says Moll, 'all the sluices of my passions: he broke into my very soul by it; and I unravell'd all the wickedness of my life to him'. The minister is by her when the death warrant arrives. Her name is upon it.

The following day, as she panics and weeps at the thought of impending death, she paces her cell, alone. Her governess has been struck down by illness, and when the minister unaccountably does not come, she has no one with whom to share her fears and her new-found repentance. It is not until four o'clock that she hears the minister's knock, and opens the door to hear that he has spent the day begging the secretary of state to reprieve her. He has succeeded! Her name has been taken off the warrant for tomorrow's executions, but she has only been granted a stay of one month. She is woken the next morning by St Sepulchre's bell, and the 'dismal groaning and crying' from the six prisoners who are shortly to die.

> This was follow'd by a confus'd clamour in the house; among the several sorts of prisoners, expressing their awkward sorrows for the poor creatures that were to die, but in a manner extreamly differing one from another; some cried for them; some huzza'd them, and wish'd them a good journey; some damn'd and curst those that had brought them to it, that is meaning the evidence, or prosecutors; many pittying them; and some few, but very few praying for them.

The six are taken away and hanged, the next sessions inexorably approaches and Moll begins to wonder how long her reprieve will last. Too old to plead her belly, there is still one way out, and she takes it: with the minister working on her behalf, she proffers 'an humble petition for transportation'. It is heard. Two weeks after her stay of execution she learns she has been pardoned on condition of transporting herself to His Majesty's plantations. Her life seems to have come full circle. Some sixty years ago her mother was taken from this prison, convicted, like her, of theft on a London street, and sent across the Atlantic to labour in an American field. Now it is the daughter's turn.

The practice of 'reprieving for Virginia' had tailed off somewhat during the Interregnum, between 1649 and 1660, when political prisoners instead of criminals tended to fill the transatlantic ships and New World plantations. Transportation to Virginia, Maryland, the Caribbean and the new American colonies of Carolina and Connecticut became common again after the Restoration in 1660, although the felons were little more welcome than Moll's mother had been in 1614. Virginia's settled population was now growing fast. It would almost triple between 1650 and 1700, for not only were native children being born and raised but indentured servants were continuing to pour in. Who, therefore, would want to buy the services of a convicted criminal, especially one hampered by sex, age or deformity, when a servant, travelling voluntarily with an unblemished record, cost the same? If the felon were young, male, healthy and apparently repentant, then the merchant who organised his passage across the Atlantic might find a buyer for him. Women, children, the old, the sick and the lame were not so easily disposed of. The best a moneyless convict could hope for was degradation and labour; the worst, abandonment on an American beach to die because nobody would buy him. There is an escape route, however, and Moll's governess knows what it is. Recovered from her illness, the old lady comes to see her protégée and is immensely cheered by Moll's news. 'Why, *you have money, have you not?*' she reminds Moll, and therefore nothing to fear from either the voyage or life in America. Money, as the wise old governess knows, talks as loudly aboard the convict ships and on the plantations as it does in the Newgate cells.

When Moll's mother was sent to Virginia in 1614, she had no say in how she travelled, nor where she arrived, nor who acquired her services thereafter; it was a matter of pure luck that she ended up as well as she did on her farmhouse in Virginia. By the time Moll herself is exiled, the system has changed. The Virginia Company, whose ship took Moll's mother to America, was dissolved when the Crown took direct control of Virginia in 1624. Since then felons ordered to leave England had generally had to arrange their own passage. There was no systematic state apparatus (as there would be when, for example, Australia became the principal penal colony) to actually take away those sent into exile. Some parishes paid for the ad hoc removal of groups of local ne'er-do-wells after sentencing, while people with funds behind them paid the costs of their own removal, but a lucrative private system had come into being for the rest. The same shipowners, syndicates, wealthy passengers and captains who had made their profit on indentured servants when Moll first went to Virginia had extended their operation to felons. Convicts who could not afford to buy a ticket across the Atlantic were obliged to lease themselves to captains or supercargoes, who sold them off in America just as they did indentured servants.

Transportation was just that: an order to transport oneself out of the kingdom. No conditions of hard labour or other punishment were attached to it, for exile itself was the punishment. If, therefore, convicts had enough money to pay for a comfortable passage and did not have to sell themselves into servitude in America in order to live, they had as good a chance as anyone else – better, indeed, than penniless indentured servants – to establish themselves comfortably in their exile. As Moll has enough money put away from her thieving, she need not fear the cargo hold and the wharfside auction. Not that she can think about all that at the moment, however, for her mind is wholly given over to Jemmy.

It is over three months before the next ship bearing convicts to Virginia leaves the Thames, and Moll devotes them to saving Jemmy, who is still unaware that his wife is in the same gaol as he. He too is living in privately rented chambers on the Master's side, and has managed to stave off trial, having 'found means to bribe or buy off some of those who were expected to come in against them'. When the prosecutors, losing patience, begin searching out new witnesses to bring their case, Moll sees her opportunity. 'Publication was made,' she writes, 'that such prisoners being taken, anyone that had been

robb'd by them might come to the prison and see them.' Pretending
that she has been robbed in a Dunstable coach and might be able to
identify these men as her attackers, she is led in to see them. Disguised
and muffled as she is, Jemmy does not know who his visitor is. Moll
immediately asserts she recognises him, and he was indeed the man
who robbed her. When Jemmy is told, he demands to see this witness
who is preparing to testify falsely against him. The keeper is prevailed
upon to leave them alone, and Moll uncovers her face. '*My dear*, says
I, *do you not know me?*'

> He turn'd pale and stood speechless, like one thunder struck, and not
> able to conquer the surprize, said no more than this, *Let me sit down*;
> and sitting down by a table, he laid his elbow upon the table, and
> leaning his head on his hand, fix'd his eyes on the ground as one stupid:
> I cry'd so vehemently on the other hand, that it was a good while e'er
> I could speak any more; but after I had given vent to my passion by
> tears I repeated the same words: MY DEAR, *do you not know me?* At
> which he answer'd YES, and said no more a good while.

When both have recovered voice and wits, Moll tells him what she
has been doing for the past decade – or some of it at least: 'as much
of my story as I thought was convenient'. This edited version
brought her

> at last to my being reduc'd to great poverty, and representing myself
> as fallen into some company that led me to relieve my distresses by a
> way that I had been utterly unacquainted with, and that they making
> an attempt at a tradesman's house, I was seiz'd upon, for having been
> but just at the door, the maid-servant pulling me in; that I neither had
> broke any lock or taken anything away, and that notwithstanding that,
> I was brought in guilty and sentenc'd to die; but that the judges, having
> been made sensible of the hardship of my circumstances had obtain'd
> leave to remit the sentence upon my consenting to be transported.

As if this misfortune were not enough, she has had the bad luck to
be mistaken for a rogue named Moll Flanders, 'a famous successful
thief, that all of them had heard of . . . and that under this name I
was dealt with as an old offender'.

Jemmy too brings his beloved up to date. When they parted, with Jemmy badly out of pocket, he had been 'obliged to put off his equipage and take up the old trade again'. He had robbed, plundered and adventured across the North Country. Here, he says, is the bullet wound from that time in Carlisle; there, the scar from a sword fight somewhere else, and she pats and soothes and exclaims. He says he made so much money on two occasions that he was in a position to move as a gentleman to Virginia and had tried to track Moll down to tell her so. Prudently, she does not mention that she received but disregarded his letters. They talk their way to the present, and he explains he expects to be hanged, and although 'he had had some intimation, that if he would submit to transport himself, he might be admitted to it without a trial' he thought this was no way for a gentleman to go.

Moll, of course, disagrees fervently, and tells him so. 'I blam'd him for that, and told him I blam'd him on two accounts; first because, if he was transported, there might be an hundred ways for him that was a gentleman, and a bold enterprizing man to find his way back again, and perhaps some ways and means to come back before he went.' It wanted only a little cash, she said, 'for him to buy himself off' when he got to Virginia. But Jemmy still demurs, for he has a horror of exile, and in particular of 'the woods and wildernesses of America'. Pages are taken up with their arguing back and forth, just as they did in the old days, as to the advantages and disadvantages of moving to Virginia. Moll insists 'that if he had money . . . he might not only avoid the servitude, suppos'd to be the consequence of transportation; but begin the world upon a new foundation, and that such a one as he could not fail of success in', for here she is to advise him how to do it. In the end Jemmy consents to her proposal. In February they are taken with fifteen other convicts to a Virginia ship waiting at Deptford.

14

Moll settles in Maryland but returns to England again, 1675–83

A young Londoner called James Revel was convicted of theft and sentenced to fourteen years' exile in Virginia in the late 1600s.[13] He returned to Britain at the end of his term and wrote a piece of doggerel called, in the unwieldy style of his times,

THE POOR UNHAPPY TRANSPORTED FELON'S SORROWFUL ACCOUNT OF HIS Fourteen Years Transportation, At Virginia, in America. IN SIX PARTS. BEING A Remarkable and Succinct History of the Life of James Revel, the unhappy Sufferer Who was put Apprentice by his father to a tinman, near Moorfields, where he got into bad company and before long ran away, and went robbing with a gang of thieves, but his master soon got him back again; yet would not be kept from his old companions, but went thieving with them again, for which he was transported fourteen years. With an account of the way the

---

13 James Revel's poem *The Poor Unhappy Felon Transported* . . . has been the subject of much discussion by historians. The earliest surviving edition is from the eighteenth century, but it is nevertheless believed to have been written several decades earlier, in the 1660s or 1670s. Nothing is known about Revel, who may have been writing under an assumed name. Some historians have therefore concluded his poem is a piece of fiction, but others are convinced it is an authentic first-person narrative because of the familiarity it displays with places and practices in seventeenth-century Virginia. The fullest discussion of its authenticity is by John Melville Jennings in *The Virginia Magazine of History and Biography*, Vol. 56, No. 2 (April 1948), pp.180–94.

transports work, and the punishment they receive for committing any fault. CONCLUDING WITH A Word of Advice to all Young Men.

'One night,' he wrote, 'was taken up one of our gang, Who five impeach'd, and three of them were hung.' Revel was one of the two who escaped the noose, and was sentenced instead to be shipped to America, 'sold,' he wrote, 'for a slave, because he prov'd a thief'. He sailed with sixty others, 'a wicked lousy crew as e'er went o'er', of whom fifty-five were still alive when they reached Virginia seven weeks later and were made ready for sale.

> Then to refresh us we were all made clean
> That to our buyers we might better seem
> The things were given that did to each belong
> And they that had clean linen put it on
> Our faces shav'd, comb'd out wigs and hair
> That we in decent order might appear.

Sluiced, primped, combed and shaved, Revel and his comrades were exposed for sale and examined by buyers like livestock.

> Some view'd our limbs turning us round
> Examining like horses if were sound
> . . .
> Some felt our hands others our legs and feet
> And made us walk to see we were complete.

This humiliation, as much as the period of hard labour which followed, is what Jemmy so dreads. There was a means to evade the auction block, however, as James Revel – himself penniless – and Moll's governess had both noted. As Moll and Jemmy's ship approaches the Virginian coast, the captain calls upon them to discuss how their savings might be deployed to mutual advantage. They must, he says, 'get some body in the place to come and buy us as servants, and who must answer for us to the governor of the country, if he demanded us'. As Moll has no acquaintance in Virginia on whom she can call for this favour, however, she asks the captain to arrange it on their behalf. For '6000 weight of tobacco, which he said he was accountable for to his freighter', he takes the case efficiently in hand, bringing 'a planter to treat with him, as it were for the purchase of these two servants, my husband and me, and there we were formally sold to him, and went a shore with him'. After toasting the deal in a local alehouse, the buyer hands over a 'certificate of discharge, and an acknowledgement of having serv'd him faithfully, and we were free from him the next morning, to go whither we would'. While the poorer convicts are led away for sale in the open market, Moll and Jemmy re-embark and sail on, looking for suitable land to buy, seed and settle on.

Moll has once again to exercise delicacy in reconciling her new and old family situations. Just as she withheld from Humphrey the knowledge that her mother was sent to America as a convict, now she must fudge the issue of colonial relatives with Jemmy. He already knows her mother lived in Virginia, but does not know in what capacity either mother or daughter arrived, nor the sorry history of the latter's incestuous marriage. She explains her reluctance to rekindle old bonds to Jemmy in terms he can sympathise with: that 'since the misfortunes I had been under, had reduc'd me to the condition I had been in for some years, I had not kept up any correspondence with them, and that he would easily believe, I should find but a cold reception from them if I should be put to make my first visit in the condition of a transported felon; that therefore if I went thither, I resolv'd not to see them.'

Privately, Moll is sure the old lady must be dead, and rather hopes that Humphrey is too. She has no wish to confront him. They travel north up the Chesapeake, leaving Moll's old home on the York River behind them. Colonial settlement has spread, carrying the distinctive mixture of Stuart English and Native American languages throughout the tidewater: Maryland, the Susquehannah; Anne Arundel County, the Potomac; Port Oxford, the Rappahannock. Moll and Jemmy land on the south bank of the Potomac River, in Westmoreland County, Virginia and the first thing Moll does on landing is to enquire after her mother and husband/brother. The news she receives is troubling, for they too have moved north from their old plantation to Westmoreland. If she settles hereabouts, she will have Humphrey as an unsettlingly close neighbour. She does not know what to do. If there were not the question of her mother's legacy, it would be easy, but Moll remembers the old lady's promise that she will leave her daughter something and is determined to get it if she possibly can. By facing Humphrey she risks revealing her past to Jemmy but will be able to claim her inheritance; by going elsewhere she will keep Jemmy's illusions intact but put no money in her purse. There was never really a choice: she opts for the first.

Heavily gowned and hooded, Moll wanders the edge of the plantation which has been pointed out to her as her former husband's and sees two male figures near the house. A passing local identifies them as father and son, both named Humphrey. Moll is taken by a fit of the vapours as she realises her own son is within speaking distance of her. 'Let any mother of children that reads this, consider it, and but think with what anguish of mind I restrain'd myself; what yearnings of soul I had in me to embrace him, and weep over him; and how I thought all my entrails turn'd within me, that my very bowels mov'd,[14] and I knew not what to do.'

She recovers from her moment of maternal passion to hear the local still chatting away. The poor old gentleman, she is saying, had the misfortune to marry his own sister, who ran away to England when the fact came out and left the family in 'such confusion, that it had almost ruin'd them all', and the mother has since died. Moll perks up at this news and 'began to enquire into the circumstances of the family, how the old gentlewoman, *I mean, my mother*, died, and how she left what she had'. The local is remarkably well informed: 'she had been told, that *my mother* had left a sum of money, and had ty'd her plantation for the payment of it, to be made good to the daughter, if ever she could be heard of, either in England, or else where; and that the trust was left with this son, who was the person that we saw with his father'.

While delighted by news of her legacy, Moll still cannot see how she is to get her hands on it and simultaneously keep her husbands apart. She decides it is too risky to stay in Westmoreland for the moment. She will return, alone, when she has formulated some plan. Jemmy, as is his custom, leaves all decisions to her even though Moll herself has, she confesses, but the vaguest idea of American geography. She knows only 'that *Maryland*, *Pensilvania*, East and West *Jersy*, *New York*, and *New England*, lay all north of *Virginia*, and that they were consequently all colder climates, to which, for that very reason,

14 Tender emotions were considered to reside in the bowels, rather than the heart.

I had an aversion . . . I therefore consider'd of going to *Carolina*, which is the most southern colony of the *English*, on the continent of *America*.'

Back down the Potomac they sail, in an uncomfortable five-day passage across the broad Chesapeake to Maryland's eastern shore. Hopes of Carolina are disappointed, however. When they arrive at a place Moll names as Philip's Point (possibly at the mouth of the Nanticoke River, Dorchester County) they find the Carolina-bound vessel has already sailed. Nonetheless, the country all about them seems 'very fertile and good' so Moll and Jemmy, weary of travelling, decide to set up their plantation nearby. There is as yet no settlement along the Nanticoke and so, on the directions of an 'honest Quaker', they travel sixty miles 'nearer the mouth of the bay'. This distance and direction would take the pair towards Somerset, Maryland's newest and southernmost county, a destination also suggested by Moll's new friendship with the helpful Quaker.

Moll tends to skate over the details of her travels, but going sixty miles through the virgin country of Maryland's eastern shore was, like undertaking a transatlantic voyage, more arduous than her short sentence suggests. George Fox, founder of the Quakers, travelled in this area a year or so before Moll and Jemmy. In February 1672 his ship ran aground on the Maryland shore in a Chesapeake storm. Continuing overland, he recorded in his journal, he and his companions travelled through woods, crossing rivers in 'Canoos (which are Indian Boats) causing our Horses to swim by'. They rested at isolated plantations but never for long; 'for we had thirty miles to ride that afternoon', Fox recalled of one occasion, 'if we would reach a town . . . [some] got to the town that night, exceeding tired; [others] were fain to fall short, and lie in the woods that night also, making themselves a fire'. He eventually reached Somerset County and spent about a month there, holding meetings in Quaker homesteads along the Annemessex, Manokin and Wicomico rivers.

The province of Maryland had been experimenting with religious toleration since its foundation in 1633. Its success, although limited, was a remarkable achievement at a time when nations were tearing themselves apart over minute differences in interpretations of scripture. Although the Calvert family had established Maryland in part as a refuge for English Catholics, George Calvert, first Lord Baltimore and first lord proprietary, specifically enjoined the colonists to leave religious dissent behind them, and welcomed Protestants into his fiefdom. George Calvert, however, was a rare man in being able to separate his religion and his public life and could not keep the madness of the Christian world at bay. An increasing number of Protestants arrived in Maryland during the 1640s, fleeing persecution in Europe but bringing it with them to America. By April 1649 Catholics and Quakers were experiencing such hostility from these cuckoos in the nest that George Calvert's son Cecilius, second lord proprietary, steered an 'Act Concerning Religion' through the colonial assembly in an attempt to uphold his own tottering government and his father's founding principle. This Toleration Act, as it came to be known, stipulated that

> whatsoever person or persons shall from henceforth uppon any occasion of offence or otherwise in a reproachful manner of Way declare call or denominate any person or persons whatsoever inhabiting, residing, traffiqueing, trading or commerceing within this Province or within any of the ports, harbors, creeks or havens to the same belonging an heritick, scismatick, idolator, puritan, independent, Prespiterian, popish prest, Jesuite, Jesuited papist, Lutheran, Calvenist, Anabaptist, Brownist, Antinomian, Barrowist, Roundhead, Separatist, or any other name or terme in a reproachfull manner relating to matter of religion

were to be fined ten shillings, or the equivalent in goods, for each offence, half to go to the person offended and half to the lord proprietary. If the fine were not paid, the offender was to be whipped, and imprisoned until ready to publicly ask forgiveness of the person insulted.

Quakers were among the Toleration Act's principal beneficiaries, and a considerable number arrived in Somerset County through the 1660s, when the sect was actively being persecuted in Europe, Virginia and New England. The British 'Quaker Act' of 1662 made it illegal to hold any religious convictions other than those of the established Church. English Quakers preaching in New Amsterdam – the Dutch colony which became New York in 1664 – were imprisoned and flogged. In 1657 the Massachusetts assembly stipulated that anyone found guilty of transporting Quakers into the colony be fined one hundred pounds, while anyone found harbouring them once there was to pay forty

shillings per hour of their presence. In Virginia, too, didactic Angli-
cans enacted the first of several anti-Quaker laws in 1659. They were,
wrote the colonial assembly, 'an unreasonable and turbulent sort of
people' whose objective was to 'destroy religion, laws, communities
and all bonds of civil society'.

The Chesapeake Quakers were not victims of bloodier persecu-
tion, in part because Maryland offered them a home. (Pennsylvania,
despite Moll's synopsis of American geography, did not yet exist;
William Penn founded it, as a Quaker refuge, in 1681.) Maryland and
Virginia both claimed the eastern shore, which bordered Accomack
County in Virginia, and Dorchester County in Maryland. In August
1666 Cecilius Calvert named a part of the disputed land Somerset
County after his aristocratic sister-in-law and drew a boundary with
Virginia. The Quakers who immediately began to arrive there, settle
and swear allegiance to the proprietary government strengthened his
shaky claim to the land.

A scattered but definable community of the dissident, the tolerant
and the land-hungry was emerging along the Manokin and
Annemessex Rivers by the time of Moll and Jemmy's arrival. There
was the Johnson family, headed by Anthony, a Negro who arrived in
Virginia in 1620 and was sold to a planter. At that date distinctions
between slavery and servanthood were fluid, and African blood did
not automatically entail lifelong slavery. Anthony was freed after
serving a term of service, in the same manner as English servants,
and had since been acquiring land, indentured servants of his own
and possibly slaves. He was a substantial landowner. There was
Ambrose Dixon, brought into Accomack, Virginia in 1649 as an indentured servant, and his wife Mary, who followed him to America in
1652. They had done well: Ambrose's trade – he was a caulker – was
a useful and profitable one in a maritime county. The Dixons moved
north into Somerset to practise their Quaker faith, and the meeting
house near their home, Dixon's Choice, was the centre of the
Annemessex community. There were sober, God-fearing artisans and
craftsmen here, most of them religious refugees from Virginia: in 1662
there was a cooper, a caulker, a carpenter and a leather dresser, all of
whom also owned tobacco fields; three chirurgeons (surgeons) and a
large group of families who devoted themselves entirely to 'planting'.
We can imagine Moll and Jemmy, therefore, guided by their new

Quaker friend, arriving somewhere near Dixon's Choice, numbed by the saddle or the hard wooden seat of a cart, covered in dust, shaken by the ruts and pits of the Maryland roads and desperate to find some place where they can rest and start making their home.

Their Quaker friend finds a warehouse for the goods they have brought from England and a temporary lodging for themselves, and directs them in their purchase of 'an *English* woman-servant just come on shore from a ship of *Leverpool*, and a *negro* man-servant, things absolutely necessary for all people that pretended [intended] to settle in that country'. They then bought 'as much land for £35, paid in ready money, as would make a sufficient plantation to employ between fifty and sixty servants, and which, being well improved, would be sufficient to us as long as we could either of us live'. Finally, it seems, prosperity is within their grasp: on fertile land, with helpful neighbours, they settle into planting life. Within a year they have fifty acres of cleared ground, some planted with tobacco and some with 'corn sufficient to help supply our servants with roots, and herbs, and bread'. Truly this is a colonial success story. Moll and Jemmy spend happy evenings totting up stock on their fingers and coming to joyous results. They are rich! No wonder they 'used to look at one another, sometimes with a great deal of pleasure, reflecting how much better that was, not than Newgate only, but than the most prosperous of our circumstances in the wicked trade that we had been both carrying on'. How horrified their Quaker neighbours would be if they knew that the quiet elderly couple which has recently moved in among them are convicted criminals, bigamously married: she, a thief and mother to illegitimate children; he, a highway robber.

Life continues pleasantly and according to the rhythm of the land. Crops are sown, crops are harvested, tobacco is packed and shipped to England. Wigs and swords and fowling pieces arrive from England for Jemmy, so he can indulge his passion for dressing up and shooting things. A request to Moll's old governess yields a more useful cargo: harness for horses, tools, clothes for servants and 'woollen cloth, stuffs, serges, stockings, shoes, hats, and the like, such as servants wear; and whole pieces also, to make up for servants'. Moll and Jemmy's American prosperity rests primarily, however, not on importing luxuries for trade but on planting, and that in turn rests on their ownership of other people's labour. The governess also buys and sends out another sort of cargo: 'three women-servants, lusty wenches . . . suitable enough to the place, and to the work we had for them to do; one of which happened to come double, having been got with child by one of the seamen in the ship'.

Convict James Revel ended up on a tobacco plantation on the other side of the Bay and the other side of the labour market. He was bought at auction by a 'grim old man', who took him to his plantation up the Rappahannock River, where conditions for the field-hands were hard.

> A canvas shirt and trowsers me they gave
> A hop-sack frock in which I was a slave
> No shoes or stockings had I for to wear
> Nor hat, nor cap, my hands and feet went bare.

Five other felons and eighteen Negroes worked in the fields with Revel, and no difference was made in the treatment of servants and slaves.

> We and the negroes both alike did fare
> Of work and food we had an equal share.

A plot was set aside for them to grow food in order to supplement their diet, where they worked on Sundays. Every other day was spent in the fields from dawn to dusk, and in the mill, grinding corn, when the light failed outside. 'Much hardship then indeed I did endure,' Revel recalled. 'No dog was ever nursed so before / More pity the poor negro slaves bestow'd / Than my brutal and inhuman master would.' Revel's grim picture is corroborated by the memoir of a French Calvinist preacher named Jean de Labadie, who travelled to Maryland from New York and was shocked by the conditions in which plantation servants laboured. American historian Annie Lash Jester quotes Labadie's comments on arriving at Bohemia Manor, the huge estate owned by businessman, cartographer and fellow Calvinist Augustin Hermann.

> For their usual food, the servants have nothing but maize bread to eat,
> and water to drink, which sometimes is not very good and scarcely
> enough for life, yet they are compelled to work hard. They are brought

from England in great numbers into [Maryland and Virginia], and sold each one according to his condition, for a certain term of years, four, five, six, seven or more. And thus they are by hundreds of thousands compelled to spend their lives here and in Virginia, and elsewhere in planting that vile tobacco [which is] fed and sustained by the bloody sweat of these poor slaves.

A few Marylanders, or publicists for Maryland, took a different view. George Alsop was an indentured servant there for four years and came back to England burning to set right those he thought calumnified the province and the way it treated its lower orders. Alsop believed ardently in the divinely decreed social hierarchy and, since the lower orders were made to serve, it was better, Alsop thought, to do so in Maryland than in London: 'the four years I served there were not to me so slavish, as a two years Servitude of a Handicraft Apprentice- ship was here in London'. His description of the comfortable terms and kind masters that govern a servant's life is rather like Moll's old mother-in-law's, as is his assurance that they will all take their place on the next rung of the social ladder when their term is up. Alsop himself was clearly treated well – although he chose to return to England – and certainly there were colonial households in which servants were treated as Moll had been in her Colchester house: with affection and some respect, as witnessed by the number of marriages contracted between indentured servants and the children of their employers. (One of the Calthrope daughters, Moll's old neighbours in Virginia, married an indentured man when his time had expired.) One hopes that Moll the mistress tended more in this direction in her dealings with her servants. And also with her slaves, for, like most Accomack and Somerset landowners, she is almost certainly a slave owner.

In 1664 Maryland passed a law mandating that black slaves could not be freed, and thereafter a distinction was made between servants, who were white and arrived from Europe, and true slaves, who were black, brought from Africa and bound in perpetuity, their offspring as well as themselves the property of their owners. The Anglo-Dutch Wars of the 1660s had ended with an equivocal victory for the British, and the transatlantic slave trade had been a spoil of war. British merchants had ousted their Dutch rivals along the West African coast, and one result was an influx of enslaved black labour into America. When Moll's free black neighbour Anthony Johnson died in 1670, the local court disregarded the thirty-five years he had lived and worked alongside his white landowning neighbours as an equal, pronouncing that 'as a black man, Anthony Johnson was not a citizen of the colony'. His land was assigned to a white planter instead.

Despite the comfortable income from her slave-worked plantation, however, another source of money is still on Moll's mind. Leaving Jemmy happily killing the colonial wildlife, she returns to Westmoreland County. From temporary lodgings there she sends a letter to her old husband, explaining she comes not to make trouble, but merely 'as a sister to a brother, desiring his assistance in the case of that provision, which our mother at her decease had left for my support'. She also expresses her 'most passionate desire of once seeing my one, and only child'. It is a happy chance for Moll that Humphrey Senior has gone blind and gives the letter unopened to his son to deal with. The young man comes galloping up to Moll's lodging, asking the messenger who delivered the letter 'which was the gentlewoman which sent him'. 'The messenger said *there she is, sir*, at which he comes directly up to me, kisses me, took me in his arms, and embrac'd me with so much passion, that he could not speak, but I could feel his breast heave and throb like a child that cries, but sobs, and cannot cry it out.'

Moll's joy at seeing her boy is not misplaced, for he has turned out a more decent man than she has any right to expect. He treats her with unreserved affection and courtesy, and when he has recovered from the shock of meeting her, explains how he has managed her legacy, a small plantation on the York River, and offers to continue managing it in such a way as she may count on an income of a hundred pounds a year. During her five-week stay with him her son treats her beautifully, and she cannot but notice that all about her are signs of wealth. A sneaky thought even crosses her mind, similar to one which briefly crossed it back in the 1630s, when Humphrey Senior lay on the verge of death. Just for a moment she begins 'secretly now to wish, that I had not brought my *Lancashire* husband from *England* at all'. But it passes; 'that wish was not hearty . . . for I loved my *Lancashire* husband entirely, as indeed I had ever done from the beginning'.

Moll's son is keen to accompany her back across the Chesapeake, but she puts him off as she has not told him about Jemmy. They also decide not to tell the older Humphrey, and so it seems Moll has pulled off the semi-miraculous feat of keeping everyone in the dark and still getting her money. One day, she decides, she will tell her son that she has met a neighbour over the bay and decided to marry him, and that will resolve that matter. Before she returns to Maryland, she gives him a gold watch as a present, desiring sentimentally that he would 'now and again kiss it for my sake'. She does not tell him she stole it in a London church.

Whatever lingering worry Moll might have had about her abandoned American family is resolved, her legacy is hers and she lives in unthought-of prosperity. Her adventurous life it seems is drawing to a close, and Moll, weary with writing, deals briskly with the eight years they spend in Maryland. Again she has no interest in what is happening around her: the breathless arrival of Virginia's Governor Berkeley on the eastern shore in 1676, pursued by Nathaniel Bacon and his mutinous band of colonists; the calling-up of the militia and the vengeful expedition against the Nanticoke Indians in 1678; the rumours of atrocity and bloodshed trickling down from the north, where white settlers are fighting the Wampanoake; the chatter and controversy as Pennsylvania is carved out of land to the north and peopled with Quakers. None of it disturbs the quiet pair who potter about their plantation and sit silent in the meeting house each Sunday, waiting to hear the Lord's voice. Moll restrains any lingering urge to pick her neighbours' pockets.

Moll might have lived out her life in America but Jemmy wants to come home. Despite the prohibition on his ever returning from exile, the couple returns to England in about 1682. Moll is nearly seventy, her husband sixty-eight. Comfortably ensconced in a house somewhere, with a colonial income to keep the fires lit, food on the table, servants in the attics to clean and cook and nurse, they finally retire from the fray. 'We resolve,' promises Moll, in her last sentence, 'to spend the remainder of our years in sincere repentance for the wicked lives we have lived.' Do you believe her?

Part III

1683–1727

15

Moll's creator, 1683–1722

In 1683, the year in which he depicts Moll writing her autobiography, Daniel Defoe was about twenty-three years old and still going by his original name of Daniel Foe (spelt ffoe in some documents). Although Defoe is now chiefly remembered as one of the first English novelists, he did not start writing fiction until he was nearly sixty. He brought to his fiction the advantage of a rich, fully lived and rackety life, spent sailing close to political winds and upsetting powerful people in an age when those were dangerous pastimes.

As a child, Defoe was educated to Protestant notions of work, sin and fear. His family, as Dissenters, lived for many years under the real threat of dispossession, exile or even death. As a young adult, he was a respectable London tradesman, a juror, a member of a guild, paterfamilias and husband. This existence, however, ran alongside a parallel and less worthy one, in which he was a dabbler in dubious business propositions, a bankrupt, a defrauder, a shuffler of bank accounts – a 'gay deceiver', as his mother-in-law called him as she saw her savings disappear. Then there was the life of the soldier and the activist, for as a young man he was either active participant or propagandist in many of the great political events of his generation.

In 1683, however, Defoe was still an eager and hopeful young man just starting out in life, the well-educated son of a Dissenting family. He was engaged to Mary Tuffley, daughter of a prosperous cooper who had promised a large dowry, and was setting himself up as a merchant in Cornhill, in the City of London. It was the start of a fitful but mostly unsatisfactory career in business which saw Mary's dowry lost and Defoe turn his hand to whatever he could to make ends meet. Two years after they married, politics intervened in the young couple's life. When Charles II died in February 1685 without a legitimate heir (although with a surfeit of illegitimate ones), the throne went to his Catholic brother, James II, whose accession was a direct threat to the Defoes. Daniel was one of thousands to take arms against the new King that July, joining a Protestant army being raised in the West Country. It was led by the Duke of Monmouth, Charles II's eldest illegitimate son, a Protestant championed by many as the true heir. Daniel, with many others, must have gone into hiding when Monmouth's rebels were defeated and hunted down on the Somerset Levels. Monmouth was taken to the Tower, where he was horribly killed by an incompetent executioner. At the Bloody Assizes which followed, 320 people were sentenced to death and 800 to exile in the colonies. Defoe slunk back to London along roads festooned with the body parts of those executed. There he resumed his business career, trading in beer, wine, liquor and fabrics, keeping his head down and hoping the King's soldiers did not come knocking at his door.

Three years later Protestantism finally triumphed in England. James II's eldest daughter, Mary, was Protestant herself and married to a dour Protestant prince, William of Orange. In 1688 a powerful faction in England invited William to invade England and depose his father-in-law. When James abdicated and fled, Mary, who did not want to govern her unruly inheritance alone, suggested she and her husband rule jointly as William III and Mary II. This combination of circumstances was known as the Glorious Revolution of 1688, of which Daniel Defoe was a noisy promoter. The new monarchs were bound by the Bill of Rights passed in 1689, which guaranteed Protestantism in England and subjected the rule of the Crown to that of Parliament in key areas, such as levying taxes and maintaining an army. The Civil War was finally won.

If the Glorious Revolution was a time of joy for English Protestants, it was also, for the Defoes personally, a time of distress. Their first daughter died, and Defoe's business ventures began to fail. He had been trying to expand his business interests and make money from the American colonies, but the move was ill timed and his partners seem to have been ill chosen.

Details of Defoe's American interests emerge from the lawsuit he started in the Courts of Chancery in 1690. The suit was against one Humphrey Ayles, mariner of Redriff, who was master and part-owner of a vessel called *The Batchelor of London*. On 18 June 1688 – five years after Moll and Jemmy return from Maryland in the novel – Humphrey Ayles signed an agreement with Daniel Defoe. He undertook to sail for America with the first good wind after 20 June and to take on board his vessel all such goods, merchandise and passengers as Defoe should in the intervening two or more days put on board. A large part of this cargo was indentured servants, who were to be exchanged in Maryland for tobacco. Defoe's instructions were that Ayles should sail as directly as winds permitted for Boston, where he should discharge a part of the cargo, and proceed 'within eight days' for New York. He was not to stay in that town for longer than ten days, but must sail on to Maryland, where the remaining cargo would be disembarked and Ayles was to take on board 'hogsheads of Tobacco and other goods and merchandizes'. Fully loaded, he was to make for the Isle of Wight or the Downs, a gathering place in the Channel for fleets, and await Defoe's instructions as to whether the American cargo was destined for London or Amsterdam.

The cargo which Defoe had been expecting the *Batchelor* to bring home by autumn did not, however, cover the costs of the voyage, and he held Captain Ayles responsible. Instead of spending only eight days in New England, Ayles had spent twenty-six – on his own account, Defoe suspected, doing his own business and neglecting that of his client, taking on unauthorised passengers and freight. When Ayles finally got to Maryland, he found the agents there had 'despaired of his comeing' and sold to other captains the tobacco which should have been reserved for Defoe. Not only did Ayles therefore fail to bring back the goods which would have paid for the voyage, but he even had the cheek to charge Defoe £144 for demurrage – a fee charged for any extra time a ship spends in harbour while waiting to load or unload cargo – as well as over £1,000 for damages.

Captain Ayles saw things differently and began his own suit against Defoe. He had promptly delivered Defoe's indentured servants to his Maryland factor, but there had been no tobacco there for him to take on board. He had wasted a great deal of time sailing back and forth, sending parties inland to deal with planters, trying to find some tobacco to bring home, but there was none to bring.

It is not clear how this lawsuit ended. Soon after, however, another ship in which Defoe had a share was taken by a French privateer, since by now England and the Netherlands were at war with France. In 1692 he went bankrupt, probably as a result of these two heavy losses. It was an early lesson to Mary Defoe that her husband would not be a steady provider. Over the next thirty years of married life, he was in turn a serial, and serially unfortunate, investor, a political agitator, a government spy, a bankrupt (again), a journalist, a pamphleteer, a convicted, imprisoned, pilloried criminal and an adviser to royalty. He began his writing career as a supporter of William of Orange and would later let it be known that he had enjoyed an intimacy with this Protestant monarch whom he so much admired and whom he saw as the principal bulwark against Catholicism and absolutism. It is possible that in the very last years of the seventeenth century he started setting up an anti-Jacobite espionage network at the king's personal request.[1] Whether for this or for commercial reasons – perhaps travelling abroad to source wine and cloth – Daniel was absent much of the time from the family home, leaving Mary and her mother Joan Tuffley to deal with creditors and their growing brood of children. Even when he was in London, Defoe spent periods living with his married sisters. In particular, he spent time with Elizabeth Defoe Maxwell, who was a widow, escaping his creditors and tutoring his little niece, also named Elizabeth. His writing career developed alongside the espionage and frequently one bled into the other. As his publications veered into satire, caricature and then very close to sedition and libel, Defoe found himself in increasing trouble. In 1702 he was imprisoned; in 1703 he was pilloried. 'In the School of Affliction I have learnt . . . Philosophy,' he wrote ruefully in 1712. 'I have seen the rough side of the World as well as the smooth, and have in less than half a year tasted the difference between the Closet of a King, and the Dungeon of Newgate.'

Queen Mary died in 1694, and William III in 1702. Since they were childless, Queen Anne, Mary's Protestant sister, succeeded to the throne. Anne's reign coincided almost exactly with the thirteen years

---

1 Jacobites were supporters of the exiled Stuart dynasty.

of the War of the Spanish Succession, a drawn-out and immensely costly conflict which spread across all parts of the globe colonised or claimed by Europeans. In 1702, the year of Anne's succession, Defoe was convicted of libel, having written a satire on Anglican bigotry against Nonconformists, *The Shortest Way with Dissenters*. He was pilloried and imprisoned for his wit, and released from Newgate Gaol only by the intervention of the secretary of state, Sir Robert Harley. Harley's interest was not benevolent: he had his eye on Defoe as an 'agent of the crown', in other words a spy. Defoe's work for Harley over the next eight years has remained for the most part shadowy and unknowable, despite the best attempts of biographers to excavate evidence. Accounts of payments to 'Alexander Goldsmith' and 'Claude Guilot', Defoe's code names, remain, but they are itemised only as 'for her Majesty's special service', 'as of Her M. Royal Bounty' and 'for secret services'.

Queen Anne died in 1714. Her reign had been a kind of extension of the previous century, dominated by personalities, concerns and politics left over from the lives of her father, grandfather and even great-grandfather, Charles I. Despite eighteen pregnancies, none of Anne's offspring lived past childhood. On her death, therefore, the British throne passed to a German dynasty, in the person of Anne's second cousin, the Elector of Hanover, the first of the four Hanoverian Georges who personified the eighteenth century.

By October 1714 the new German king had taken up residence in St James's Palace, but his accession was not accepted by everyone. In 1715 the Jacobites attempted to invade England and were defeated. About 640 Jacobites, mainly Scots, were sent to America and the Caribbean. Although the Jacobite threat would not completely disappear for three decades, it seemed after the failed invasion in 1715 that England and Scotland, united by Act of Parliament in 1707, could at last begin to settle into a new, peaceful status quo. The next two decades saw the struggles of Whigs and Tories, court and country; the rapid ascent of Robert Walpole, Britain's first prime minister; and, under his influence, the flowering of an unstoppable culture of money-making, rapaciousness and consumer excess.

Daniel Defoe was back in London by the time of George I's accession. In 1714 he was in his mid-fifties and generally regarded as a sly and untrustworthy old dog: someone with a finger in every pie, earning his dirty shilling, abandoning each patron as soon as another paid better. After his provocative pamphleteering and clandestine political work, not everyone in the coffee houses of the City would share a pipe and a bowl with him. He was openly accused of apostasy, of prostitution, of being a writer for hire. The anonymous writer of *Judas Discuvr'd, and Catch'd at last: or, Daniel de Foe in Lobs Pound* (1713) described him as 'an *Animal* who shifts his Shape oftner than *Proteus*, and goes backward and forward like a hunted *Hare*; a thorough-pac'd, true-bred *Hypocrite*; an *High-Church Man* one day, and a *Rank Whig* the next'. There was truth in the accusation.

Daniel Defoe

The Whigs and Tories were the political parties which emerged from the seventeenth-century debates over limitations on royal power. Broadly speaking, Whigs were in favour of the monarchy's subservience to Parliament and toleration for Protestant dissent. Tories, on the other hand, believed in the divine right of kings and supported the Anglican Church. Defoe's patron under Queen Anne, Robert Harley, was a Tory, and thus associated with everything Defoe had been fighting and writing against in the decade before his imprisonment in Newgate. When George I took the throne in 1714, however, the Whigs replaced the Tories in power and Harley's career was effectively over. Daniel Defoe smoothly and swiftly switched allegiance to Charles Delahaye, under-secretary of state and head of the embryonic Hanoverian secret service. Delahaye placed Defoe as an undercover agent on the staff of the bookseller Nathaniel Mist, editor of the *Weekly Journal*. Mist was a Tory of rabid heat and passion, in love with Stuarts dead and exiled and constantly scalding his toe in Jacobite waters. Defoe was told to keep an eye on him, but when his day job was done, he, like the other hacks, came to the coffee house to eavesdrop, gossip, drink, dream, eat jellies and scribble. Later he coached home to the comfortable country house in Stoke Newington which he had recently acquired and where his patient wife Mary waited, hoping he would be home before nightfall.

A family upset lurked behind this cheerful picture. Daniel's niece Elizabeth Maxwell had recently disappeared. Her mother had been angered when she learned that her eighteen-year-old daughter had betrothed herself to a young man of whom she did not approve, and forbade the match. It was a common enough situation, but young Elizabeth's reaction was extreme. She ran away from home, telling no one where she was going. The best her family could hope for was that she had obtained a respectable position as an upper servant or companion, and would let them know where she was when her anger subsided. At the back of the collective Defoe mind, however, must have been the dread of receiving news of her downfall, for it was not easy for a woman to make a safe way through life unsupported and unprotected by her kin. Everyone knew the dangers of the streets. Mary had locks installed on every door of the Defoe house in Stoke Newington, and checked each one every night before taking herself and her rattling great bunch of keys to bed, her children all breathing in their beds, her silver safe in the sideboard downstairs, her maid-servants – she thought – chaste in the attics above. Terrible things happened outside, and even inside one's own house when the wrong people entered, and Mary could not but know about them for her husband reported their doings in his newspapers.

Among the things that most interested the Hanoverian metropolis and its commentators was the turbulent urban underclass, semi-visible all around them, which had been 'bred up to crime' and knew nothing but gangs and thieving. Their territory was the dangerous area around the squalor of Seven Dials, the dank alleys of the Mint in Southwark and the docks in Shadwell and Wapping, where a man was advised to go armed and a lady not at all. One of the most popular genres for the reading public was criminal biography: the lives and deaths of these people, sensationally written up from their appearances in court and last confessions. Leading the way in the genre were the Ordinaries of Newgate Gaol, one of whom Moll Flanders had met and disdained. Their job was to save the souls of the almost-damned who lived within the prison's walls. Their perk was to write and sell titillating accounts of the state of those souls and the weak frightened bodies which enclosed them. Each hanging day the Ordinary accompanied the condemned in their death carts from Newgate to Tyburn, gave them the last sacrament, took down their dying words and rushed home to immortalise these in cheap prose, delivered to the printer that night and sold to a hungry public at eight the next morning. They were devoured by a society fascinated by its own seamy underside.

Newspapers always kept a corner free for indecency and violence, and there were hacks among the Tyburn crowds to watch the condemned swing and note their fear, fortitude or indifference. They haunted Newgate and the Old Bailey, offering bribes for gossip; they dredged up information on widows, children, relations with parents, childhood (well or ill spent), youth, first indications of wickedness and descent into hardened crime, and returned to the coffee houses of St Paul's Churchyard to write up their nasty stories. This was the hub of London's burgeoning press, overshadowed by the great new dome of the cathedral and lined with printers, mapmakers and booksellers pumping out pamphlets on South Sea dreams, scandal, theological argument, accounts of travels more or less fabulous, political infighting and the wonders of the colonies. In 1714 a popular work was produced by 'Captain' Alexander Smith: *The History of the Most Noted Highway-men*, an anthology of mini-biographies including the 1662 *Life of Mrs Mary Frith*. It went through five editions by 1719.

Defoe, like most jobbing writers, could turn his hand to criminal reporting when required, but he had other interests as well. A theme to which he turned time and again was the need to exploit the colonies, despite his own sad history of colonial trade. He was fascinated by the earliest explorations of Virginia, writing *A General History of Trade* in 1713 and *A Historical Account of the Voyages and Adventures of Sir Walter Raleigh* in 1720. Virginia (by which Maryland was also under-stood) appears in these as a land of fabulous but undeveloped riches, eagerly awaiting its divinely ordained fate: British capital and British settlement.

Along with the pamphlets, the espionage and the bread-and-butter work of newspaper reporting, Defoe was also writing his first work in the developing Hanoverian style of 'false memoir'. He produced five of these over the next five years: *Robinson Crusoe, Captain Singleton, Moll Flanders, Colonel Jack* and *Roxana*. *Robinson Crusoe* was published in 1719 but was set a half-century before, at the time of Defoe's own childhood, and purported to be the autobiography of an adventuring Scot. Defoe had cribbed from the recently published account of Alexander Selkirk, a Scottish seaman marooned for four years on a Pacific isle, rescued by chance when a British man-o'-war put in for water and spotted the wild man in goatskins. Defoe gave his hero some perfunctory adventures on the high seas and a brief career slaving in West Africa, and brought him to the tobacco plantations of Brazil. He sent him out a cargo of goods from England with which Crusoe 'bought me a Negro slave and an European servant also'. Fifty rolls of tobacco resulted, and his ambitions swelled. One Negro was not enough; neighbouring planters 'told me they had a mind to fit out a ship to go to Guinea; that they all had plantations as well as I, and were straitened for nothing so much as servants'. Off went Crusoe to Africa to buy some, 'standing away to the northward' and unaware of the horrors his creator had planned for him.

By the time *Robinson Crusoe* was published in 1719, Defoe's next fictionalised hero was already taking shape: 'Captain' Bob Singleton, bought as a toddler by Gypsies, taught to beg and steal before he runs away to sea, turns pirate and is left on another unfriendly island. And behind Bob Singleton were the fainter outlines of a hero and heroine adrift on other tides. The first, Colonel Jack, was a boy-thief who became a Virginian planter, returned to Britain to participate in the Jacobite uprising of 1715 but saw the error of his ways and became a loyal Hanoverian subject. And then there was Moll, soiled by seduction and felony but redeemed by colonial adventure, drawing to her the sights and sounds of Defoe's everyday life and memories of his youth. Among those memories was the death of Mary Carleton, who was hanged at Tyburn when Defoe was in his teens. Convicted of theft in February 1671 and transported to Jamaica, she had secretly returned to England before her time was up. A few months later she was arrested again for some petty crime. Someone at the Old Bailey recognised her at her trial, and she was charged with being illegally returned from transportation. She pled her belly, but the panel of matrons could find no sign of life and she was hanged.

Trawling through the lurid criminal biographies of the early 1700s, one can find many other echoes of Moll Flanders, or perhaps they are better called presentiments. Another famous Moll was hanged at Tyburn in 1703, her story and last confession on sale the day after. This was Moll Raby (alias Jackson alias Brown), an offender, said the Newgate Ordinary, with 'almost as many names as the fabulous hydra had heads'. Her particular skill was in 'bilking her lodgings' and she had practised it all over London. 'One of her adventures was at a house in Great Russell Street, by Bloomsbury Square, where, passing for a great heiress, who was obliged to leave the country by reason of the importunate troublesomeness of a great many suitors, she was entertained with all the civility imaginable.' One day, when the family was out, she sent a servant to cash a fraudulent bill of £150 and asked the maid to go with him in case he was minded to run off with the money. By the time they returned, having been told the bill was a forgery, the house had been robbed of £80 in cash and £160 worth of plate. Marrying an honest butcher, Moll Raby persuaded him to 'go upon the pad in the daytime' (become a mugger),

> while she went upon the 'buttock and twang' by night; which is picking up a cull or spark, whom, pretending she would not expose her face in a public-house, she takes into some dark alley, where she picks his fob or pocket of his watch or money, and giving a sort of Ahem! . . .

the fellow with whom she keeps company, blund'ring up in the dark, knocks down the gallant and carries off the prize.

On the death of her butcher, Moll Raby went 'upon the night sneak' – or became a common burglar – and was informed against by two accomplices after breaking into a house in Soho Square. Her last speech was brief and pathetic: she had been well brought up at first, she told the crowd, and knew good things, but did not practise them, having given herself up to all manner of wickedness and vice . . . She had a husband, she thought, in Ireland, if still alive, but she was not certain of it, because it was now six years since he had left her. Then she stepped off the platform to her death.

And what of thief Moll Hawkins, also hanged that year, having given birth to the child which at first reprieved her? Hawkins had, she said, 'gone upon the question lay': dressing herself well and then

taking an empty Bandbox in her Hand, and passing for a Milliner's or Sempstress's Apprentice, she goes early to a Person of Quality's House, and knocking at the Door, asks the Servant if the Lady is stirring yet: for if she was, she had brought home, according to order, the Suite of Knots (or what else the Devil puts in her Head) which her Ladyship had bespoke over Night.

Then she robbed the house while the servant went upstairs to fetch his mistress.

These were the sorts of cases which brought crowds to the Old Bailey and provided copy for London's writers. One in particular would feature in a newspaper edited by Daniel Defoe. Her name was Moll King.

16

The last Moll, 1718–21

On a Sunday morning in London, June 1718, Moll King alias Gold alias Gilstone tucked a pair of false hands into her pocket and headed for St Anne's, Soho, the most fashionable church in London. A rumour that the Prince of Wales, the eldest son of George I, would soon be renting a St Anne's pew was bringing every pretty lady on the up to these aristocratic streets, mincing along on high fashionable heels, or hiring a chair with a fellow either end to carry her if she had the money. Every penniless gallant who was awake this early would soon swagger in to display himself here, and the congregation would resemble less a pious flock than a Drury Lane audience or the louche late-night crowd from Vauxhall Gardens. And for each pretty lady who stalked the court, and each pretty youth who stalked a rich widow, there were others who stalked them, following them here from the theatres and the pleasure gardens.

Mrs King was one of these: like Moll Flanders, she was an autem diver. Choosing her neighbours carefully, she slid into her mid-pew seat and clasped her false hands in prayer. Unknown to the ladies who eased their tight shoes to either side, her real hands were diving into the slits cut in the seams of their skirts, extracting their purses. Once the watches, coins and trinkets these contained were sorted and removed, the purses were deftly replaced.

A seventeenth-century lady's purse

Moll King was a criminal of many years' standing: one of the hands fingering a neighbour's pocket had been scarred by the branding iron in October 1693, when, under the name of Mary King alias Godman, she was convicted of 'robbing the House of one Joseph Bayly of St Giles Cripplegate' – Daniel Defoe's boyhood parish – 'and carrying away one Alkereene Petticoat, val. 7 s., three yards of Hair-fringe, a Hood, and three yards of White Flanders Lace'.

A quarter-century of experience separated the teenager caught with an armful of fripperies in St Giles and the middle-aged lady in St Anne's. Moll King had since taught herself, or been taught by some mentor, to glance at a lady and come away with a complete mental inventory of her worth. She knew whether a lady's ribboned cap sat atop real hair or false; whether her gown was of silk, damask or the fashionable 'Indian cotton' or calico; whether the lace which trimmed her cuffs, ruffles and lappets was home-made or from Valenciennes, or the more expensive variety from Flanders. She had gained subtler skills too. She could read character, or at least mood: who was alert and who distracted; who was likely to shout for a constable and who to become flustered and self-doubting, and let a thief flit away. This continual calculation of wealth and its availability marked out an experienced thief like Mrs King from the inexperienced who tumbled in and out of the compters, bridewells and gaols of London. To steal a handkerchief worth a shilling risked the gallows, but so did stealing a watch worth thirty pounds, and she who took the latter saved on risk and work, could put money by for her retirement when her fingers had stiffened and her eyesight was weak, and when – if – she was eventually taken, could bribe the gaoler and procure false witnesses for her trial.

Moll King did not only come to St Anne's, Soho each Sunday to rummage in other people's pockets. A dashing young man about thirty years younger than her, of an age which can survive a debauch and still appear fresh in the morning, had also taken to worshipping here. 'Captain' John Stanley – most young men about town assumed the title, whether or not they had any right to it – was a gallant with a long sword, a seductive pout and too little money to live the life he wanted. He was a veteran of duel and adulterous intrigue, despite his youth, and Moll King was one of many smitten by his charms. She did not know, perhaps, that Stanley already had a long-term mistress and illegitimate child living in a house at the corner of Old Bailey and Ludgate Hill. John Stanley, like Moll King, had found a home from home in the cattle market of St Anne's, 'where some madams pray in their paint and see their Heaven in Man'. He was a luscious youth, as keenly watched as watching, and Moll King was poised to get him in the best way she knew.

Squeezing past the young man when she entered the church, Moll had eased the watch from his pocket and slipped a gold box worth twice its value into its place. According to a *Life of John Stanley* written by the Newgate Ordinary, Thomas Purney, in 1723, the captain looked for his watch at the end of the service and found it missing. Mrs King then approached 'and said, if he'd go with her, she'd bring him to the Woman that took it'. Off they went to a Soho tavern, to share a bottle of wine 'which he offer'd her for her civility', though surely wondering whether the thief might not get away as they drank. Lifting her glass with one hand, she replaced the watch in his other pocket with the

other and 'told him, instead of being robb'd, he had robb'd her'. Captain
Stanley stared in confusion; Moll called other customers to help,
described her gold box and accused her escort of having taken it.
When he was searched and the box was found in his pocket, he 'lay
at her Mercy', a frightening game for him, for its value was enough
to hang him. But 'she desiring all to withdraw, threw herself about
his Neck, and embracing him, declared how long how much she lov'd;
and instead of his being made a Prisoner, own'd herself a Captive to
his Beauty. After many Kisses and Caresses, she presented the Box to
him with two Diamond Rings; and offer'd him much more for the
continuation of his Friendship.' So at least went the story told at the
time about the odd couple who emerged from a Soho tavern one
sunny summer morning, having struck their bargain.

Captain Stanley told the Newgate Ordinary something of his life
five years later, and the reverend gentleman wrote it up and sold it
the day after Stanley's execution. His version described a small-time
thug, a weak man whose looks were greater than his talents. Son of
an army officer who had fought in Spain, young John was given a
good start in life but went off the rails when he discovered drink and
women. It was a standard Newgate morality tale: John Stanley, wrote
his biographer sadly, 'gave himself too much up to pleasure'. His
parents, seeing the way their son was going, made several attempts
to separate him from a certain Hannah Maycock, but none was
successful. Most recently, his father had obtained for him a post with
the Royal African Company, working at Cape Coast Castle on the
west coast of Africa. It was a place where a young man might clear
his head, forget his attachments and make good money from selling
on black captives. At the last moment, however, Hannah Maycock had
persuaded him to renege on the deal.

Like many of the females glimpsed in the margins of seventeenth
and eighteenth-century documents, Hannah Maycock seems to share
many of the characteristics of Moll Flanders. Seduced by John Stanley
when both were still in their teens and then left to bring up a baby
single-handed, she determinedly followed him to Portsmouth, tracked
him down to the ship bound for Africa, and brought him back to
London. Despite the 'extream Grief and Affliction' this caused his
parents, John stayed with Hannah, who soon had another child.
However, when John could no longer afford to support her, his father

having apparently disowned him, she threatened to find another keeping-cully who could. This was his situation when Moll King ensnared him, caught between the fading grip of a gentle birth and the lure of vicious living, desperately needing an income and not too concerned about how it was earned. Moll King was not the only one to buy his favours. While she exchanged diamond rings for love, at least one other married lady had already 'made him handsome Presents in return for his Endearments'.

Moll King left no confession, and so almost nothing is known of her life before Captain Stanley entered it – the names of her parents, her birthplace, whether she married young or had children, not even her date of birth. She was probably a native Londoner, born in the 1670s. Captain Stanley's biographer believed her to be married to a City officer in 1718, but the man played no part in her story after that date and may have been dead, abandoned or merely a useful fiction. No one knows whether she had slipped into crime in some youthful crisis of destitution or defiance and never slipped back out, or whether she was bred up to it from infancy. All that is known is that she was a professional thief, able to move disguised among her prey.

Crime increased after the Spanish wars ended in 1713. In particular, crime against property rose, and the old system by which London managed its policing and the enforcement of public morality seemed to be unable to deal with the situation. After the peace treaty of 1713, 157,000 fighting men returned to Britain: 1 per cent of England's population, and a far higher percentage of that part of the population which was male and had to earn its living. Their former commander the Duke of Marlborough was engaged in building Blenheim Palace, a gift from a grateful nation (or its gratitude as interpreted by its queen), but the grateful nation made little provision for the thousands who had fought and trudged behind him. Many gravitated to the cities and brought brutality and instability with them. The new military hospitals at Greenwich and Chatham took a few of the injured; parishes here and there supported others; but the majority were looking for work, not finding it and doing what they needed to survive. Every hanging day in London saw old sailors and soldiers among those swinging at Tyburn – broken, dispensable men like twenty-three-year-old burglar Matthew Cornwall, who spent nine years with the army and was 'so ignorant that he could not so much as read, nor say the

Lord's Prayer'; twenty-seven-year-old Richard Bell, who fought for the Queen in Flanders and was hanged for stealing five shop books; James Johnson alias Fishpond, who went to sea with Her Majesty's fleet when he was ten, and was hanged at the age of sixteen for stealing seven dozen hats.

Demobilised fighters and the camp followers who returned with them were not the only turbulent stream sucked in by the capital's currents. City life was so unhealthy that the birth rate would not exceed the death rate for decades, but so many young men and women alighted from provincial coaches each day that London's population was increasing nonetheless. There were 'strange Beggars everywhere,' wrote a London paper in March 1716, 'some wheedling and some demanding,' as well as 'Cripples, lusty Men and Women, Vagabonds, Blind People, pretended and real Mad Folks'. Londoners were renting out spare rooms, attics, cellars, cupboards, pallets and outhouses to the immigrants who came to serve them in shops, inns and private houses, heft brick and stone at building sites or unload ships in the Pool. Most of the work was temporary and ill paid but still great numbers arrived, lured by the prospect of more money and a better life. There was possibility in the capital's air. Victory abroad and a solution (even if a disputed one) to the dynastic question brought expansion, speculation and trade, renewal and change, investment and optimism to George I's first years. But London was a hard place for immigrants as well as an exciting one. The law of the market governed their chances here, not the law of the parish or the family they had left behind. In Hanoverian London, as Defoe knew, everything was for sale: a place in Parliament, a favour at court, a tip at the Exchange or a tip-off to the magistrate, stolen silver, third-hand clothes or, if you were really hard-up, ten minutes against a wall with your skirts over your head. There was temptation everywhere, and little encouragement to respect other people's property other than the brutality of punishment for the 'giddy and unthinking people' who swarmed London's streets: drunkards, desperates, opportunists, those who pinched laundry hanging out to dry or knocked a joint from a butcher's stall or reached into a shop to lift a hat hanging just within; blank-eyed veterans who had seen horrors on the battlefields; men too quick with their fists, and casual criminals who were law-abiding one day and thieves or whores the next.

Law enforcement was inadequate, and so was legislation. Criminal law was not designed for the reform and rehabilitation of criminals, but for their punishment or elimination. Retribution was given high visibility: from being tied to a post and publicly whipped from Newgate to Smithfield, through the humiliation of the pillory, to the moment at which the cart was kicked away and the criminal swung above the crowd at Tyburn. All these spectacles were as much for public edification as individual punishment, but even this harsh system was not working as well as it had. Exhibitions of pain and death no longer inspired just terror but also defiance and the creation of martyrs and heroes. So in 1718, the year Moll King went thieving in St Anne's Church, the authorities decided again to turn to the colonies.

'Suppose,' wrote Daniel Defoe,

I should propose a place in the world, where, if the English could plant at this time any numbers of their people, even the poorest and meanest, supposing them to be the only inhabitants, and willing to live . . . where 100,000 people may immediately plant and build, find food, and subsist plentifully, the soil fruitful, the climate comfortable, the air healthy, unmolested by savages and cannibals . . . wanting nothing to be inhabited by Christians, and ally'd to the rest of the Christian world by commerce and navigation.

This was Defoe's dream. The manifesto set out above was included in his *A Plan of the English Commerce*, written six years after *Moll Flanders*. This was the most concentrated and coherent of Defoe's many suggestions for colonisation and the energetic state regulation of colonial trade and settlement. Expanding colonial trade was a long-term project, however. In 1718 the colonies were more immediately useful for the reception and recycling of British rubbish.

But the seventeenth century's ad hoc system of exiling undesirables had fallen into confusion. War, demobilisation, a glut of labour and overcrowded gaols had clogged the system's wheels at home, and overseas some uppity colonials had declared they no longer wanted the mother country's rejects. The detritus of 'voluntary' transportation had been left to swill about the gaols of England, taking up space required by the rise in recent convictions. Some unwanted males had been absorbed into army and fleet when the country was at war, but that safety valve had been screwed down by peace. Some others had died in gaol; some were quietly released, whatever the condition of their pardon required; some were taken to America by speculative agents and captains who thought the gamble worth a try, and abandoned when colonial buyers would not buy them.

In May 1718 Sir William Thompson MP grasped this mess and shook it into a new order by pushing a piece of criminal justice legislation through Parliament. Handily serving the interests of three of Sir William's positions – recorder of London (in which capacity he acted as Old Bailey judge), solicitor general and propertied Englishman – the 'Act for the further preventing Robbery, Burglary, and other Felonies, and for the more effectual Transportation of Felons, and unlawful Exporters of Wool; and for declaring the Law upon some Points relating to Pirates' introduced a dramatic change.

> Whereas it is found by Experience, That the Punishments inflicted by the laws now in Force against the offences of Robbery, Larceny and other felonious Taking and Stealing of Money and Goods, have not proved effectual to deter wicked and evil-disposed Persons from being guilty of the said Crimes . . . and whereas in many of his Majesty's Colonies and Plantations in America, there is great Want of Servants, who by their Labour and Industry might be the Means of improving and making the said Colonies and plantations more useful to the Nation.

Previously, judges had had to sentence convicted felons to death or, if clergyable (entitled to benefit of clergy), to branding. Sir William's act provided a new primary sentence, and moreover made it a government responsibility to see that sentence carried out. From now on men and women convicted of felonies in English and Scottish courts could be punished by periods of transportation to His Majesty's Plantations, their passage paid for by His Majesty's government. Offences which had previously been clergyable would be punished with seven years' exile, those previously non-clergyable by fourteen. Offenders reprieved from death to be pardoned on condition of transportation were generally sentenced to exile for life.

Sir William found the right man to help him in a London slave trader and tobacco merchant named Jonathan Forward. Already expert at calculations in flesh, Mr Forward had spotted the opportunities

offered by the new Transportation Act. He dispatched 170 British criminals to Maryland in 1717 with great efficiency and promised Sir William
that he would convey as many more convicted felons from London
and the Home Counties as the courts might see fit to exile to America.
For this, he would charge the government three pounds per convict,
all in. A. Roger Ekirch quotes Sir William Thompson in *Bound for
America: The Transportation of British Convicts to the Colonies, 1718–1775*
(1987) as finding Forward's fee 'really cheap . . . no one else is ready
to take them at so low a rate'. In April 1718 sixty-six of Mr Forward's
next cargo were brought down an alley from Newgate to stand in the
Sessions Yard.

Judgments were swift. Frances Jacob, shoplifter, and Hugh Alford,
mugger, transportation. Eleanor Wade, who lifted a silver spoon from
a washing-up bowl, transportation. Sixteen-year-old Samuel Whittle,
pickpocket, transportation. William Cutler of Hillenden, for stealing
laundry left to dry on a hedge, transportation. John Ellis of St Giles
and John Ellis of St Margaret's Westminster, both thieves, transportation. Thomas Warman, for stealing his landlord's 'Stuff Curtains
and a Curtain-Rod', transportation. Robert Perryman, for mugging
Lydia Ashley on Ludgate Hill, transportation. Gerrard Pell, for stealing
two brass cocks from a pub cellar, transportation. Three boys, Christopher Matthews, John Pierpoint and John Shippy, for breaking open a
draper's and stealing therein, transportation, and there'd be a fourth
if he hadn't turned informer. Twenty-seven were given the new
sentence of transportation in April. Another twenty joined them at
the sessions in May.

Some of those who received the new sentence had nothing to say
in their defence, nor any 'friend' to support their case against the prosecutor. A handful could not recollect their crime nor their part in it,
for they had been too drunk. A few were feisty or defiant and put up
excuses or denied what they had previously confessed to a magistrate.
Elizabeth Portor, Fenchurch Street maidservant, charged with stealing
a China perfume pot set in silver, value five pounds from your master,
what do you say? 'I was going into the cellar to fetch Coals, the Silver
catch'd hold of my Coat, and I looking found it half covered with
Earth, and thinking it had been a thing buried there that belong'd to
no body in the House, I thought I had as much right to it as any body
else.' Transportation. Rose Knight, prostitute and thief, charged with

stealing from Joseph Gilder, 'said that the Prosecutor would have done what she would not let him, and because she would not comply, charged her with picking his Pocket'. Transportation. Bridget Noland, mugger-prostitute: punter John Williams 'was upon the Bed with her with his Breeches unbutton'd, but would not lie with her, saying she had the Pox, but gave her a Shilling to fetch Rods to Slogg him with, and that when he came to pay his Reckoning it was 5 s. and he said he had lost his Money'. Transportation. Elizabeth Lawlor, who stole 'the Carcass of a Lamb': 'I was disorder'd in my Head and crazy, I do not know what I did nor how I came by it.' Transportation. Mary Cooper, stopped with nine yards of stolen muslin in her apron: 'It was given me by a Woman, but I cannot tell who the Woman was.' Transportation.

On 23 August 1718, with no fanfare, four horse thieves, fifteen muggers, twelve shoplifters, eight pickpockets, three coiners (all female), one receiver, ten burglars, fifty-five thieves and twenty assorted others were packed into low boats and taken eighteen miles out of London into Kent, to where the former slave ship *Eagle* waited in deep water off Gravesend. She was bound for America. Only one of London's newspapers, the *Historical Register*, remarked briefly on the fact. To those not directly affected by Sir William Thompson's gaol clearance programme, the advent of penal transportation in its new form was a matter of singularly little importance.

Moll King was not distracted from her career either by the new threat of the colonies or her love affair with Captain Stanley, tempestuous though that seems to have become. However many women Captain Stanley was entertaining on the side, he seems to have fully earned whatever money Mrs King was giving him. 'Some time their Love remain'd,' wrote the Reverend Purney in full purple flow. 'No Jove could be fonder of Ganymede, tho' the Thunderer was chang'd into Strephon, than was Madam of Mister. She was a perfect Venus, and he as Adequate as Adonis. Love darted from her Eyes, to snatch the Beauty that dwelt in his.' Moll's luck in thieving did not match her luck in love, however. 'Not many Days did the sunshine last, for Madam was apprehended for privately taking things (as I remember from a mercer) and sent first to the Compter, and from thence to Newgate.' Only the detail of the mercer was wrong.

Moll King attended the evening service at St Anne's, Soho on 19 October 1718, sitting in her usual meek and inconspicuous position.

She was working with a partner that day, a 'tall Gentleman seeming to be well drest in Black', perhaps Captain Stanley himself. He lighted on Mrs Ann Earnly, a rich elderly lady who had left the evening service with her granddaughter and was waiting for her coach. When it came, the gentleman 'was very officious in assisting her to get into her Chariot, and she taking him to be some Neighbour that knew her, did not suspect him' until he 'lift[ed] up both her Arms higher than was necessary'. She 'cast her Eye down to see for her Watch' and it was gone. The black-dressed man had disappeared too, but the grand-daughter had seen him pass the watch to Moll King. Mrs Earnly's footman marched Moll into an alehouse, and when she was pulled to her feet again to be taken before the constable, the watch was found lying on the floor.

However, the 'tall Gentleman' had not deserted Moll. When Mrs Earnly's coachman turned up to see what had become of the footman, he found the 'Man in Black . . . with another . . . resolutely pressing into the Room where the Woman was, swearing and cursing, saying what did they take that Woman for? She was an honest Woman.' There was a fight. The coachman was knocked down, but took one of Moll's defenders with him. But it was all to no avail. 'Not being able to force their way in, they ran away,' and Moll was carried off to the magistrate with the evidence of the granddaughter, the footman, the landlord and the bleeding coachman against her. She was charged under the name of Mary Goulston with 'privately stealing a Gold Watch, Chain, &c. value 30l. from the Person of Mrs Ann Earnly', bound over for appearance at the December sessions and sent into Newgate to await her trial.

She was an old thief and knew that if the jury found her guilty of stealing to the real value of the watch, she would be sentenced to death. The Old Bailey did not sit in November, so she had to wait in Newgate until the first week of December. At some point during the dank dark months of October and November 1718, Moll King realised that the old delaying tactic might save her.

Five judges arrived at the Old Bailey on 18 December 1718 ready for the usual dreary procession of accused felons: thieving maid-servants, pickpockets, muggers, shoplifters, the odd highwayman, forger, coiner and murderer. One person had been sentenced to death and thirteen to transportation before Moll King emerged into the freezing Sessions Yard, scarred hand upon her belly. Mrs Earnly was there to testify against her, and although Moll King 'denied the Fact', it 'being plain, the Jury found her Guilty'. As expected, she was sentenced to death. 'My Lord', she said, and they must have sighed. They knew what was coming. The Transportation Act had conferred an unintended but distinct benefit on the Newgate Wags, and the impannelling of matrons now interrupted the Old Bailey Sessions a dozen times each month. A reluctant posse took Moll King away, lifted her petticoats to press their hands on her stomach and confirmed she was with quick child. Her sentence was respited, and she was returned to gaol.

As Moll's belly grew, the convict ship *Eagle* arrived in the booming frontier town of Charleston, carrying nine convicts fewer than had left London. Those who had not died on the passage out were auctioned off. In March 1719 the *Sophia* of Bideford reached the quieter shores of Annapolis, Maryland, where her surviving convicts were also sold. In February 1719 the *Worcester* sailed for Maryland with ninety-seven more (three of whom died en route), and in May 113 were loaded aboard the *Margaret* in London, 104 of whom reached the Chesapeake shore and disembarked into the humidity of a Maryland summer and another wharfside auction. Some time that spring or summer Moll King's baby was weaned and taken away. Instead of seeing her name on the death warrant, however, she found it on a pardon: she was to escape death on condition of transportation to the colonies. In October 1719 she went aboard the *Susannah and Sarah*, Captain Wills, bound for Annapolis.

17

Moll King's Annapolis, 1722

Moll King's ship took the same route from London to the Chesapeake as Moll Flanders' had done: catching the trade winds off Portugal which took them to Canary, then the north-easterlies to the West Indies, where water and food was taken on, then north up the coast of Florida through the bumpy stretch where the warmth of the Gulf Stream collides with cold waters from the north, and north again until an easterly arrived to push them between the Capes. Same route, same discomfort and same fears: first of a physical defect in the vessel or some spiteful combination of weather and second that they might be overhauled by pirates.

Moll Flanders feared the Barbary corsairs, but Moll King was in greater danger from the piratical flotsam thrown up by the Spanish wars. The pirate Blackbeard was a rogue Royal Navy man, demobilised in 1713 but not ready to go home. In June 1718 he attacked Charleston harbour, taking hostages and demanding heavy ransoms. The convict ship *Eagle*, making for Carolina a few months later, was stopped by pirates who forced some of the convicts to join them, and put the nine who refused 'a-shore in a Desart Island wholly without Inhabitants'. The *Susannah and Sarah* was more fortunate, safely entering the Chesapeake in late 1719 or early 1720 and sailing the 195 miles upriver to where fresh water lapped at the wharves, warehouses, mud streets, empty lots and dispiriting cluster of huts which was Annapolis.

The city of Annapolis did not exist when Moll Flanders cast her last glance up the Chesapeake nearly forty years before. America's immigrant population (free and bond) had more than doubled since then: to 250,000 in 1700 and 475,000 in 1720. Some settlers went west, trekking off to find cheaper land further from the bay and closer to the shrinking lands of the indigenes. Small settlements linked them to the coast, sometimes no more than a tavern, a meeting house or a plantation. Carters, peddlers, travelling preachers, runaway servants and wanderers seeking work or refuge kept these isolated folk in touch; gossip was carried on carts and ferries, coastal smacks and oyster boats. But cities were beginning to appear on the shoreline, with the infra-structure of urban living and newspapers, entertainments, shops, hotels and populations rivalling those of provincial English towns. New York had a population of 7,000, Philadelphia of 10,000. Maryland's total population was about 80,000, of whom Annapolis itself housed only a couple of hundred.

The *Susannah and Sarah* was the fourth ship to bring unwanted British labour to Annapolis in two years, and surely any novelty which had originally attached to the arrival of these grubby, malnourished people had worn off. Sir William Thompson had devised the Trans-portation Act in part to address the colonies' need for white labour. What it threw up, however, pleased the colonists of 1720 little more than Elizabeth Handsley and Moll Flanders' mother pleased the godly Virginian farmers of a century before. The men and women who rode into Annapolis to inspect the cargo came reluctantly, for no one wanted to take home a convict. Nonetheless, they came. Someone had to till the fields, tend the livestock, cook and clean, and there were too few white servants to do it.

What the colonists of Maryland really wanted were strong single young men of good character and certified Protestant faith, who had chosen to make the crossing and brought with them some skill at the hoe, the anvil, the helm of a coasting vessel or the hoop of a barrel. If they had to take women, they wanted trained cooks, maids, seam-stresses, washerwomen or nursemaids, or the makings of sturdy brides who could calve a cow, heft an axe, shoot an intruder and bear a stream of babies. They did not want felons, and they did not want Negroes, yet increasingly they were being obliged to take both: cica-trised, trembling fellows trafficked in the African hinterland and brought in European ships from Guinea, sullen, unusable criminals from Seven Dials and Shadwell. The problem was that blacks and convicts were readily available, and free white Protestant males were not.

When Moll Flanders and Jemmy retired to live on their colonial income, most field hands had been white. Now the majority was black, for the slave trade was bringing increasing numbers of Africans into America, while white servants from Europe were becoming scarce. American opportunity had lessened for the British labouring classes. Tobacco was a less profitable crop, and what had been a relatively socially mobile culture had become more rigid in all ways: race, class and gender.

Nor did Hanoverian England produce the same numbers of hopeful emigrants which Stuart England had thrown up. The lumpen seventeenth-century hordes of potential field hands no longer sought their fortunes in America, despite inducements. In 1698 Carolina had offered a thirteen-pound bounty to shipmasters who brought free white male servants for sale. Still too few came. In 1716 it was decreed that there must be one white servant for every ten African slaves. It was not possible, however, to enforce the ratio. The bounty on a white man was raised to twenty-five pounds, but even this had little effect, and nor did offers of tax relief, land grants and shorter periods of indenture. Virginia found itself in a similar situation, exacerbated by its attempts to ban potentially subversive groups including Quakers, Catholic priests and 'jaile birds'. Maryland too tried to restrict the import of African slaves, yet their number had soared from 3,000 in 1697 to 8,000 in 1710, and the change had sown the seeds of a different culture. Huge landed estates were being established; a handful of extremely rich families had emerged and were laying the foundations of the Old South.

Convicts might be one solution to the dearth of white labour but they brought their own problems with them – so much so that in 1680 the General Court of Virginia attempted to ban them, citing the 'danger to the Colony caused by the great number of felons and other desperate villains sent over from the prisons of England'. Female convicts were particularly unwanted. In 1697 the Council of Trade and Plantations in London had tried to relieve prison overcrowding by shipping a consignment of women to the colonies. A farce had ensued.

Carolina refused to take them, saying its government had 'from their first settlement earnestly desired to be excused from entertaining criminals. But,' they added helpfully, 'it is well known that they will be willingly entertained by Virginia, Maryland, Barbados, Jamaica or the Leeward Islands.' Those colonies did not agree. The Virginia agent in London said that both Virginia and Maryland had 'found the entertainment of convicts to be prejudicial' on the grounds that they were 'on the Continent and several Governments joining on each other', and recommended Jamaica and Barbados for their reception, 'who will bid them welcome, as they most properly may, being confined under one Government and enclosed within the Island'. Jamaica, however, only wanted men and told the council via a petition of merchants that 'they would not receive [the women] except on condition of receiving one hundred and fifty male convicts with them'. Barbados was no more welcoming, but thought that 'in places where white women work in the field, as Virginia and Carolina, such women as those may be useful and acceptable'. In the end, only the Leeward Islands agreed to take them, and off they went.

No free white Protestant males disembarked from the *Susannah and Sarah*, which disgorged instead eighty thieves and a handful of receivers into the bitter cold of a Maryland winter. And if the colonists of Annapolis regarded the wares laid before them with disappointment, the convicts looked around with a similar lack of admiration.

> A City situate on a Plain
> Where scarce a House will keep out rain
> The Buildings framed with Cyprus rare
> Resembles much our Southwark Fair
> But Stranger here will scarcely meet
> With Market-place, Exchange or Street
> And if the Truth I may report
> Tis not so large as Tottenham Court.

Such were the contemptuous words of Eden Cook, who visited Annapolis in 1707 or 1708, the year the city was chartered, and wrote up his impressions in a fatuous piece of verse called *The Sotweed Factor*, sotweed being a derogatory term for tobacco. When Moll King arrived over a decade later, Annapolis still existed more in theory than in timber, let alone in bricks and mortar. About forty houses had been built and empty lots had been pegged out for more on Powder Hill. Governor Nicholson had invited artisans to take them up and build their homes and yards there, but few as yet had accepted. Work had started, but not finished, on a church, and there was a very basic marketplace. The only building worthy of note was the Capitol, a two-storey affair in brick. Around this were the houses owned by planters who lived on their farms but came into town every so often for business or the rudimentary pleasures which Annapolis offered. There were warehouses down by the river, where the convicts were housed, cleaned and auctioned off, and that was the end of town. It was not a place to make a Londoner feel at home.

The Transportation Act had in part been underpinned by the assumption that penitent convicts could be assimilated into colonial life without too much friction, forming thereafter a productive white labour force. Some in England (although not those on the receiving end) even considered a spell in the colonies a bracing way to reclaim wayward youth. Young John Ellis's uncle had insisted on prosecuting him, despite knowing seven years in America might result. Benjamin Larkin, brought up 'from a Child' by one Captain Buckland, 'prov'd an untoward Boy' and eventually stole and sold the captain's 'Silver Tankard, value 38 s'. He could have been sentenced to death if convicted, but 'the Indictment was laid favourably, with a Design to prevent his receiving a heavier Sentence hereafter, hoping that going abroad may reclaim him'.

Many of those caught up in Sir William Thompson's calculations, however, did not want to be 'reclaimed', did not want to assimilate and certainly did not want to labour, even with the potential reward of a future within the free white colonial hierarchy. 'The Law was not,' objected Henry Davis, convicted of stealing four brass candlesticks from a London inn, 'that they should be in such a manner sold for Slaves, which was worse than Death, being Christians by Baptism'; even 'the Negroes,' he thought, wrongly, 'after they were Baptised were no longer Slaves'. The Act did not deal with passive colonial building blocks; it dealt with people, and they did not always share Sir William's vision. They wanted to go home, they did not give twopence for colonial development and they did not believe in the official rosy view of a period of repentant servitude laying the ground for a future of colonial prosperity.

We do not know what, exactly, happened to Moll King alias Gilstone when she disembarked from the *Susannah and Sarah*. Documentation regarding convicts in early colonial America is extremely scarce. In order to claim his fee, the captain of each convict ship was obliged only to retain a Landing Certificate for each man or woman who had survived the passage and disembarked. The government did not need or wish to know to whom he had sold them, at what price and for what purpose. However, a rare set of sales records has survived for the convicts of the ship *Margaret*, which arrived in Annapolis a few months before the *Susannah and Sarah*, and we can infer Moll King's likely fate from these. Included were: Sarah Naggs, sold to Peter Galloway, a Quaker on the Western Shore; Elizabeth Dobbs, sold to Joseph Pettibone, merchant; and Ann Peirce, Mary Perkins, Susan Read, Jane Scott alias Holloway, Mary Thirty alias Kirby, Mary Wilson (and more than a dozen men), sold to Patrick Sympson and William Black, planters, merchants and 'sotweed factors'.

A few of the *Margaret* convicts were sold singly or in pairs to local tradesmen: a butcher, a tailor, a miller, a wig maker, a magistrate; a couple of widows also took a woman each off the captain's hands. One, Thomazin Elby, was sold to Dr Charles Carroll, physician, planter, businessman and patriarch of what was becoming the wealthiest clan in Annapolis. Two years later he began construction of a brick mansion on the shore, where Thomazin presumably spent her seven years in domestic service. But the largest group of women went to what Eden Cook called the 'planting rabble', and at whom much of his scorn was aimed.

> A Herd of Planters on the ground
> O'er-whelm'd with Punch, dead drunk, we found
> Others were fighting and contending
> Some burnt their Cloaths to save the mending
> A few whose Heads by frequent use
> Could better bare the potent Juice
> Gravely debated State Affairs.

These were the men who probably also bought the convicts off the *Susannah and Sarah*. They owned small tobacco plantations outside the city and had a particular interest in buying female white servants.

This was not the 'respect of wives and children', which the Virginia Company had hoped might do its settling work in 1619, but an exercise in tax avoidance. Planters paid tax on male white servants and on black slaves of both sexes working in the fields, but white females were exempt.

There survive few testimonies from convicts brought to the Chesapeake in the years just after the Transportation Act was passed, but they give a little detail about the conditions in which they lived. Mary North, a contemporary of Moll King, was reprieved from death in London on condition of her consenting to be experimentally inoculated against the smallpox. In America she and twenty others 'were Sold for 50 l. to walk into the Sea to the middle to find Oysters in Winter time, and the like'. Seventeen-year-old Edward Mires of Maidstone 'fell,' he would later relate, 'to a severe Master on the Coast of America, having only a Shirt and Skins ty'd for Shoes, and Indian Corn to eat'. He was sold to a Carpenter, for 15 l. and with him 'travell'd from one Plantation to another'. Perhaps James White left the most pathetic tale of all. He and six others were abandoned by the supercargo of their ship on the American shore, presumably because they seemed unlikely to fetch any money at auction.

He being one of them, travel'd several hundred Miles about the Country, living upon whatever he could get, as sometimes Hens, Chickens, Pigs, &c. sometimes on Basses, Hollibuts, Clams, &c. which he found by the Rivers and the Sea Shores. He said, he was above six Months in this manner independant; till he met with some Indians, who liv'd he believ'd always in Woods, and they reliev'd him. Soon after he assisted some English Servants in their Work, and telling them how he was Transported, and knew not which way to turn himself, they frequently brought him Victuals, without acquainting their Mistress at home with it. But he was soon after, hired by a Planter, and tho' he labour'd very hard, 'twas a comfortable Life, for he had Food sufficient, and all Necessaries; till his Employment being to carry fresh Water over the Rocks, for the use of Ships, that were bound for England, the sharp Stones so cut his Legs; That the Salt Water and the Gravel prejudicing the Wounds. He lost the use of his Feet; and tho' the Planters Wife heal'd one Legs for a time, it grew again so bad that he was unable to Work, and his Master was therefore unwilling longer to maintain him. After this, he said, he suffer'd again a World of Misery.

Probably most convicts did not suffer so badly. Not all masters and mistresses were neglectful or cruel, but the few testimonies we have inevitably record more bad experiences than good. The *American Weekly Mercury* newspaper ran endless advertisements for runaways, and the fugitive servant already figured in Chesapeake folklore. Eden Cook enquired of a 'surley peasant' for a lodging, who

> ask'd from whom I'de run away
> Surprised at such a saucy word
> I instantly lugg'd out my Sword
> Swearing I was no fugitive
> But from Great Britain did arrive.

There was another way for a convict to secure his or her liberty, however. It was the same one that Moll and Jemmy had taken in the 1670s, when they were nominally sold to a planter, who then discharged them in return for '6,000 weight of tobacco'. The experience of convict John Filewood may reveal a cynical variation on this practice: buying a convict at a low price in order to charge him a higher one for his own redemption. Filewood, a former highwayman, was transported aboard the *Eagle* for fourteen years, but returned to England before that time had elapsed. Rearrested and sentenced to die, he told the Newgate Ordinary that 'he died for the Fault of the Planter in America he was sold to; for he invited him, for a Sum of Money, to accept of his Liberty, and when he had his Freedom, the Love of England was natural'. Perhaps this also explains the movements of Moll King alias Gilstone. She had no intention of staying in cold shabby Annapolis or the lonely plantations around it. We do not know exactly how she did it, but by summer 1720 Moll King was back in London.

On 4 June 1720 Daniel Defoe's novel *The Life, Adventures and Piracies of the Famous Captain Singleton* was published, and advertised in the *Weekly Journal*. On Saturday 16 July 1720 an article appeared in *Applebee's*, another paper to which he regularly contributed. This was ostensibly a letter written by 'Moll of Rag Fair', a crime-sodden district of London just east of the Tower. In fact, the letter was almost certainly written by Defoe himself, having heard that the notorious Moll King was back in London and up to her old tricks. The writer of the letter, she/he informed *Applebee's* readers, was 'an Elder, and well known Sister, of the *File*: – a pickpocket of many years standing', who after several happy and successful years had come to grief.

> I was unhappily drawn a-side out of my ordinary and lawful Calling into the dangerous Business of Shop-lifting, and being not half so clever and nimble at that as I was at my own Trade, I was nab'd by a plaguy Hawks-Ey'd Journey-Man Mercer, and so I got into the Hands of the Law. It went very hard with me upon this Occasion, and to make my Story short, I run thro' all the several Ways of being Undone; I mean the Newgate Ways, for I was Try'd, Condemn'd, pleaded my Belly, had a Verdict of the jades they call Matrons in my Favour, and at length having obtain'd a suspicion of Hanging, I got to be Transported.
>
> Whether I was transported, what Adventures I met with abroad, *if I was abroad*, and how I came hither again, I say, are too long for a Letter.

Was this Defoe's hint that another 'false memoir' was being prepared for publication?

18

The end of Moll, 1723–7

By the time of Moll King's illegal return from America in the summer of 1722, the unintended effects of the Transportation Act on criminal London were starting to be seen. Newgate Wags, slave shipowners, venal matrons: all these had benefited from the new law. Another group now finding a lucrative angle were London's infamous thief-takers, and Moll King had come up against the most dangerous of them all.

'As my being here,' continues Moll of Rag Fair in her letter to *Applebee's*,

> is a new Trespass [i.e. crime] and may bring me back to the gallows, from whence it may be *truly* said I came, I am not quite so easie as I was before, tho' I am prudently retir'd to my first Employ, and find I can do pretty well at it; but that which makes me more in danger is the meeting Yesterday with One of my old Acquaintance; he salutes me publickly in the Street, with a long out-cry, *O brave Moll*, says he, *Why what do you do out of your Grave? Was not you Transported? Hold your Tongue, Jack*, says I, for God's Sake, what have you a mind to ruin me? D—— me, says he, *you Jade* give me a Twelver than, *or I'll tell this minute*; I was forc'd to do it, and so the Rogue has a Milch Cow of me, as long as I live.

Mary Frith was long dead and gone, but her 'brokery' operation had been taken up and expanded by others, thief-takers. The 'Jack' who blackmailed Moll out of twelve pounds was the most famous of them all, Jonathan Wild, the self-styled Thieftaker-General of Great Britain and Ireland. His 'Office for the Recovery of Lost and Stolen Property' was at 68 Little Old Bailey, a crooked offshoot which ran north-west just below the Sessions House. It was famous, open long hours and 'as full as if it had been an Exchange', for this was where Londoners came to retrieve their stolen goods.

Wild, like Mary Frith, was respectable in the eyes of his customers but lived a double life. Underground London knew him as a gang-master, heavily involved in organised crime. In 1725 he was finally unmasked and executed. There was the usual spate of biographies, one of them written by Daniel Defoe himself, who described the facade Jonathan presented to the world.

> The People who had been robb'd, it may be suppos'd were always willing enough to hear of their Goods again, and very thankful to the Discoverers, and so readily gave an Account of the Things they had lost, with such proper Descriptions of them as were needful; The next Day, they should be told, there was such or such part of their Goods stopt among other Goods, which it was supposed were stolen from other People, and so upon Assurance given on both Sides to make no Enquiry into the particular Circumstances of stopping the Goods, and a Consideration [payment] to the Person who went between, for helping the Loser to his Goods again, the Things were restor'd, and the Person receiv'd abundance of Thanks and Acknowledgments for their Honesty and Kindness. [Jonathan] always pretended he got nothing for [his] Pains but the Satisfaction of having help'd the People to recover their own again, which was taken by a Company of Rogues.

It was all theatre. Jonathan, like Mary Frith, already knew where the stolen goods were, who had stolen them, where and when. The thieves had either brought them straight to him and were awaiting their cut from the victim's redemption fee, or they were stolen to Jonathan's order in the first place and were logged and stored in a warehouse in Newington Butts or the sinister house he owned round the corner in Chick Lane. Men and women who disobeyed Jonathan were brought to the Chick Lane house to be questioned in a warren of rooms and corridors and windowless cellars which ran behind a bland facade. There were trapdoors and secret ways in and out, and men standing guard with guns and knives. The walls of the inner rooms were too thick for passers-by to hear the screams and Fleet Ditch ran beneath, swallowing into its filth what Jonathan did not want to leave by the door.

Wild had been working towards his position since 1713, when the City's marshal, Charles Hitchen, recognised his talents and plucked him from small-time crime to teach him the business. Like members of Parliament, civic officials, gaolers and everyone else who bought himself a public or private office in Hanoverian Britain, Mr Hitchen regarded his position principally as a means of making money. There were at least 2,000 people in London, Mr Hitchen believed, who lived solely from theft, and his own activities were a sort of tax on their profits. 'I must first tell you,' he advised his apprentice, 'that you'll spoil the trade of thief-taking in advancing greater rewards than are necessary. I give but half a crown a pocketbook and when the thieves and pickpockets see you and I confederate, they'll submit to our terms and likewise continue their thefts for fear of coming to the gallows by our means.' Since then Jonathan Wild had left his mentor far behind. By 1722 he was the most powerful thief-taker in the city.

Wild recognised the opportunities offered by the Transportation Act. The penalty for convicts returning before their time was death, and a bounty of forty pounds was due to whoever turned them in to the authorities. For a thief-taker, it was a bonanza: once Wild knew a convict had returned and had tracked her down, he could decide how best to use her. He could put her to work and take a cut of the proceeds, knowing she would not dare betray him, or he could use her to 'impeach' members of rival gangs. Impeaching was giving evidence against a defendant in court, and was Jonathan Wild's preferred method of dealing with enemies. Either they would be set up, with a couple of Wild's people infiltrating their gang and later turning King's evidence, or he would track down gang members and threaten or bribe them into informing on their comrades.[15] If the returned convict refused, her work was not up to standard or she

---

15 This method became so notorious that when the writer John Gay used Jonathan Wild as the model for the wicked gaoler in the *Beggar's Opera* of 1728, he gave the character the name Peachum. Peachum, however, was also the satirical representation of another towering Hanoverian figure: Sir Robert Walpole, George I's first minister, who was notoriously adept at lining his own pockets with public money. The sequel, *Polly Peachum*, featured the adventures of the gaoler's daughter in the West Indies and was banned, partly through Walpole's influence.

became dispensable in order to save someone else, she could be turned in for a useful sum and hanged. The reference in Moll King's letter to being a 'Milch Cow' for a 'Rogue' was therefore a brutal but accurate summary of her relationship with Jonathan Wild.

Daniel Defoe wrote up various cases in his 1725 biography to demonstrate how Wild worked. One of these anecdotes seems to be an expanded version of the incident already referred to in the *Applebee*'s letter, and demonstrates how Moll and others in her vulnerable position ended up in Wild's employ. A gold watch had been stolen and its lady owner called on Mr Wild at his Office. 'Mr Wild,' wrote Defoe,

> after the usual Enquiries of when it was lost? And where? And being told it was at St Ann's Church Westminster, paused a while and calls up a Servant, and asks aloud, 'Where was M—ll K—g last Sunday?'
>
> 'About Westminster,' says the Man, 'but the Bi—h would not tell where.'
>
> 'She is a dextrous jade at the Work,' Mr Wild told his client, 'but I'll have her safe before Morning.'

Wild then told his client that he would persuade Moll to give the watch back in return for twenty guineas, refused any payment for his own part in the deal and promised the lady an anonymous man would bring her her property a couple of days later. As soon as the lady had gone, Wild's men brought in Moll King, 'who he frighted out of the Watch,' wrote Defoe, 'with threatening to have her put into Newgate for the stealing of it'. She was also forced to pay him eighteen guineas for his silence. A few days later the lady client returned to 68 Little Old Bailey and positively insisted Mr Wild accept a further fifteen guineas for his kindness.

The details of Moll King's employment by Wild thereafter are unclear, but it seems the first task he had in mind for his milch cow was a dirty business. Wild was involved in gang warfare which he would ultimately lose, paying with his life in 1725. Penal transportation had become a tool as important in the gangmaster's armoury as a shotgun, an attack dog or a cudgel. If one of the enemy could be entrapped in a crime by false comrades who would then impeach him or her, that person would soon be out of sight – dead or in America – and the opposing gang would be one member down. Among Wild's fiercest enemies in 1720 was a woman called Elizabeth Harris, whose husband had been transported after he had been impeached by Wild's people. Mrs Harris was now planning to hit back at Jonathan Wild by entrapping and impeaching the Fields, a thieving couple who had worked for Wild for many years. Having carried out a robbery along-side Mr and Mrs Field, Elizabeth Harris showed her hand, turning King's evidence and impeaching them. When the constables went to arrest William Field on Mrs Harris's evidence, he escaped them and did not appear in court. His wife was acquitted for lack of evidence, but another of the robbers (and Mr Wild's employees), Ann Merritt, was sentenced to death. Found with quick child, she was later trans-ported to America. Tit for tat.

When Jonathan took Moll King into his employ in the spring or summer of 1720 he was concentrating on destroying Elizabeth Harris's gang and Moll King was to be one of his weapons. Among Mrs Harris's associates was one Richard Trantum (or Grantham), who stood accused in July 1720 of housebreaking and theft. Moll King was one of the three witnesses who testified in court that they had found Trantum with the stolen goods. Trantum was transported, and the ball lobbed back into Mrs Harris's court. Moll King then disappeared from the records for a year, probably thieving with a cut for Wild, perhaps engaged in dirtier tasks, with the threat of being turned in for a bounty hanging constantly over her head.

There had been a change in her personal life. If she had hoped that Captain Stanley would wait faithfully for her return from America, she was mistaken. John Stanley had taken up again with Hannah Maycock, and the couple now had three children. Their relationship, however, was volatile and sometimes violent, and Stanley was still making periodic attempts to leave. In 1720 or 1721 his father died and the event had a profound effect on John: whether because of some personality disorder or because of his wandering childhood and preco-cious promiscuity, he started to lose his mind. The grim advance of venereal disease is another possibility. Attempting to reform, he spent a brief period on the Continent but could not stay away from Hannah. As Moll King resumed her life around Soho and Covent Garden, so John Stanley returned to Hannah Maycock and their growing brood of children.

If Captain Stanley had moved on, however, so had Moll King. During

her brief time in Annapolis she had taken up with transported felon
Robert Bird, and returned to England as Mary Coulston (or Gilstone)
alias Bird alias King. Robert Bird himself returned illegally from
America in 1720 or early the following year, and by the summer of
1721 the two were together in London, working and presumably living
as a couple. On 12 July 1721, a year after she impeached Richard
Trantum, Moll appeared under her new name at the Old Bailey. The
indictment was that she, Humphrey Burton and Richard Bird (Robert's
brother) had attempted to burgle a house in Covent Garden. Richard
had not been caught when they went to trial, and Moll and Humphrey
were acquitted for lack of evidence. Perhaps this was a vengeful entrap-
ment by Mrs Harris's gang; perhaps the two really had been attempting
to burgle a house, although it was not Moll King's preferred modus
operandi. In any case, it seems Jonathan Wild played the same role in
subverting the prosecution as Moll Flanders' governess had attempted
in the 1670s. Two of the witnesses to the alleged burglary were known
to have previously worked for Wild. Presumably by the time they
reached the witness stand, they had been bribed or threatened into
forgetting everything they originally told the prosecutor they had seen.
Both Moll and Humphrey were acquitted. Moll King, however, faced
a second indictment: 'for that she having been formerly Convicted of
a Felony and transported among other Convicts from Newgate for
the same, had returned into Great Britain without any Lawful Cause'.
To this she had no option but to plead guilty. She received her second
death sentence and returned to Newgate.

On 28 July, however, her death sentence was inexplicably commuted.
Instead, she was to remain imprisoned 'at His Majesty's pleasure'.
Either the government had taken pity on an elderly, possibly enfee-
bled, woman, or Jonathan Wild had exerted pressure on some vulnerable part of the sentencing system. A belated thanks for Moll's
impeachment of Richard Trantum? More probably the expectation of
her being useful to him in the future.

The month before Moll King was reprieved a second time from
death and returned indefinitely to Newgate, a more distinguished prisoner also entered the prison. Nathaniel Mist, Daniel Defoe's editor at
the *Weekly Journal*, became an inmate on 10 June 1721. Mist was in hot
water again. Government thugs had been periodically raiding his offices
for over a year, hunting for seditious material. (Defoe's role in these

raids is unknown.) They need not have bothered. Mist obligingly published an openly seditious article (Defoe's role once more unknown) and was arrested. Defoe remained at large, writing and covering for Mist's absence at his various papers. He also regularly visited Mist in prison. As interrogator? As friend? As co-conspirator? This aspect of Defoe's life, like so many others, can only be guessed at.

Nathaniel Mist's imprisonment in Newgate therefore coincided almost exactly with Moll King's. During the seven months both prisoners spent there Daniel Defoe came and went, came and went, visiting Mist and bringing gossip in and out of the gaol. Is it impossible that this is when the idea for *Moll Flanders* entered his brain, and that during these months he detoured from Mist's private apartments on the Master's side to the less comfortable quarters of Moll King on the other, jotting down her memories of crime and the colonies, adding them to his notes on Mary Carleton and Mary Frith (as well as his fears as to what might be happening to his niece, Elizabeth Maxwell)?

Moll Cutpurse, Mary Carleton, Elizabeth Maxwell, Moll Raby, Moll Hawkins, Moll King – and one other, final lady who may have influenced, at the last possible moment, the novel on which Defoe was working in 1721. Her name was Moll Harvey, and she was tried at the Old Bailey that December for picking the pocket of Daniel Cassel. The story was an old one. She was walking in Bishopsgate with a friend when she bumped into a drunken man with a valuable watch. Off they went to a lodging in Petty France, where the man may or may not have paid for sex and Mary Harvey may or may not have pinched his watch and passed it to a woman known as squinting Abigail. There is little here that was not alleged, denied, embroidered upon and judged dozens of times each year. The minor detail which makes me wonder if Daniel Defoe heard it and went back to his desk, inspired and chortling, to put the final touches to his manuscript was that the drunken punter was a Dutchman, perhaps a citizen of Flanders. The Old Bailey scribe waggishly took down his testimony verbatim. 'The Prosecutor depos'd,' he wrote,

> That As he was going along von Night, very merry vid Liquor, dese two Vomen (de prisoners at de bar) fell in his vay, and Mary Harvey ask a him to go vid her to her loshing, and ven da came dare, she no find de key of de door. Den Ann Parker told a him she had got a

loshing in Petty France; and so he vent vid em to dat loshing, and vent up von pair of Stairs, and dare Mary harvy and he tumbel upon de Bed togeder; and den Harvy pick a his Vash out of his Pocket, and give it to Parker [and run away] but his Breeshes vare down and he could no run after dem to cash'em.

Flanders. There have been hints all through Moll's story – contraband lace, immigrant weavers and now drunken punters. Could Defoe's developing heroine have been given her final name in December 1721? On 27 January 1722 *The Adventures and Misadventures of Moll Flanders* was published by W H Chetwood, whose premises were at Cato's Head in Russell Street, just a couple of doors along from where Moll King had been arrested. Two days later Moll King's indefinite sentence of imprisonment in Newgate ended – at whose behest is not known, nor for what reason – and she was sent aboard the *Gilbert* at Tilbury, bound for Annapolis on her third Atlantic voyage.

It would be a neat ending to the story if she had stayed there, but by 16 June 1722 she was irrepressibly back in London. By 19 September she was back in Newgate. 'Moll King,' announced the *Daily Journal* wearily, 'a most notorious Offender, famous for stealing Gold Watches from ladies' Sides in the Churches, for which she has been several times convicted, being lately returned from Transportation has been taken and is committed to Newgate.' This time it is unclear who arrested her and claimed the bounty. It was not Jonathan Wild, so maybe some other thief-taker got there first. Nor is it clear why she was not tried again for returning from transportation, given a third death sentence and sent to the gallows. Instead she was simply returned to America in June 1723, and that is the last definite news we have of her. We do, however, know exactly what happened to two of the men in her story, Captain John Stanley and Jonathan Wild. By 1725 both were dead.

When John Stanley returned to England and Hannah Maycock, he also returned to his old vices of gaming, whoring and fathering illegitimate children. 'Had he been Master of a competant Fortune for his Subsistance,' he would petulantly tell the Newgate Ordinary, he would have lived a worthier life. Alas he was penniless, and his mental state deteriorated fast after his father's death. 'He had been fitter for Bedlam,' his mother sobbed, 'than to walk the streets,' and his madness was punctuated by violent rages. In October 1723, when Hannah replied to some suggestion with what he interpreted as insolence, he stabbed her under her left breast. She died a few hours later, and on 23 December 1723 Captain Stanley was hanged for her murder.

The ignominious end of Jonathan Wild is well known. By the time of his death in 1725 Wild had made a huge number of enemies. It is estimated he had been personally instrumental in sending sixty people to the gallows, and they all left friends, confrères or loved ones behind who bore a grudge. A couple of years after his dealings with Moll King public opinion was turning against him. The truth about his parallel career as extortionist and taker of bribes was beginning to emerge. His public-servant disguise was wearing thin and self-interest was clearly visible through the tatters. In early 1725 he overreached himself, arranging a gaol-break to allow one of his men to escape. When it became clear the authorities were not going to be bribed or bullied into dropping the charges against him this time, the enemies he had made in his long vicious career came out to testify against him. In a last-ditch attempt to demonstrate how effectively he had sought to bring criminals to justice rather than operate for any private gain, Jonathan published what became known as 'Wild's List': the names, offences and ultimate fates of all those he had turned in for returning from transportation, with Mary King at number 74. He was convicted on a run-of-the-mill charge of theft of lace – one of dozens which might have served the purpose – and hanged at Tyburn in 1725. Daniel Defoe saw him die and noted the crowd was larger than any he had ever seen.

Did Moll King, then, have the last laugh? We do not know exactly what happened to the woman Wild had 'frighted' out of her watch and used for a year before seeing her returned to America. It is possible that she returned to London again. If she did, perhaps she was the 'Mary Gold of London, Spinster' who went shoplifting in 1727, stealing a length of 'Cherry colour'd Riband' from the shop of John Towers and '2 Pair of Women's Leather Shoes' from Thomas Hyram, and was sentenced to transportation. And if, indefatigably, she returned from that trip, perhaps we catch our last glimpse of her in August 1729, the latest date one could reasonably expect her to be alive and working. Was she, like Moll Cutpurse and Moll Flanders' governess, semi-retired and working as a landlady in Aldgate with her friend Ann

Goodrick at that date? Mary King and Ann Goodrick were both, the
Old Bailey noted, 'former convicts' who could not resist a last heist.
When one of their lodgers fell ill, they stole her possessions, sneaked
out and pawned them. The lodger recovered her health and her goods,
however, and prosecuted. Both her landladies were transported.

A gallows ticket to view the hanging of Jonathan Wild on 24 May 1725

Afterword

There is a happy footnote to the story of how and why Daniel Defoe came to write his history of Moll Flanders. Daniel had enjoyed a close relationship with his niece Elizabeth Maxwell since his days hiding from arrest in the house of Elizabeth's mother. Seven years after the girl disappeared, angry that her betrothal had been blocked, the Defoe family at last received a letter. Aged only eighteen, she had run away to the docks, made arrangements with a ship's captain and sailed for Philadelphia. There, she and the other immigrants disembarked to be sold by the captain at auction. Elizabeth, however, being a feisty girl, took matters in hand herself. 'In the crowd around the auction block,' she remembered as an old lady, was a man wearing the broad-brimmed hat of a Quaker. Elizabeth believed one of the Friends would make a kind master, and boldly approached him, asking him to acquire her. As Andrew Job (or Jobe) had five sons but no daughter, he obliged, paying off the captain and taking her home to his land near the Brick Meeting House on the Pennsylvania border, there to help Mrs Job with the tasks of keeping six males fed, clothed and clean. Elizabeth did not write home for the whole seven years of her service. When she finally contacted her family, her name had changed. She had married one of the five sons and was now Mrs Thomas Job. Their many descendants still live in Maryland and Pennsylvania.

Bibliography

Many editions of *Moll Flanders* have been published since 1722. I have used the Broadview Editions version published in 2005 and edited by Paul A Scanlon, which reproduces Defoe's original spelling and punctuation.

Alsop, George, *Character of the Province of Maryland*, London, 1666
—— *American Weekly Mercury*, Philadelphia, 1719–27
—— Old Bailey Sessions Papers and Newgate Calendar, www.oldbailey.org
—— The County of Middlesex Calendar to the Sessions Records, New Series, Vol. 2, www.british-history.ac.uk
—— Items from the Gaol Delivery Register Temp. James I
—— *The Life and Death of Mrs Mary Frith, commonly called Moll Cutpurse*, London, 1662
Backscheider, Paula R, *Daniel Defoe: His Life*, Johns Hopkins University Press, 1989
—— *Moll Flanders: the Making of a Criminal Mind*, Twayne Publishers, 1990
Bailey, Nathan, *A Dictionary of Thieving Slang*, London, 1737
Ballagh, James Curtis, *White Servitude in the Colony of Virginia*, Johns Hopkins University Press, 1895
Baseler, Marilyn, *Asylum for Mankind: America, 1607–1800*, Cornell University Press, 1998
Bernbaum, Ernest, *The Mary Carleton Narratives, 1663–73; A Missing Chapter in the History of the English Novel*, Cambridge University Press, 1914
Beverley, Robert, *History of Virginia*, London, 1722
Black, Benjamin and Lave, Jonathan M, 'The Dismal Science of Punishment: The Legal Economy of Convict Transportation to the American Colonies', *Journal of Law and Politics*, Fall 2002

Blewitt, David, 'Changing Attitudes towards Marriage in the Time of Defoe: The Case of Moll Flanders', *Huntingdon Library Quarterly*, Vol. xliv, No. 2

Brugger, Robert J, *Maryland – A Middle Temperament, 1634–1980*, Johns Hopkins University Press, 1988

Carr, Lois Green, 'Emigration and the Standard of Living: the 17th-Century Chesapeake', *Journal of Economic History*, June 1992, pp. 271–91

—— 'The Planter's Wife', *William and Mary Quarterly*, 3rd series, Vol. 34, No. 4, pp. 542–71

—— and Morgan, Philip D, *Colonial Chesapeake Society*, University of North Carolina Press, 1991

Christianson, Scott, *With Liberty for Some: 500 Years of Imprisonment in America*, Northeastern Publishing, 1998

Clemens, Paul G E, *The Atlantic Economy and Colonial Maryland's Eastern Shore*, Cornell University Press, 1980

Coldham, Peter Wilson, 'The Transportation of English Felons', *National Genealogical Quarterly*, Vol. 63, No. 3, September 1975

—— *English Convicts in Colonial America, 1617–1775*, Vols 1 and 2, Banner Publishing, 1975

—— *Emigrants in Chains: A Social History of Forced Emigration to the Americas*, Sutton Publishing, 1992

Committee of State Library, *Colonial Records of Virginia*, Clearfield Co., 1998

Cook, Eden, *The Sotweed Factor, or a Voyage to Maryland*, London, 1708

Culpeper, Nicholas, *Directory for Midwives*, London, 1651

Davies, Stevie, *Unbridled Spirits: Women of the English Revolution 1640–1660*, Women's Press, 1998

Defoe, Daniel, *The Family Instructor*, London, 1715

—— *Captain Singleton*, London, 1720

—— *Robinson Crusoe*, London, 1720

—— *The Adventures and Misadventures of Moll Flanders*, London, 1722

—— *Colonel Jack*, London, 1722

—— *Roxana: The Fortunate Mistress*, London, 1724

—— *The True and Genuine Account of the Life and Actions of the late Jonathan Wild, Not Made up of Fiction and Fable, but taken from his own Mouth, and collected from PAPERS of his own Writing*, London, 1725

—— *A Plan of the English Commerce*, London, 1728

—— *Augusta Trimphans: A Proposal to Prevent Murder, Dishonour and Other Abuses, by erecting an Hospital for Foundlings*, London, 1728

—— *Conjugal Lewdness, or, Matrimonial Whoredom*, London, 1727

—— (attrib.) *The History of the Pressyard*, London 1717

Dod, John and Cleaver, Robert, *A Godly Form of Household Government: for the Ordering of Private Families, According to the Direction of God's Word*, London, 1598

—— *The Duties of Husband and Wife, A Plaine and Familiar Exposition of the Ten Commandments*, London 1603

Dolan, Frances E, *Dangerous Familiars: Representations of Domestic Crime in England 1550–1700*, Cornell University Press, 1994

Earle, Peter, *The World of Defoe*, Scribner's, 1977

Ekirch, A Roger, *Bound for America: The Transportation of British Convicts to the Colonies, 1718–1775*, Oxford University Press USA, 1987

Erickson, Robert A, 'Moll's Fate: Mother Midnight and Moll Flanders', *Studies in Philology*, Vol. 76, No. 1, pp. 75–100

Evenden, Doreen, *The Midwives of Seventeenth-Century London* (Cambridge Studies in the History of Medicine), Cambridge University Press, 2000

Fogleman, Aaron S, 'From Slaves, Convicts and Servants to Free Passengers: The Transformation of Immigration in the Era of the American Revolution', *Journal of American History*, Vol. 85, No. 1, June 1998, pp. 43–76

Forbes, Thomas R, 'The Regulation of English Midwives in the 16th and 17th Centuries', *Medical History*, July 1964, 8(3), pp. 235–44

Fox, George, *Journal*, Rufus M Jones (ed.), 1908

Fraser, Antonia, *The Weaker Vessel*, Knopf, 1984

Fraser, Walter J, *Charleston! Charleston! The History of a Southern City*, University of South Carolina Press, 1991

Galenson, David W, 'The Rise and Fall of Indentured Servitude in the Americas: An Economic Analysis, *Journal of Economic History*, March 1984, pp. 1–26

Gay, John, *The Beggar's Opera*, London, 1728

—— *Trivia: or the Art of Walking the Streets of London*, London, 1716

Gifford, George E, 'Daniel Defoe and Maryland', *Maryland Historical Magazine*, 53, 1957

Gragg, Larry Dale, *Englishmen Transplanted: The English Colonization of Barbados 1627–1660*, Oxford University Press USA, 2003

Grovier, Kelly, *The Gaol: The Story of Newgate, London's Most Notorious Prison*, John Murray, 2008

Hall, Clayton Colman, *Narratives of Early Maryland, 1633–1684*, Scribner's, 1925

Harriot, Thomas and de Bry, Theodore, *A briefe and true report of the new found Land of Virginia*, London, 1588

Hatch, Charles E, Junior, *The First Seventeen Years of Virginia, 1607–1624*, Jamestown 150th Anniversary Historical Booklets No. 6, University Press of Virginia, 1997

Howson, Gerald, 'Who Was Moll Flanders?' *Times Literary Supplement*, 18 January 1968

—— *Thieftaker-General: Jonathan Wild and the Emergence of Crime and Corruption as a Way of Life in Eighteenth-Century England*, Transaction Publishers, 2006

'HT', *A Glimpse of Hell*, London, 1715

Jennings, John Melville (ed.), 'James Revel: The Poor Unhappy Transported Felon's Sorrowful Account of His Fourteen Years' Transportation at Virginia in America, *Virginia Magazine of History and Biography*, 56, 1948, pp. 189–94

Jester, Annie Lash, *Domestic Life in Virginia in the Seventeenth Century*, Virginia 359th Anniversary Celebration Corporation, 1957

Jones, Reverend Hugh, *The present state of Virginia*, London, 1724

Kolchin, Peter, *American Slavery 1619–1877*, Hill and Wang, New York, 1993

Korda, Natasha, 'The Case of Moll Frith: Women's Work and the All-Male Stage', *Early Modern Culture*, 2004

Kulikoff, Allan, *Tobacco and Slaves: the Development of Southern Culture in the Chesapeake, 1680–1800*, University of North Carolina Press, 1986

Langley, Batty, *An Accurate Description of Newgate. With the rights, privileges, allowances, fees, dues, and customs thereof*, London, 1724

Lupton, Donald, *London and the Country Carbonadoed and Quartred into Several Characters*, London, 1632

Macfarlane, Alan, *Abortion Methods in England*, 2002, http://www.alanmacfarlane.com/savage/A-ABORT.PDF

Main, Gloria L, *Life in Early Maryland, 1650–1720*, Princeton University Press, 1982

May, Geoffrey, 'Experiments in the Legal Control of Sex Expression', *Yale Law Journal*, 1929

McMullan, John, *The Canting Crew: London's Criminal Underworld 1550–1700*, Rutgers University Press, 1984

Middleton, Arthur Pierce, *Tobacco Coast: A Maritime History of Chesapeake Bay in the Colonial Era*, Mariners' Museum, 1953

Moore, John Robert, *Daniel Defoe: Citizen of the Modern World*, University of Chicago Press, 1958

Moore, Lucy, *Conmen and Cutpurses: Scenes from the Hogarthian Underworld*, Penguin Classics (new edition), 2004

Morgan, Edmund S, 'The Labor Problem at Jamestown 1607–18', *American Historical Review*, LXXCI, 1971, pp. 595–611

Newman, Karen, *Cultural Capitals: Early Modern London and Paris*, Princeton University Press, 2007

Norton, Mary Beth, *Founding Mothers and Fathers: Gendered Power and the Forming of American Society*, Alfred A Knopf, 1996

Novak, Maximilian, *Daniel Defoe: Master of Fictions: His Life and Work*, Oxford University Press, 2003

Perry, James R, *The Formation of a Society on Virginia's Eastern Shore, 1615–1655*, University of North Carolina Press, 1990

Picard, Liza, *Restoration London*, Wiedenfeld and Nicolson, 1997

Pollak, Ellen, *Incest and the English Novel*, Johns Hopkins University Press, 2003

Purney, Reverend Thomas (attrib.), *The Life of John Stanley*, London, 1723

Quaife, G R, *Wanton Wenches and Wayward Wives: Peasants and Illicit Sex in Early 17th-Century England*, Croom Helm, 1979

Quinn, David B, *Explorers and Colonies: America 1500–1625*, Hambledon Continuum, 1990

Ransome, David R, 'Wives for Virginia', *William and Mary Quarterly*, Third Series, Vol. 18, No.1, January 1991, pp. 3–18

Rawlings, Philip, *Drunks, Whores and Idle Apprentices: Criminal Biographies of the 18th Century*, Routledge, 1992

Richetti, John, *Cambridge Companion to Daniel Defoe* (Cambridge Companions to Literature), Cambridge University Press, 2009

Riddle, John M, *Eve's Herbs: A History of Contraception and Abortion in the West*, Harvard University Press, 1999

Ridgely, David and Washington, George, *Annals of Annapolis, comprising sundry notices of that old city*, Baltimore, 1841

Riley, Elihu Samuel, *'The Ancient City': A history of Annapolis, in Maryland, 1649–1887*, Record Print (Office), Annapolis, 1887

Risjord, Norman K, *Builders of Annapolis: Enterprise and Politics in a Colonial Capital*, Maryland Historical Society, 1997

Rude, George F E, *Hanoverian London, 1714–1808*, University of California Press, 1971

Severin, Timothy, *Seeking Robinson Crusoe*, Macmillan, 2002

Sharp, Jane, *The Midwives Book, or the Whole Art of Midwifery Discovered*, London, 1671

Smith, Abbot Emerson, *Colonists in Bondage: White Servitude and Convict Labor in America 1607–1776*, University of North Carolina Press, 1947

Smith, 'Captain' Alexander, *A General and True History of the Lives and Actions of the Most Famous Highwaymen*, London, 1714

Smith, Captain John, *The Generall Historie of New England, Virginia and the Summer Isles*, London, 1624

Smith, Warren B, *White Servitude in Colonial South Carolina*, University of South Carolina Press, 1961

Sollers, Basil, 'Transported Convict Laborers in Maryland during the Colonial Period', *Maryland Historical Magazine*, 2, 1907, 43, pp. 17–47

Speed, John, *The Theatre of the Empire of Great Britaine: Presenting An Exact Geography of the Kingdomes of England, Scotland, Ireland, and the Iles adioyning: With The Shires, Hundreds, Cities and Shire-townes, within ye Kingdome of England*, London, 1611

Steele, Ian K, *The English Atlantic 1675–1730: An Exploration of Communication and Community*, Oxford University Press USA. 1986

Stone, Lawrence, *The Family, Sex and Marriage in England, 1500–1800*, Oxford University Press, 1987

—— *Road to Divorce: England 1530–1987*, Oxford University Press, 1990

—— *Uncertain Unions: Marriage in England 1660–1753*, Oxford University Press, 1992

Sutherland, James R, 'Some Early Troubles of Daniel Defoe', *Review of English Studies*, Vol. 9, No. 35, July 1933, pp.275–90

Symonds, Matthew Thomas, 'Grub Street Culture: the newspapers of Nathaniel Mist 1716–1737', unpublished thesis

Thomas, Keith, 'The Puritans and Adultery: The Act of 1650 Reconsidered', *Puritans and Revolutions: Essays in 17th-Century History Presented to Christopher Hill*, K Thomas and D Pennington (eds), Oxford, Clarendon Press, 1978

Todd, Janet and Spearing, Elizabeth (eds), *Counterfeit Ladies: The Life and Death of Moll Cutpurse and the Case of Mary Carleton*, Pickering and Chatto, 1993

Tomalin, Claire, *Samuel Pepys: The Unequalled Self*, Viking, 2002

Torrence, Clayton, *Old Somerset on the Eastern Shore of Maryland: A Study in Foundations and Founders*, Clearfield Co., 1979

Turman, Nora Miller, 'The Eastern Shore of Virginia, 1603–1964', *Eastern Shore News*, Virginia, 1964

Wallenstein, Peter, *Cradle of America: Four Centuries of Virginia History*, University Press of Kansas, 2007

Waller, Maureen, *Scenes from London Life*, Hodder and Stoughton, 2000

—— *The English Marriage: Tales of Love, Money and Adultery*, John Murray, 2009

Walsh, Michael and Kirkland, Don, *White Cargo: The Forgotten History of Britain's White Slaves in America*, New York University Press, 2007

Watt, Ian, 'The recent critical fortunes of Moll Flanders', *18th Century Studies*, Vol. 1, No. 1, Autumn 1967

West, Richard, *The Life and Strange, Surprising Adventures of Daniel Defoe*, Carroll and Graf Publishers, 1999

White, Father Andrew, *A Briefe Relation of the Voyage unto Maryland*, London, 1634

Wildman, Edward E, 'Elizabeth Maxwell Defoe', *The General Magazine and Historical Chronicle*, April 1933

Woolley, Benjamin, *Savage Kingdom*, Harper Perennial, 2007

Ziegler, Edith, 'The Transported Convict Women of Colonial Maryland, 1718–1776', *Maryland Historical Magazine*, Spring 2002, pp. 5–32

Index